Black Leaders
TEXANS FOR THEIR TIMES

The publication of this book was made possible through financial assistance from the Harris and Eliza Kempner Foundation and the Texas Historical Foundation, and in cooperation with the Center for Studies in Texas History, University of Texas, Austin.

Black Leaders
TEXANS FOR THEIR TIMES

Edited by
Alwyn Barr and
Robert A. Calvert

Texas State Historical Association

© Copyright 1981 Texas State Historical Association.
All rights reserved.
Library of Congress Catalog Card No. 81-51226
ISBN 0-87611-056-1 paper
        087611-055-3 cloth

First printing: 1981
Second printing: 1985
Third printing: 1990

Contents

ILLUSTRATIONS

INTRODUCTION

Alwyn Barr and Robert A. Calvert

Until the midtwentieth century black history stirred little interest among white historians and laymen, with the exception of topics or periods such as slavery and Reconstruction which sharply influenced the entire nation. Concern with civil rights in recent years, however, has stimulated an increased desire to explore and understand the history of black people. Yet the wave of new studies generally has focused upon mass movements or upon a few national leaders, while devoting less attention to the more numerous and perhaps equally crucial leaders who functioned effectively in a variety of settings on state and local levels. It is hardly surprising then to find that widely read college textbooks for Texas history seldom mention black leaders.[1] The primary purpose of this volume is to recognize some of those black Texans who, in the words of Frederick Douglass, led the movement to "devise and carry out measures for their own social advancement, and for the general improvement of their condition."[2]

From the long list of black leaders in Texas, selections for inclusion in this volume have been made with several goals in mind. Although many blacks from Texas, such as Scott Joplin and Emmett J. Scott, rose to prominence after departing the state, those included here lived a major portion of their lives within its boundaries and influenced its history.[3] To insure that this volume will expand upon existing knowledge of black leaders in Texas, most of those selected for inclusion have not been the subjects of earlier biographical studies. The few essays which are exceptions represent efforts to present new information about the individuals or to analyze their careers from new perspectives. Leadership has been defined in broad terms to reflect both the wide range of possible activities and also the limitations which existed in different periods. Finally, this volume is an attempt not to designate the most important black leaders of the state but rather to select from among the most significant Negroes in Texas history a representative group worthy of greater attention than they previously have received.

In the twilight of his long career as a scholar and civil rights leader, W. E. B. DuBois sought to briefly describe national black leadership in these words:

> In the 18th century, the Negro slaves and freedmen were guided within by Negro religious preachers in church units. Then, in the 19th century, they developed leaders in the Abolition movement. After emancipation they had the intelligent leadership of preachers, teachers and artists who, together with philanthropic black men of affairs, guided and advised the group.
>
> But from 1910 until after the First World War, Negro businessmen forged to the front and today they form the most powerful class among Negroes and dominate their thought and action.[4]

Other historians have added to his list of leaders for each period. For the antebellum era, fraternal leaders and artistic figures should be recognized. Yet the frontier experience in Texas emphasized more individualistic possibilities for free blacks which varied from the dominant national patterns. During Reconstruction and beginning again in the 1930s, politicians and civil rights leaders joined the ranks of black leadership, as did sports and military figures in the twentieth century.[5] Black Texans rose to prominence in all of these realms of activity.

The variety of leadership roles represented here also emphasizes the diversity of viewpoint and approach to black individual and community needs which has existed in most periods. While black leaders on the national and local levels frequently have sought Negro unity on specific issues, recognition of diversity in all eras of black history is important to an understanding of the complexity of Negro society and leadership.

While exploring the activities of black leaders included in this volume, the odds against which they struggled should be kept constantly in mind to fully understand their significance. What might have seemed successful but not outstanding achievement in the larger society often represented a remarkable level of accomplishment by a

Negro because of the limitations and restrictions resulting from discrimination which sharply circumscribed opportunities.

The contributions of black leaders to the Negro community have been extensive: as examples of individual perseverance and success, as voices of protest against white discrimination, as guides to collective black uplift, as organizers for political influence, and as expressers, through music and art, of the deepest hopes and frustrations of their people. Moreover, recognition of their efforts and achievements by white society represents a crucial breakthrough in the development of a more realistic and balanced perspective on race relations.

For a general history of black people in the state, see Alwyn Barr, *Black Texans: A History of Negroes in Texas, 1528-1971* (Austin, 1973), which contains an extensive bibliographical essay. The only recent collection of biographical essays on black leaders in Texas is Effie Kay Adams, *Tall Black Texans: Men of Courage* (Dubuque, 1972). It contains brief sketches of thirty individuals, including some who left the state early in their lives and others whose significance existed primarily on the local rather than the state level. The essays tend to be more eulogistic than analytical. There are several important studies of individual black leaders in Texas. Two concerning Estevan, the black explorer of the Spanish period, are Jeannette Mirsky, "Zeroing In on a Fugitive Figure: The First Negro in America," *Midway*, VIII (June, 1967), 1-17, and John Upton Terrell, *Estevanico the Black* (Los Angeles, 1968). A major Reconstruction political figure is discussed in Randall B. Woods, "George T. Ruby: A Black Militant in the White Business Community," *Red River Valley Historical Review*, I (Autumn, 1974), 269-280. Theodore D. Harris (ed.), *Negro Frontiersman: The Western Memoirs of Henry O. Flipper, First Negro Graduate of West Point* (El Paso, 1963), describes service with a black cavalry regiment in West Texas. The black leader of the Republican party in Texas during the late nineteenth century is the subject of Maud Cuney Hare, *Norris Wright Cuney: A Tribune of the Black People* (New York, 1913; reprint ed., Austin, 1968). Jack Abramowitz, "John B. Rayner—A Grass-Roots Leader," *Journal of Negro History*, XXXVI (Apr., 1951), 160-193, concerns a prominent black member of the Populist party in the 1890s. There are two accounts of D. W. ("80 John") Wallace: Hettye Wallace Branch, *The Story of "80 John": A Biography of One of the Most Respected*

Negro Ranchmen in the Old West (New York, 1960), and R. C. Crane, "D. W. Wallace ('80 John'): A Negro Cattleman on the Texas Frontier," *West Texas Historical Association Year Book,* XXVIII (1952), 113-118.

Several biographies recount the early twentieth-century career of heavyweight boxer Jack Johnson, including Finis Farr, *Black Champion: The Life and Times of Jack Johnson* (New York, 1964), and *Jack Johnson Is a Dandy: An Autobiography* (New York, 1969). The plaintiff in major civil rights cases of the 1920s and 1930s is the central figure in Conrey Bryson, *Lawrence Nixon and the White Primary* (El Paso, 1974). James W. Byrd, *J. Mason Brewer: Negro Folklorist* (Austin, 1967), analyzes the career of the most important black literary figure in twentieth-century Texas. The career of the most prominent midtwentieth-century black political leader in Texas is the subject of Ira B. Bryant, *Barbara Charline Jordan: From the Ghetto to the Capitol* (Houston, 1977); James Haskins, *Barbara Jordan* (New York, 1977); and Barbara Jordan and Shelby Hearon, *Barbara Jordan: A Self-Portrait* (New York, 1979).

NOTES

1. Rupert Norval Richardson, Ernest Wallace, and Adrian N. Anderson, *Texas: The Lone Star State* (3rd ed.; Englewood Cliffs, N.J., 1970), and Seymour V. Connor, *Texas: A History* (New York, 1971), mention N. W. Cuney, Charles Bellinger, L. A. Nixon, and R. L. Smith. For a recent analysis of Afro-American leadership, see the essay by Nathan I. Huggins in *Ethnic Leadership in America,* ed., John Higham, (Baltimore, 1978), 91-118.

2. Philip S. Foner (ed.), *The Life and Writings of Frederick Douglass* (4 vols.; New York, 1950-1955), II, 33-34.

3. Richard Bardolph, *The Negro Vanguard* (New York, 1959), includes nineteen prominent blacks born in Texas, though most won acclaim after leaving the state.

4. Julius Lester, (ed.), *The Seventh Son: The Thought and Writings of W. E. B. DuBois* (2 vols.; New York, 1971), II, 631.

5. Bardolph, *Negro Vanguard,* passim.

I

DAVE: A Rebellious Slave

Paul D. Lack

Slavery in the United States and in Anglo-Texas prior to the Civil War sharply limited opportunities for black leadership because the laws regulating slave life generally prohibited education and weapons and restricted travel and meetings. Yet slaves succeeded in carving out some time and activities for themselves in which individuals rose to various levels of leadership. Slave preachers could provide guidance for their fellow bondsmen, especially in secret meetings where they spoke of morality, self-respect, and the hope of freedom. A slave driver, or foreman, might become an intermediary representing both the field hands under his supervision and the slaveholder who had selected him for a position of some authority. House servants, because of their more advantageous positions and skills, could lead through the information and goods they acquired and passed on to other bondsmen. Occasionally a slave sought to lead a group in revolt or escape, though the odds against success limited the number of attempts.

Other bondsmen led by example. Slave craftsmen acquired skills, produced artistic as well as practical goods, and some earned their own money and achieved a degree of education. Field hands might show the way to dignity through the productivity of their labor or by refusal to accept whipping. Many slave mothers set a standard for family life by their opposition to the sale of their children. Dave represents this type of leadership. Although he lived in a town, unlike 90 percent of the slaves, his experiences ranged across the spectrum of slave life from accommodation to resistance when change threatened his attractive situation in an urban setting.

The roles of some Texas slave leaders may be explored through the brief autobiographical accounts contained in Ronnie C. Tyler and Lawrence R. Murphy (eds.), *The Slave Narratives of Texas* (Austin, 1974). Good general accounts of slave leadership may be found in Eugene Genovese, *Roll, Jordan, Roll: The World the Slaves Made* (New York, 1974); and John W. Blassingame, *The Slave Community: Plantation Life in the Antebellum South* (New York, 1972).

The Editors

This sketch of a slave known only as "Dave" seeks to provide an intimate picture of slavery. His life has been written in spite of vast gaps in biographical data and the complete absence of material left by the subject himself. Even the most basic facts—birth date, birthplace, surname—remain a mystery. So does any knowledge of his life after slavery; however, some information about this man in bondage can be pieced together.[1] It reveals a life full of pathos and tragedy resulting from a struggle to maintain some command of his destiny.

In the process of asserting his rights as a human being, Dave assumed a place as a leader within the slave community, even though he apparently acted from self- rather than group-oriented motives. A recent student of the slave social structure has noted that leadership among the bondsmen came from a variety of sources. Those entrusted with responsibility for their fellows—conjurers, physicians, teachers—occupied high positions in the slave hierarchy, as did slaves with special verbal or manual skills. Others achieved leadership status because of their clever or rebellious traits of character.[2] Dave, as well as other slave rebels, led by example. He provided a model of courage, tenacity, and cunning, which served as an alternative to the submissive qualities demanded by the ruling class.

Although Dave was in many respects an uncommon man, his life was not unrepresentative—he serves as the prototype of the urban slave. During the slavery era and into the middle of the twentieth century, the life of most black Texans centered around a rural environment. Yet Texas Negroes also have an urban heritage, which dates from the establishment of the first cities on the southwestern frontier. Slaves often preferred city life, in part because it meant a better standard of living but also because it promised increased leisure and a variety of social contacts. The town environment helped mold slaves with unservile characteristics of self-awareness, assurance, and pride. Though small in number, city bondsmen throughout the South had great influence by helping create a tradition of resistance to oppression.[3]

Whatever the social setting, the quality of slave life depended in part on the character of individual owners. Sometime before 1860 Dave had become the property of Galveston lawyer William Pitt Ballinger, who, like many other urban dwellers, considered himself a model master. Moderation dominated his thoughts about slavery and his relationship with his bondsmen. Though a defender of the institution, Ballinger consistently ridiculed "the necessity of being ultra on the negro question." Accordingly, he defended the liberty of several free blacks during an era when sectional and local social tensions threatened the existence of this class.[4] He also believed that slaves had limited rights that should be respected by the law. Ballinger acted as agent for many absentee slaveowners, and he frequently provided the legal defense for bondsmen who became embroiled with the authorities.[5] His own words suggest firm support for slavery as an institution and a paternalistic form of racism:

> I think slavery has its evils, & I am not prepared to say that I consider the best social state of slavery preferable to the best social state of free institutions—But it has also its blessings—its "ennobling" influences....if the hand of Providence be visible in any thing in this world it is the American slavery—necessary, I believe, in the first place to the development of this country—"elevating" to the African race & promising redemption hereafter.[6]

There emerged from the Galveston lawyer's thoughts a reassuring conclusion—that "kind" treatment of one's "charges" would soften the harsh features of the system and result in pleasant, mutually acceptable relations between master and slave. It was Dave's fate to challenge this assumption.

The Ballingers made considerable demands of their domestic

workers. Essentially, they expected servants to be attractive, capable, and dutiful.[7] But in return for his labor, Dave received a few meaningful rewards. His owners' quest for pleasant relations with their slaves probably meant that Dave escaped some of the harsh physical abuse of bondage, especially since the public scrutiny of urban life often discouraged unseemly treatment of slaves. The fact that the Ballingers maintained one of the most substantial households in town may also have resulted in some material benefits for the family slaves.[8] Furthermore, in the opinion of his owners, Dave enjoyed the personal relationships inherent in his household duties, especially caring for the children.[9]

Undoubtedly, Dave also found his social condition mitigated by being part of a large black contingency in the Ballinger household. His master owned several slaves, working four or five in the residence in addition to those he hired out.[10] The Ballinger slaves included Dave's mother and perhaps other relatives. Living with his family provided Dave with both emotional and physical comfort. His mother gave special attention to fitting her children with decent clothing. She probably accomplished this chore by doling out apparel discarded by her masters; blacks in the coastal town often wore such garments.[11]

Dave's life to this point almost seems to be drawn from the southern white mythology of contented "darkies" cheerfully performing light domestic duties at the behest of benevolent owners. Yet, in reality, rebellion comprises a central theme of his life, and his environment served as a major source of discontent. From his perspective probably the most significant advantage of working for the Ballingers was the opportunity of living in Galveston. There Dave joined a large slave community with vastly expanded opportunities for recreation and fellowship. Even had his labor been confined to the family estate, significant contacts with other blacks would have been unavoidable. Then in November, 1860, Ballinger hired Dave to the Island City House, an act which inextricably thrust the young bondsman into the most cosmopolitan atmosphere in Texas.[12]

Galveston's population of over 7,300 included almost 1,200 slaves.[13] The size and complexity of the urban milieu shielded the bondsmen from constant oversight and allowed them to create a vital social life. Galveston afforded slaves ample outlets for religious expression. Most local bondsmen scorned worship with white congregations in favor of attendance at one of two substantial black churches.[14] The white community tolerated slaves' spiritual activities and some other events such as supervised dances,[15] but many masters worried about the effects of illicit social gatherings on the discipline of blacks. At these clandestine activities slaves indulged in social convivialities such as eating, drinking, singing, dancing, and card playing. Bondsmen often congregated at suburban "groceries" where they could purchase liquor, a practice which the authorities attempted to suppress but without noticeable success.[16] Alarmed slaveowners also railed against masters who allowed their chattels the privilege of hiring their own time and "living out" in separate houses. Although the law eventually forbade both these practices, some slaves continued to live outside white control and, in many opinions, exercised a bad influence on more tightly governed bondsmen.[17] To whites the underground social life of Galveston signified indecent, insubordinate, and disorderly conduct on the part of quasi-free slaves.[18] To blacks the city offered a superb opportunity to seize increased pleasure and independence even while remaining in slavery.

In the manner of many town bondsmen, including the other Ballinger servants, Dave became deeply enamored with life in an urban setting. In the words of his future employer, Dave "has Sworned not to work on any plantation & says he will not live out of a city or town."[19] He also developed the ability and nerve to counteract efforts to send him to the country. His emergence as a recalcitrant derived from a basic exigency of urban bondage, the hiring system. Though hiring served as an economically profitable enterprise, Ballinger and other masters learned too of its hazards. Slaves rented to other masters frequently achieved an independence and self-assurance which occasioned subsequent disharmony. Dave acquired these traits and also the skills and habits of a thief. On several occasions Ballinger unwittingly hired his slave to a man named Ferguson, a member of a gang of thieves headed by a daredevil known as Nicaragua Smith. From Ferguson, Dave learned to make lock-picking implements. Ballinger later discovered that with two wires his bondsman could open doors and trunks "as easily as I could with the key." Several times Dave went on robbing expeditions with Ferguson, carrying keys, holding a dark lantern, and carting off valuables.[20]

For a time Ballinger remained ignorant of the influences which

Dave had encountered. The slaveowner failed to suspect that the urban environment had produced a bondsman capable of rebellion. Instead, Dave impressed the Ballingers as a respectable, pleasant person. Even at the height of subsequent tribulations with the servant, Ballinger stated, "I feel sincerely attached to him. He has many good & kind traits of character." Others acquainted with Dave apparently shared these feelings since they spoke of him as a "faithful boy" or "a favorite boy with me."[21]

The catalyst which ended the apparently tranquil relations between Dave and his masters was the Civil War. In 1862 a Union navy threatened, blockaded, and occupied Galveston. This turn of events forced Ballinger to move inland, establishing his wife and children near Waco and his legal practice in Houston, and caused him to dismantle his extensive slave household. Accustomed to hiring out his bondsmen for profit, the Galveston lawyer now hired them out haphazardly in an effort to avoid both invading Union troops and Confederate impressment officers. Though ultimately he scattered them to several parts of the state, in the spring of 1862 Ballinger sent a large group of chattels, including Dave, to a plantation operated by Aaron Coffee.[22]

Both Ballinger and Coffee expected the hire to be mutually profitable and pleasant. Neither understood that the bondsmen would undermine the venture both by subtle and by overtly rebellious measures. All the Ballinger slaves preferred life in urban surroundings; Dave possessed the boldness to make concerted efforts to regain his favorite environment and provided a model of protest for the others. Beginning with conservative intentions—an unwillingness to accommodate himself to plantation life and a desire to preserve the quasi freedoms offered by town conditions—Dave's rebellion progressed inexorably to a strike for full liberty.

Aaron Coffee's initial report on the slaves sought to reassure Ballinger: "Dave Agnes and Fanny and Aleck [are] all well." Soon, however, the owner began learning that his arrangement with the planter had resulted in considerable dangers and dissatisfactions. Failing to gain a military exemption, Coffee became a part of the Confederate army. He later wrote to Ballinger that,

> my presence is indispensable upon my place to keep my negroes in subjection & to run them off if it becomes necessary [to pre-

vent their escape to an invading Union army]. Such things as these don't warrant my getting [just] any sort of man to take charge of my negroes. In fact all the men that are trusty are either employed or in the war. Your own negroes will suffer also if mine are lost.[23]

Coffee's stint with the army meant that the Galveston slaves received little supervision, a problem which the planter unsuccessfully attempted to remedy by shuffling back and forth from camp to Halcyon, his plantation. His military status had a particularly important impact on Dave. In June, 1862, to lessen the discomfort of army life, the planter took along a servant. Coffee chose Dave because, as he later explained, "Dave is a favorite boy with me . . . he had been a good boy and very faithful to me."[24] Not satisfied with living anywhere outside the city, Dave found army life especially unpleasant. In a letter written on his behalf to his owner, he complained of physical deprivation: "Your boy Dave says he is entirely without clothing and begs you to be kind enough and send him" pants, shirts, and shoes. Dave "says the clothing he has will not last him three days."[25] He tolerated camp conditions for seven or eight months before in late 1862 he escaped and returned to the Ballinger residence in Houston.

Dave's dissatisfaction with rural conditions proved infectious. Along with the remaining hired slaves, whom Coffee returned to their owner about this time, Dave presented a ragged appearance. Responding to an inquiry from Ballinger concerning treatment of the hired bondsmen, Coffee vehemently denied maltreatment. "It has been my pleasure to treat your negroes well," he wrote, "and to say that I have done my duty as a friend to your property is true." More specifically Coffee exclaimed, "I am truly mortified to hear your negroes went home scarce of clothing." The planter charged that the Ballinger slaves had deliberately destroyed their apparel because, in the words of one of them, "he did not care a damn for such old field nigger clothing as Master William and Master Tom Jack will give him city clothing." Coffee interpreted the actions of his hired slaves as part of a clever plot: "I am aware of the fact that your negroes hate a farm or plantation so much they go to you in the condition you state in order that you will retain them in town having no other way to

misrepresent me to you." Coffee maintained that Dave especially
had been well provided—"I gave him 2 shirts 2 pair pants & 2 coats
all goods of my wardrobe" in addition to four blankets and "the best
hat I had." According to Coffee, "the cause of Dave going to see you
is to get to live in town." The planter admitted that leaving Dave in
the army camp had not been wise. Though the slave had been "put
in charge of a kind gentleman," Dave allegedly had stolen something
from a soldier and had received a whipping.[26]

Ballinger, who knew of the difficulty of provisioning slaves in a
wartime economy of inflation and shortages, accepted Coffee's explanation. The planter promised to convert Dave from a military at-
tendant to a carriage driver and gardener at Halcyon. Coffee further
assured Ballinger that "if you return [Dave] he *shall* be looked
after." In assuming that his hire in the country could be made successful, they failed to appreciate the depths of Dave's alienation from
nonurban life, the daring of his character, and the escape techniques
he had learned. Dave especially understood the importance of bluff.
For example, after leaving Camp Bates on his initial runaway effort,
he spent the night at a ranch owned by Coffee's sister, coolly convinc-
ing her that he was on his way to report to Coffee.[27] Similar boldness
characterized all his future escape efforts.

Dave quickly resumed his quest for independence. Sent back to
Halcyon in February, 1863, he remained for less than two weeks
before returning to Houston, where he had the misfortune of bump-
ing into Coffee. The planter doggedly put the slave on board a train
with the intention of taking him back to the farm, but Dave rode only a short distance before he jumped off the speeding cars and
escaped, badly mashing his hand in the process. His goal was not yet
complete freedom, but he would accept slavery only in a town setting. His determination, daring, and skill finally nullified Ballinger's
efforts to hire him in the country. Coffee refused to take back the
rebellious slave, explaining to Ballinger in exasperated tones:

> Dave left . . . [without] the least provocation. So under the
> circumstances I should prefer you to hire him to some one else.
> If ever a man tried to take care of your negroes I have & no
> man ever regretted more the trouble Dave has given you. He has
> Sworned not to work on any plantation & says he will not live

out of a city or town. It is truly unpleasant to have him act so badly giving you & Mrs. B. so much concern about him. I think it upon the whole decidedly best that you hire him or dispose of him as you See fit.[28]

Dave won an important victory in a battle of wills—Ballinger in frustration granted his bondsman's wish to live in an urban setting. Dave had spent less than a year away. For the remaining ten months of 1863 and all of 1864, he worked in domestic capacities at the Houston residence of the Ballingers, and on occasion he toiled elsewhere at day labor.[29] Accepting Dave back into the Houston household, Ballinger tacitly acknowledged not only the superiority of the slave's willpower but also the legitimacy of his methods; thereby, the owner unwittingly contributed to Dave's growth as a rebel.

A few months after regaining the town enviornment, Dave presented further evidence of a deep and growing rebelliousness. When, in early August, 1863, the Ballinger family discovered that a large amount of money had been stolen from a "safe" place, suspicion fell on Dave, who "confessed" after a severe whipping and a threatening lecture. Declaring that he had "been thoroughly satisfied a long time of [Dave's] dishonesty," Ballinger feared the implications of his slave's "very bold and ingenious procedure" and considered selling him. Several factors saved Dave from the auction block. Ballinger knew that a sale would entail a financial loss, and Hally, his wife, would not agree to it because of what he described as her sentimental attachment to Dave and his family. Furthermore, despite a conviction that "I don't believe we ought to keep him . . . . We can have no confidence in him," Ballinger hoped that "punishment and exposure" would effect a change in Dave.[30]

The owner did not yet know that Dave had received an apprenticeship in burglary from Ferguson. More important, with his slaveowner's point of view, Ballinger could not understand that, in the words of one historian, "thieving and deception seem to be normal human responses to unjust treatment and confinement."[31] Furthermore, slaves believed it illogical for a bondsman as one form of property to be able to steal other varieties of the master's property, and they interpreted slavery itself as a form of theft.[32] Along with many other slaves, Dave perceived lawlessness as a normal, legitimate means of furthering his material welfare and personal liberty. In fact, breaking the law often supplied the only means of accomplishing these goals. Expediency—the prospect of detection and punishment, not moral pangs about "dishonesty"—provided the only meaningful restraint on his career as a thief.

In response to his growing dissatisfactions with Dave, Ballinger decided to hire or sell the bondsman to Thomas M. Jack, an in-law living in Mississippi. Jack promised to "treat [Dave] well—control him strictly" in an effort to transform him into a "good servant," but the arrangement fell through, apparently because of the owner's apprehension that Dave would resist and undermine such a transaction. Once again Dave had frustrated a plan to remove him from his preferred environs.[33]

Perhaps chastened and restrained by the initial detection and by the prospect of sale into the country, Dave worked in and out of the Ballinger home in Houston for over a year without further incident. However, in early November, 1864, his master wrote that he once again became suspicious of Dave and "arranged things to trap him." Ballinger failed to discover decisive proof, so on November 23 he confronted his bondsman and "charged it on him." Dave "denied everything" until, in his owner's words, "I tied his hands & stripped him & was about to commence on him when he said he would tell all." The slave admitted having taken over five dollars in specie and some liquor. He then demonstrated the ease with which he could open locks, and he related the story of how he acquired his techniques and daring from Ferguson, Nicaragua Smith, and their gang. To the consternation of his owner, Dave "became very animated & evidently felt quite heroic in his narrative." Perhaps to avoid the sale with which Ballinger had already threatened him, Dave appears to have tried once more to "put on ole Massa." As his story unraveled, he reproached Ferguson "'as the author of every species of crime & the worker of his own ruin." The slave further maintained that he had failed to report the gang only because he feared them and that he had refused an opportunity to run away to Mexico out of his attachment to the Ballinger family.[34]

This episode set in motion a series of dramatic events which resulted in Dave's imprisonment a month later, but his life unfolded more in the form of an adventure story than in the orderly manner

envisioned by Ballinger. The slaveowner inadvertently contributed to
his slave's rebellion by angrily and forthrightly telling Dave "that he
couldn't live with us," thereby alerting him to the need to con-
template some action to avoid being sold. Though giving Hally the
final decision about disposing of Dave, Ballinger urged her to sell the
bondsman, despite their mutual attachment to him and his "many
good & Kind traits of character." On November 25 Ballinger made
the tactical error or sending his defiant chattel on an unsupervised er-
rand to Hally.[35] Instead of taking the prescribed journey, Dave set
out on a trek of his own. He returned to the Ballinger residence in
Houston, where, finding the master gone, Dave searched for com-
modities which would further his escape. He took a kind of survival
kit which included weapons (a pair of pistols, shot, caps, and
powder), matches, a ham, a saddle bag, and a bridle. His motive, he
later told Ballinger, "was to prevent being sent to the country." As
Ballinger explained to his wife, Dave "thought you would sell him
up the country probably at once . . . and determined to brave the
consequences."

The precise destination of the runaway remains a matter of conjecture. Initially the slaveowner identified three places as likely goals
of the fugitive: to the interior where his mother resided during the
war, to Mexico and freedom, or to the coast where he might escape to
the Yankees. Ballinger became quite pessimistic: "I doubt however a
good deal if we get him. He is very smart—and may succeed in getting off." The slaveowner took vigorous measures to locate the
runaway, since anything less than a full-scale effort would probably
fail. He notified friends, authorities, and "faithful darkies" all along
the fugitive's most likely routes, impressing on everyone the need for
vigilance by giving them "a vivid idea of Dave's ability to rob."

Ballinger's determination to find the runaway derived from
more than a desire to retain his monetary value. "If I knew he was
gone for good," Ballinger wrote to his wife, "I should feel an-
noyed—but easy." But with Dave on the loose, he continued, "I feel
real uneasiness about him. There is no lock we have but he can easily
open . . . . Dave can come into the premises any moment & help
himself. What he may take, I have of course, no idea, and nothing is
secure from him." Though Ballinger foiled the runaway effort, Dave
succeeded in making himself an economic and psychological burden

to those who continued to restrict his freedom.

His flight failed largely because of the tightened security measures arranged by Ballinger. Although a group of railroad workers detained Dave shortly after he left Houston, he temporarily avoided arrest by concocting a story for a judge who was acquainted with the Ballinger family. The judge, saying that "certainly he had knew [*sic.*] Dave always—that he was a faithful boy & was telling the truth," ordered the slave's release. Still, Dave remained free only a short while before a law officer, alerted by a telegram from Ballinger, discovered the mistake and had the fugitive reapprehended.

"I feel relieved at having caught him," wrote Ballinger, "as I felt he was in the vicinity—& that I was powerless against him." Ballinger exaggerated the dangers somewhat since Dave had intended to gain his liberty rather than to terrorize his owner. The runaway apparently hoped to catch a horse, ride to the coast, and find the Union army and freedom. Though failing in that goal, he had succeeded in reducing his worth as a piece of property. In making plans about what to do with Dave, Ballinger knew that he could neither keep him nor gain his former market value. He decided on one course of action even before the runaway had been recaptured: "I shall make his punishment an example & terror to him, . . . have him thoroughly whipped two or three times—not unmercifully or enough to injure him, but enough to impress him the balance of his life with the deed of punishment."

Beyond that immediate treatment, Ballinger considered three alternatives in "disposing" of Dave. First, the slave could be sold "to the country where he will not be likely to return here." He concluded against that possibility because of a belief that it would be impossible to sell a slave with such a proclivity to steal and run away. Second, Ballinger thought about letting the law "run its course" by prosecuting Dave on the charge of housebreaking and stealing pistols. That alternative the lawyer rejected as too expensive because "inevitably" it would result in Dave's execution. Finally, Ballinger decided to hire Dave to the state prison at Huntsville, where he would be "worked and treated as a convict." The advantages of this plan, Ballinger believed, were that society would be safe from the rebellious bondsman, Dave might learn a useful trade, and the hire would pay the slaveowner three hundred dollars per year in cotton cloth manufactured by the inmates.[36]

To his master's surprise Dave seemed "very little effected [*sic*]" either by the harrowing "scrapes" of his adventure or by his confinement in a Houston jail.[37] His outwardly placid attitude may have been because he had no intention of remaining imprisoned. He stayed in jail just over a week when, on December 7, with four other inmates, he broke out and again became, in Ballinger's words, "the subject of excitement." Dave proceeded to the Ballinger residence in a vain effort to gain assistance from his slave acquaintances. He escaped detection for about ten days before again returning to the family estate, professedly to turn himself in but possibly to renew his search for provisions. There he fell into the hands of the authorities who once again placed him in custody. On Christmas Eve, Ballinger wrote with satisfaction, "the Sheriff carried Dave to the Penitentiary where he is now safely."[38] The slaveowner still had not learned sufficient appreciation for the resourcefulness and elusiveness of his bondsman.

For Dave the last days of 1864 must have been a bitter period. He stayed in solitary confinement the entire week from Christmas to New Year's Day, normally a time of celebration even for slaves. After January 1 he began a life of unrelenting labor. The penitentiary superintendent believed that hard work and close supervision would transform Dave into a valuable laborer. "I will endeavor to make him quite useful as I doubt not he has heretofore been ornamental,"[39] the official wrote to Ballinger. Dave soon demonstrated his "enterprising" nature to the prison authorities. Less than a month out of solitary, he obtained a rope, scaled the walls of the penitentiary, and for a few days refamiliarized himself with what one official called "the benefits of freedom and fresh air." After his recapture, however, Dave's life resembled that of any other "convict." He labored in the factory rather than at a trade as his owner had requested, and the officials watched him with special care to assure that "he will not be likely to escape again."[40] Dave remained incarcerated during the rest of the spring. In late April, Ballinger received the ample sum of $120 in specie from the penitentiary as payment for the hire of his chattel for the first half of the year. Perhaps Dave secured his release in the early summer of 1865. The names of neither Dave nor Ballinger appear in the payroll ledgers or receipts of the penitentiary after April, 1865, though by some subterfuge other blacks labored in the prison for a few additional months while payments for their work continued to go to their former owners.[41] On this rather anticlimactic note, Dave disappears from the annals of history.

What place, then, does Dave's life occupy in the history of black Texans? In the most obvious respects, he hardly represents the "typical" Texas slave. Most bondsmen lived in rural isolation; Dave grew up in an urban atmosphere with a life-style comparatively privileged. Furthermore, he engaged in a personal struggle which, had it been fully emulated by the majority, would have rendered slavery impotent as an institution. Yet, however atypical in some respects, his life suggests a number of important conclusions. Many bondsmen, like Dave, preferred the city over the country. After slavery the number of urban blacks rose steadily, and a movement for freedom and equality accompanied urbanization. Though hardly a palliative for the squalor and injustice which black Texans have suffered, urban life even during slavery produced a class of people freer than their rural counterparts from the strictures of white oppression. His life also demonstrates the disruptive nature of the Civil War for both master and slave. The wartime experience presented increased possibility for a slave to grasp his liberty, but it brought too a greater amount of displacement and physical suffering.

Dave's life also yields some insights into the nature of slave rebellion. Scholars often have couched their questions on the black response to slavery in terms of absolutes—accommodation to the system or alienation from it. Yet Dave's rebellion suggests no such dichotomy. It originated conservatively from a desire to remain an urban bondsman and to further his material comfort. In a sense he desired freedom within the institution of slavery. Likewise, to attain his goals he first adopted a variety of moderate pressures, such as running away from his hirer to his owner and alleging physical maltreatment as the source of his discontent. As his subsequent life dictated to him the ultimate irreconcilability of freedom and slavery, he became progressively more radical in both means and ends until he finally sought to escape from slavery. To Dave, and perhaps to many other bondsmen, a concept of freedom through revolution seemed far less crucial than the immediate realities of survival and securing a better life-style. Only when the system clearly denied his ambition and when he became aware of his abilities to confute the established order did Dave become a full-scale rebel. As other recent historians have suggested, the mainstream of American slaves created means of protest without developing a full-scale revolutionary tradition. Slaves like Dave interpreted bondage as a system of reciprocal rights and duties, clearly defined the limits of their responsibilities and the owners' privileges, and fought courageously in asserting their position.[42]

Historians have come to treat slaves, slaveholders, and the institution of slavery as complex, many-faceted subjects. In this sense Dave aptly personified the slave. His white contemporaries saw Dave as a pleasant, attractive, likable person; yet they also understood that his perceptive, quick, bold, ingenious, and persistent qualities of character made him a grave discipline problem. One central theme—an insistence upon some control of his own destiny—best explains his enigmatic personality. His master once wrote of Dave "I felt . . . that I was powerless against him." Dave failed in his goal, but even in bondage he succeeded in denying complete victory to those who would control him.

NOTES

1. Recent scholarship has rightly emphasized the need to evaluate the slave experience from the slave point of view and has discovered a surprising amount of material left by slaves. Where these sources are nonexistent, the scholar is faced with the choice of using the extant materials, in this case the papers of slaveowner William P. Ballinger, or leaving the story untold. My decision to write this biographical sketch of Dave is based on the belief that his life was meaningful, that it yields insights into the slave response to bondage, and that it deserves to be known. In constructing this portrait I have attempted to transcend the acknowledged limitations of the sources and to present a narrative showing Dave as an active participant in forging his own life.

2. John W. Blassingame, "Status and Social Structure in the Slave Community: Evidence from New Sources," in ed. Harry P. Owens, *Perspectives and Irony in American Slavery,* (Jackson, Miss., 1976), 137-151. In contrast to Blassingame's conclusions, the more conventional view maintains that those with high status jobs—house servants, drivers, artisans—occupied the most respected positions in slave society. At the same time other scholars have recognized that slaves often respected rebels and that runaways contributed to a spirit of resistance. Eugene D. Genovese, *Roll, Jordan, Roll: The World the Slaves Made* (New York, 1974), 324-398; Kenneth M. Stampp, *The Peculiar Institution: Slavery in the Ante-Bellum South* (New York, 1956), 333-340.

3. Richard C. Wade, *Slavery in the Cities: The South, 1820-1860* (New York, 1964), 209-242.

4. William Pitt Ballinger Diary, Jan. 2, 1857, Jan. 31, 1860, Jan. 13, 14, 1864 (typescript; Archives, University of Texas at Austin); J. S. Murrow to Ballinger, Jan. 14, Feb. 8, 27, 1863, Harriet Lad to Ballinger, May 1, Aug. 17, Dec. 24, 1864, William Pitt Ballinger Papers (Archives, University of Texas at Austin); Earl W. Fornell, *The Galveston Era: The Texas Crescent on the Eve of Secession* (Austin, 1961), 92.

5. Ballinger Diary, Mar. 20, 1857, Oct. 17, 1860, Apr. 24, 25, 27, 28, May 30, 1863; B. W. Eve to Ballinger, Nov. 20, 1862, William Eichelbergh and W. A. Thompson to Ballinger, Apr. 20, 1864, M. E. Wilkins to Ballinger, Sept. 6, 1864, B. S. Viser to Ballinger, Sept. 20, 1864, C. G. Walker to Ballinger, Oct. 2, 1864, Ballinger papers (UT).

6. Ballinger Diary, June 21, 1860.

7. For Ballinger the search for suitable domestic slaves was a troublesome chore. Ballinger Diary, Jan. 13, 19, 25, Aug. 11, 12, 1860.

8. Fornell, *Galveston Era*, 92.

9. Ballinger to "My dear Mother," June 10, 1863, Ballinger to Lucy Ballinger, Sept. 22, 1863, William Pitt Ballinger Papers (Rosenberg Library, Galveston, Texas). According to Eugene Genovese, slaves often recognized the need to show affection for their masters in order to prevent cruelty. But outward cheerfulness did not necessarily signify abject dependence, for "to the tendency to make them creatures of another's will [slaves] often counterposed a tendency to assert themselves as autonomous human beings." Genovese, *Roll, Jordan, Roll*, 91.

10. One scholar estimates that Ballinger had as many as twenty slaves at one time; according to census records he owned six in 1860. Fornell, *Galveston Era*, 119; United States Eighth Census (1860), Schedule 2: Slave Inhabitants, Galveston County, Texas, 9 (microfilm; Texas Tech University Library, Lubbock, Texas).

11. Fornell, *Galveston Era*, *116-117;* Aaron Coffee to Ballinger, Jan. 17, 1863, Ballinger Papers (UT). That Dave had a strong attachment to his mother is attested to by Ballinger's belief that the bondsman would seek reunion with her during one of his runaway efforts. Ballinger to Hally Ballinger, Nov. 26, 1864, Ballinger Papers (Rosenberg).

12. Ballinger Diary, Nov. 19, 20, 1860.

13. United States, Bureau of the Census, *Population of the United States in 1860; Compiled from the Original Returns of the Eighth Census . . .* (Washington, D.C., 1864), 486.

14. Fornell, *Galveston Era*, 84-86; Galveston *Civilian*, Mar. 23, 1858; Kenneth W. Wheeler, *To Wear a City's Crown: The Beginnings of Urban Growth in Texas, 1836-1865* (Cambridge, Mass., 1968), 132; Charles Hooton, *St. Louis' Isle, or Texiana: With Additional Observations Made in the United States and in Canada* (London, 1847), 139-140; Ben C. Stuart, Scrapbook: A Series of Articles of Historical Interest Relating to Galveston and Texas Published in the Galveston *News* (Rosenberg Library, Galveston), 185, 186.

15. Fornell, *Galveston Era*, 116, 117; Emanuel Henri Dieudonné Domenech, *Missionary Adventures in Texas and Mexico: A Personal Narrative of Six Years' Sojourn in Those Regions* (London, 1858), 223; Ferdinand Roemer, *Texas: With Par-*

ticular Reference to German Immigration and the Physical Appearance of the Country, trans. Oswald Mueller (San Antonio, 1935), 48; Proceedings of the Mayor and Board of Aldermen for the City of Galveston, Mar. 30, 1850, Dec. 1, 1854, City Secretary's Office (Municipal Building, Galveston, Texas); Galveston *Civilian and Galveston Gazette,* Apr. 16, 1842; Galveston *Weekly News,* Jan. 21, 1850.

16. Stuart, Scrapbook, 232, 233; Galveston *News,* Aug. 1, 1854, Apr. 10, 1855, June 10, July 29, Sept. 30, Oct. 2, 1856, Apr. 18, June 30, 1857, Mar. 6, 1860.

17. Fornell, *Galveston Era,* 92, 93; Charles Waldo Hayes, "The Island and City of Galveston" (typescript; Rosenberg Library, Galveston), 334; Proceedings of the Mayor and Aldermen, Galveston, May 1, July 14, 21, 1854; Galveston *Civilian and Galveston Gazette,* Nov. 2, 1844, July 22, Sept. 23, 1851.

18. Galveston *Civilian and Galveston Gazette,* Nov. 2, 1844; Galveston *Weekly News,* Sept. 30, 1856.

19. Coffee to Ballinger, Jan. 9, 17, Mar. 2, 1863, Ballinger Papers (UT). Ballinger to Hally Ballinger, Nov. 26, 1864, Ballinger Papers (Rosenberg).

20. Ballinger Diary, Nov. 25, 1864; Fornell, *Galveston Era,* 123. The exact date of Dave's employment by Ferguson is unknown but must have occurred before July, 1862, when the "notorious" burglar Smith escaped from authorities in Galveston. Galveston *News,* July 5, 10, 1862.

21. Ballinger Diary, Nov. 25, 1864; Coffee to Ballinger, Jan. 9, 1863, Ballinger Papers (UT); Ballinger to "My dear Mother," June 10, 1863, Ballinger to Hally Ballinger, Nov. 28, 1864, Ballinger Papers (Rosenberg).

22. Ballinger Diary, Oct. 17, 1862; Coffee to Ballinger, May [?], 1862, J. S. Thrasher to Ballinger, Nov. 4, 1862, Ballinger to Guy M. Bryan, Dec. 31, 1863, D. Bradley to Ballinger, Apr. 1, 1864, Jno. B. Earle to Hally Ballinger, May 31, 1864, Ballinger Papers (UT).

23. Coffee to Ballinger, May [?], Nov. 14, 1862, Ballinger Papers (UT).

24. Ibid., Jan. 9, 1863.

25. H. Herrick to Ballinger, June 18, 1862, ibid.

26. Coffee to Ballinger, Jan. 9, 17, 1863, ibid.

27. Ibid.

28. Ibid., Feb. 16, Mar. 2, 1863; Ballinger Diary, Mar. 4, 1863.

29. Ballinger to "My dear Mother," June 10, 1863, Ballinger to Hally Ballinger, Nov. 11, 1864, Ballinger Papers (Rosenberg).

30. Ballinger Diary, Aug. 5, 1863.

31. Gilbert Osofsky, "Introduction: Puttin' On Ole Massa: The Significance of Slave Narratives," in his *Puttin On Ole Massa: The Narratives of Henry Bibb, William Wells Brown, and Solomon Northrup* (New York, 1969), 27-28.

32. Genovese, *Roll, Jordan, Roll,* 602. The concept that slave "crime" indicates a drive for freedom and tendency toward resistance conforms closely to the view presented by Wade, *Slavery in the Cities,* 155-160.

33. It is not clear why Ballinger changed his mind about this project, but Jack, who had declared himself satisfied that "Dave will answer every purpose," eventually expressed relief that "under the circumstances, you did not send me Dave." It seems probable that the "circumstances" referred to concerned the likelihood of fur-

ther rebellion by Dave. Ballinger to "My dear Daughter," Oct. 11, 1863, Ballinger Papers (Rosenberg); Thos. M. Jack to Ballinger, Nov. 27, 1863, Jan. 5, 1863 [1864], Ballinger Papers (UT).

34. Ballinger Diary, Nov. 11, 25, 1864.

35. Ibid., Ballinger to Hally Ballinger, Nov. 26, 1864, Ballinger Papers (Rosenberg).

36. Ballinger Diary, Nov. 28, 1864; Ballinger to Hally Ballinger, Nov. 26, 28, 1864, Ballinger Papers (Rosenberg).

37. Ballinger to Hally Ballinger, Nov. 28, 1864, Ballinger Papers (Rosenberg).

38. Ballinger Diary, Dec. 10, 24, 1864; Ballinger to Guy M. Bryan, Dec. 19, 1864, Guy Morrison Bryan Papers (Archives, University of Texas at Austin).

39. Thomas Carothers to Ballinger, Dec. 21, 1864, Ballinger Papers (UT).

40. S.B. Hendriks to Ballinger, Feb. 8, 1865, ibid.

41. Receipt, Hendricks to Ballinger, Apr. 27, 1865; Sub Abstract "A" Pay Roll, Officers and Employers, Special Boards and Departments, Penitentiaries, 1846-1865 (Archives Division, Texas State Library, Austin).

42. That no clear distinction existed between slave accommodation and resistance is a major theme of Genovese, *Roll, Jordan, Roll;* see especially 132, 587. Blassingame emphasizes protest as a more significant theme than submission, but he too suggests the great variety of means used by slaves in expressing their hostility to the suppressions of slavery. John W. Blassingame, *The Slave Community: Plantation Life in the Antebellum South* (New York, 1972), 184-216.

II

WILLIAM GOYENS: Free Negro Entrepreneur

Victor H. Treat

Before the Civil War half a million black people lived as free persons, rather than as slaves, in the United States. About equal numbers of those free blacks resided North and South, with the largest concentrations in the older states along the Atlantic coast and in Louisiana. Although some achieved middle-class status and a few became wealthy, most found themselves members of the working class and faced considerable economic, political, and social discrimination. To combat those problems some free black leaders created black churches, schools, and social organizations. Others turned to protest and political action, as newspaper editors and through the abolitionist movement and separate black conventions. Still others promoted emigration to Canada, Latin America, or Africa. As a variation upon the last theme, scattered individuals turned to the western frontier.

William Goyens became an early example of potential success for other black frontiersmen who came to Texas, as well as a leader in some aspects of frontier society such as Indian relations. During the Spanish and Mexican periods while Texas remained a frontier under authorities less sensitive on the subject of race, he and other free blacks found much of the freedom and opportunity they sought. But restrictions on black people developed rapidly after Anglo-Americans rose to power following the Texas Revolution. Thus, the free black population of Texas remained only 355 in 1860.

Extensive biographical information about other free blacks in Texas is contained in Harold Schoen, ''The Free Negro in the

Republic of Texas," *Southwestern Historical Quarterly*, XXXIX
(Apr., 1936), 292-308, XL (July, Oct., 1936, Jan., Apr., 1937),
26-34, 85-113, 169-199, 267-289; and in four articles by Andrew Forest Muir, "The Free Negro in Harris County, Texas,"
ibid., XLVI (Jan., 1943), 214-238, "The Free Negro in Fort
Bend County, Texas," *Journal of Negro History*, XXXIII (Jan.,
1948), 79-85, "The Free Negro in Jefferson and Orange Counties, Texas," ibid., XXXV (Apr., 1950), 183-206, and "The
Free Negro in Galveston County, Texas," *Negro History
Bulletin*, XXII (Dec., 1958), 68-70. For general accounts of free
blacks, see Ira Berlin, *Slaves without Masters: The Free Negro in
the Antebellum South* (New York, 1974), and Leon Litwack,
North of Slavery: The Negro in the Free States, 1790-1860
(Chicago, 1961).

The Editors

Negro slavery was a legal institution in the United States and in Texas
from the seventeenth century until 1865. Free Negroes, usually a
small minority of the black population, were caught somewhere between the world of the white man and the world of the slave. They
varied greatly in numbers from only a hundred in Arkansas in 1860,
to tens of thousands in some of the states on the Eastern Seaboard.
How did free Negroes in Texas differ in life-style, legal status, and
economic achievement from those living in the Deep South and the
Eastern Seaboard? Was there an appreciable difference in the life-
style of the free Negro in Texas? If so, why? The life of William
Goyens should help to explain and answer some of these questions.

The United States census for 1850 reveals there were 434,495
free Negroes in the United States; Texas ranked fifteenth among slave
states with 397.[1] By 1860 the national figure was 487,970, and while
the number in Texas declined during the decade to 355, the state rose
to fourteenth place because of the tremendous decline in the number
in Arkansas from 608 to 144.[2] At this time Maryland led all states
with 83,942 manumitted slaves. Even though Texas was a slave state,
it had one of the smallest free Negro populations, not just in actual
numbers but in percentages as well, of any state in the union, slave or
free.[3] In fact, the Texas total is probably less than the figure given

due to the tendency on the part of some enumerators to count "Mexican elements" as mulatto. Undoubtedly, some of those with Spanish surnames were mulattoes originating during Spanish rule, but that would not account for the inconsistent manner of their enumeration.

The actual number of free Negroes in Texas prior to 1836 is even more difficult to establish than after independence and statehood. Spanish and Mexican records are incomplete and vague.[4] In his Texas travels Benjamin Lundy, a famous abolitionist, reported in 1834 a number of well-established landowning free Negroes in and about San Antonio and Nacogdoches, including William Goyens; however, most of his observations cannot be corroborated by other contemporary accounts. Also, because of his abolitionist views, Lundy cannot be considered an unbiased observer. On the other hand, his visits and friendship with William Goyens of Nacogdoches are well documented.[5]

According to the census of 1850, William Goyens was born in North Carolina in 1794.[6] The census of 1790 for North Carolina enumerated a free Negro named William Going who was married to a white woman. He was one of those slaves who enlisted in the Revolutionary army in order to win manumission and later was granted a pension for his service.[7] Evidence substantiating North Carolina as the place of origin for William Goyens, and William Going as his father, comes in the form of a legal petition by John M. Goings in 1845. Goings, a nephew of William Goyens, in attempting to establish his legal status as a free Negro of Moore County, North Carolina, stated:

> . . . that he was born & brought up in this County, and is now a citizen there-of the age of twenty-seven years; that his grandfather William Goin was a respectable citizen of this County not of altogether white complection. But also a free man and exercised the privileges as such while he lived, that his wife, the grandmother of your petitioner (mother of William Goyens), was a free white woman & their daughter Leah (sister of William Goyens) was the mother of your petitioner.

William Goyens acknowledged that the petition was true, a copy was filed in Texas, and another was returned to North Carolina.[8] It is interesting to note that this transaction indicates Goyens had maintained some contact with his family in North Carolina.

Goyens was a rather light-skinned mulatto, but the statement on his father's complexion indicates he was a quadroon or had some Indian blood on his father's side. Indian family ties going back to North Carolina Cherokees would help explain his later great success as an Indian Agent.[9] Accounts stating that Goyens was born in South Carolina and that he was a runaway slave, are erroneous.[10]

Goyens always maintained he arrived in Texas in 1820, and there is little reason to dispute his word. "How and exactly why William Goyens came to Texas in 1820 has to remain, at least to a limited extent, an unanswered question."[11] The first documented date we have for Goyens in Texas is July 5, 1824, when he was involved in a lawsuit; his name was spelled Going.[12] That same year on September 1, he participated in the selection of the alcalde in Nacogdoches.[13]

When Goyens arrived in Texas, then under either Spanish or Mexican rule, he had much more latitude in his political, economic, and social life, than he would have later under Anglo-American domination.[14] Under Spanish law and custom, any white blood at all made the individual more socially acceptable and for all practical purposes legally white, whereas in the United States the opposite was true.[15] In any event, Goyens prospered from the beginning. The Mexican census of 1828 for Nacogdoches gave Goyens' occupation as blacksmith, but he was also involved in gunsmithing, land speculation, money lending, freight hauling, wagon manufacturing and repairing, carpentry, Indian trading, and sawmill and gristmill operations.[16] A year later the census lists him again, but this time three white people are living with him: a twenty-one-year-old man, a twenty-seven-year-old widow named Mary Lindsey, and her eleven-year-old son, Henry. Goyens entered the boardinghouse business quite early and always had several boarders in his home.[17] He ran a way station or inn when he lived in Nacogdoches, as he did later when he lived on the outskirts of town on Goyens Hill. The United States census of 1850 enumerated several white boarders with him at the later date, when he certainly no longer needed the income.[18]

There is no question that William Goyens' main source of income, or certainly his most reliable and constant one, was his trade of blacksmithing, and to some extent gunsmithing:

William Goyens' wealth was based upon his blacksmith shop, the actual labor in which he relegated to slaves and hired white men while he himself engaged in land deals, amateur detective work, racing horses, and litigation in connection with his varigated business and social activities.[19]

Blacksmithing was a common occupation for free Negroes. Whether he acquired the skill before or after arriving in Texas will likely never be known. There are a number of local stories touching on his work as a blacksmith. Most describe accounts of buried treasure or vast sums of money held by William Goyens, and most are of doubtful validity.[20] Goyens continued to work as a blacksmith to the end of his life, as is illustrated by the inventory of his estate at his death in 1856. Included were such items as iron, strap iron, bellows, various tools, and other materials used in connection with a blacksmith's forge. Also, his gunsmithing was attested to by such items as gun barrels, damaged guns, gun locks, and stocks in varying degrees of preparation. Like most blacksmiths, he manufactured and repaired wagons. Special woods and iron materials relating to wagons and their maintenance were included in the inventory.[21]

One of the boarders in 1829, Mary Lindsey, became his legal wife in 1832, and her son, Henry, became his ward. It is likely that she had been his common-law wife prior to their legal marriage. In either case such marriages were illegal under later Texas law.[22] Following the death of Goyens and his wife in 1856, there were several years of litigation between the executor of the estate, H.C. Hancock, and numerous claimants. One of the witnesses in this litigation, Juan J. Sanchez, swore in an affidavit in 1859 that he had witnessed the marriage of William and Mary in 1832 by the local Roman Catholic priest. Most of the leading figures in the Nacogdoches area, including Sam Houston, accepted Mary as the wife of Goyens; so there is no reason to challenge the marital status of the couple. The couple were childless. Had there been children they would have been mentioned earlier in the business activities of Goyens or in the estate litigation.[23]

Mary Goyens is variously identified in surviving documents. Spanish census records are vague and downright contradictory at times, and Goyens himself did not help matters when he gave different dates and details for his marriage and claim to family life in petitions to the state and, earlier to the Republic of Texas.[24] The United States Seventh Census listed her as illiterate.[25] She was a widow from Georgia with a young son from a previous marriage. Her name appears in various places as Maria, Mary, Polly, Lindse, Linsey, Mose, Pate, Sanchez, Sibley, and of course Goyens. Local legends say that Mary Goyens married several times and that she had several children other than Henry.[26] If she had other children, they did not appear when the estate was probated after Goyens's death; only the heirs of Henry, who had died in 1847, appeared to claim Mary Goyens's part of the estate through their father.[27]

Benjamin Lundy, while visiting in the Goyens household on July 14, 1834, reported:

> I went about four miles into the country, to the house of Wm. Goyens, a very respectable coloured man, with whom I became acquainted here in 1832 [no other historical record of this visit]. He still takes a deep interest in my enterprise. He has a white wife, a native of Georgia. They appear to live happily together, are quite wealthy, and are considered as very respectable, by the people generally.[28]

Lundy also records that several brothers of Mary Goyens were visiting at the time and seemed pleased with the lot of their sister. Since we are reasonably certain that Mary Goyens was illiterate, the material success of their sister might well have been pleasing to the men. And after all, Goyens was very light-skinned, and although there is little evidence he tried to cross the color line, it certainly must have been easier for him to exist in antebellum white society with a lighter skin.[29] Lundy also describes a dance attended by Goyens and himself, mentions that Mary Goyens did not attend, and writes that all the women present were Mexican. Under Mexican authority, Goyens was thrown more into Mexican social life than into Anglo-American, where even though he was known for his honesty, endeavor, and generosity, he still was not fully accepted. A visitor to Nacogdoches during this time, William Fairfax Gray, reported little social intercourse between Americans and Mexicans.[30] We may also conjecture that perhaps the Goyenses moved to the country because of the mixed marriage; the marriage and the move took place about the same time.

The question of miscegenation or mixed racial marriages invariably arises when discussing the free Negro. There were at least sixteen mixed marriages in Texas in 1850, and the number increased to twenty-one in 1860, a rather high percentage of free Negroes in the state. There was laxity in the enforcement of the Texas laws which forbade such unions.[31] One of the more common causes for legal problems among free Negroes was the charge of moral turpitude arising from living illegally with someone the person could not marry. Most such charges, however, were eventually dismissed, and they almost appear as a mild form of legal harassment. The most notable example of this would be the large, rather wealthy, free Negro family named Ashworth of Jefferson and Orange counties. Muir reported that several of the men were married to white women and were frequently called before the bench to explain their actions. They were often censured for their behavior, but, more punitive steps were seldom taken or enforced.[32]

By the standards of the day, most free Negroes in Texas were literate, although a better description would be semiliterate. Census records indicate that more than 40 percent of all adult free Negroes were illiterate.[33] In the case of William Goyens, there is considerable controversy. The census of 1850 lists Mrs. Goyens as illiterate, and it implies by omission that William Goyens could read and write. This could mean anything from a mere ability to sign one's name to facility in the written language. Robert B. Blake felt he was barely literate, "able to write little more than his own name," while Harold Schoen, working somewhat earlier and in less depth, argued he "wrote reasonably well" in both Spanish and English.[34] To date no manuscripts credited to Goyens have come to light. All that survives are a number of isolated signatures on legal and business documents. There are a number of printed documents and letters signed by Goyens and attributed to him, but whether he wrote the original or one of his better-educated white friends composed the report and Goyens merely signed his name will never be known.

Some evidence of Goyens's literacy appeared in the *Telegraph and Texas Register* in a letter addressed to Sam Houston. If this letter was written by Goyens, then there can be no question of his literacy. It began, "During the week last past I was notified by Bowles of his return, and of his wish that I should attend a talk at his village Satur-

day last," and closes, "I have the honor to be with respect your obe-
dient humble servant, William Goyens." Henry Millard, a highly
respected man and associate of Goyens in Indian affairs closed the
report with the statement ". . . in regard to Mr. Goyen . . . I can add
nothing to it."[35] Millard's closing remark would seem to give
credence to Goyens's authorship of the report.

Daniel J. Kubiak feels that Goyens could not only write
beautiful English composition and legal documents but he could with
equal facility read Thomas Aquinas and the great philosophers.[36]
Goyens could read much better than he could write, a not uncommon
trait. The success Goyens achieved in the business world and in public
life further demonstrates that he had to be able to read and cipher
with at least some accuracy and express himself to some degree on
paper, although writing would not have been of paramount importance. Some of Goyens's signatures are written awkwardly and
unevenly, as if inscribed by one unaccustomed to signing his name,
while others appear in a smooth and sure script.[37] Goyens engaged
the most influential attorneys in Nacogdoches, and indeed Texas, as
legal counsel (included were Thomas J. Rusk and Charles S. Taylor),
and presumably left most of his writing chores to the professionals.

In 1840 the Congress of the Republic of Texas called for an
enrollment of all white males over twenty-one years of age and every
property owner. This so-called census thus lists some free Negroes
since it was also a property enumeration, but the entries make no
mention of color with one exception. Peter Martin, the slave given his
freedom for services rendered in the Texas Revolution, was the only
person designated "a colored man."[38] William Goyens was listed in
the census and was obviously a man of substance, holding some 5,067
acres of land, a town lot in Nacogdoches, fifty-five head of cattle,
several horses, a silver watch, and a clock—the latter two items reveal-
ing real wealth.[39] In fact, it has been said that he was one of the
wealthiest men during the era of the Revolution and the Republic.
National, state, and county records report him as a large landholder,
rancher, blacksmith, owner of a varying number of slaves, and mill
operator.[40]

One of the unusual phenomena of the Old South was the ownership of slaves by free Negroes. It is difficult for present-day Americans
to believe that in the antebellum South Negroes owned other

Negroes for strictly economic motives. We can assume from the fluctuating number of slaves Goyens held, the variety of workers, ages, and sexes, that he not only owned slaves for his own use but bought and sold them as part of his many business enterprises. There are frequent references to individual slaves bought and sold by Goyens. Prince believed he acquired some of his slaves for humanitarian reasons, but the materials available would not seem to substantiate this thesis.[41] Ira Berlin in *Slaves without Masters,* proposes that free Negroes living under French or Spanish control retained certain feelings of superiority over Yankee blacks, free or slave, who came into the South during American domination. Thus, it might have been easier and quite natural for Goyens, affected by this sort of mentality, to own slaves. He owned slaves in Texas in the Spanish, Mexican and American periods.[42]

William Goyens purchased his first slave in 1826 to avoid slavery himself. A man named Bele English claimed Goyens as his property, which of course Goyens denied. To satisfy English and avoid further trouble, Goyens bought a slave from a Señor Llorca and transferred title of ownership to English, who then relinquished claim to Goyens. The documents are hazy at best but serve as a good example of the danger faced by every free Negro in the United States: resale into slavery.[43] Another purchase was of a twenty-six-year-old male slave named Jerry, in January, 1829, for seven hundred pesos from John Durst.[44] That same year Goyens was involved in a lawsuit with Elijah Lloyd over the ownership of a female slave previously owned by Susan Calier. The court ruled against Goyens on November 6, 1829.[45] Goyens purchased several slaves on November 6 from Susan Calier, among them a thirty-five-year-old Negro woman named Salle and her six-year-old daughter Luisa.[46] Yet another reference to early ownership of slaves by Goyens is found in the diary of Adolphus Sterne, well-known Nacogdoches postmaster and attorney, who related how a slave named Jake, owned by Goyens, was severly punished for his part in a plot to poison a local family in 1829. Sterne made one of the very few derogatory remarks about Goyens discovered, and yet at other times Sterne supported him.[47] Most of the slaves purchased by Goyens were quickly resold, which would seem to indicate a pecuniary interest. Undoubtedly, some of the people were employed by him in his various enterprises, especially in the blacksmith shop, but personal use cannot explain such large numbers.

Evidence also indicates that Goyens was careful to cooperate with legal authorities, even when other black people were involved; but that would have been necessary for his own survival.[48] On the other hand, the friendship and assistance given to Benjamin Lundy, who never mentioned that Goyens held slaves, indicates he was not insensitive to the moral questions associated with slavery.

The two most interesting and probably most remunerative business activities Goyens participated in were money lending and land speculation. There are records of numerous promissory notes either owned by him or owed by him and deeds of either purchase or sale of land. He frequently borrowed money to buy land or had a separate note cancelled as part of a land disposition. Several such transactions are so complex it is difficult to ascertain what exactly was being completed.[49] More than fifty different pieces of property were bought and sold by Goyens through the years, and undoubtedly there were some which have not been detected. Some of his land deals were with such notables as Thomas J. Rusk, Charles S. Taylor, and Henry Raguet. In a majority of the court cases in which Goyens appeared, and there were dozens, either a question of land ownership or a failure to honor a debt were the usual causes.[50]

The first recorded land transaction made by Goyens was on May 7, 1827, when he purchased a lot in Nacogdoches on Banita Creek from Pierre Mayniel for seventy pesos. Blake belived the lot was where the Nacogdoches County Courthouse now stands. Goyens built a house on the site adjacent to his blacksmith shop and lived there a number of years. It was there he began to operate an inn, or at least took in boarders.[51]

In 1832 he purchased a tract containing over a thousand acres four miles west of Nacogdoches on El Camino Real, present State Highway 21. He built his home on what was said to be the highest hill in Nacogdoches County. Still known as Goyens Hill, the crest is now occupied by the Goyens Hill Baptist Church.[52]

He was well established there by 1834 according to Lundy's report. Lundy went on to describe his visit in the Goyenses' home and how Goyens procured a pony from the Cherokees for him to use on the remainder of his journey.[53]

By the early 1840s the Goyenses' home was a large two-story

frame structure which served as a way station or inn for travelers on the Old San Antonio Road, formerly called El Camino Real. During this period he also operated a sawmill and gristmill on Ysleta Creek, several miles from his homestead.[54]

On December 13, 1841, Goyens began to divest himself of part of the mill operations, but the deal was so complex it took a year to complete. On that date he sold to Henry Raguet, for the sum of seven thousand dollars, over one thousand acres of land designated as the Mill Tract, including all buildings and improvements. Remains of the diversion dam and millrace can still be detected. Later Goyens's mill operations must have been on a much smaller scale than at Ysleta Creek.[55]

Goyens consistently maintained that in 1835 he began the legal paperwork for his claim to a league and a labor of land that he was entitled to receive as a Spanish or Mexican citizen, but before he could prove title the Texas Revolution intervened. He petitioned the Republic of Texas and later the state a number of times, claiming he had resided in the country and state since 1820, was married and had a family, and thus under Spanish, Mexican, and Texas statutes, was entitled to land.[56] He also petitioned for recognition for his service in the Texas Revolution which would also have entitled him to land. Congress passed several bills for his relief, but they failed in one house or the other, or for want of implementation.[57] He then appealed to the Nacogdoches County Land Commission to help by recognizing his Mexican citizenship, but it refused. Legal action was then brought to force the Land Commision to validate his land warrant, but the court declined to issue the writ and, in effect, denied Goyens's citizenship.[58] Recognition of bona fide free Negro land claims were uneven at best. William Goyens never had his valid claim honored by the local authorities. Others, with no better evidence than Goyens, such as Hendrick Arnold, William Ashworth, and Logan Greenberry, were granted all they were entitled to under the law.[59]

The amount of land held by Goyens was never the same for any length of time, fluctuating up and down as he bought and sold various parcels. In 1840 he held 5,067 acres; in 1842, 11,466 acres; in 1846, 12,846 acres; and at his death in 1856, 12,423 acres.[60]

Obviously, William Goyens was practicing the time-honored

business of land speculation, buying land when it was inexpensive and holding it until it accrued in value, or improving it to make it more attractive. As already mentioned, some of the transactions were very complex, involving several persons several tracts of land, and various types of payments, including cash. Without a doubt William Goyens was a sterling example of the American free enterprise system in the most idealistic sense.

Although Goyens was free to act in financial situations, he was not so free in other instances. Antebellum southern history is replete with instances in which unscrupulous white men seized free Negroes and sold them back into slavery.[61] While northern literature has tended to exaggerate such occurrences, it cannot be denied that free blacks were safe only when they were under the protection of some prominent white man. Goyens was aware of the inherent danger of his position and went before Erasmo Seguin in the early 1820s, and had himself declared a freeholder of Nacogdoches.[62] Somewhat later, in 1826, while Goyens was on a freight-hauling trip to Natchitoches, Louisiana, Bele English attempted to sell him into slavery but was bought off when Goyens purchased a slave from Llorca and gave it as payment for his freedom.[63] Later Llorca attempted to take advantage of the situation and claimed Goyens as his property. Goyens returned home and appealed to the Nacogdoches courts for protection. In his petition he referred to his earlier meeting with Seguin and maintained that he had resided in Nacogdoches for a number of years as a free man. The Nacogdoches alcalde ruled that William Goyens was in fact a free man and entitled to the rights and privileges as such under Mexican law.[64]

William Goyens and other free Negroes in Texas faced another major problem, perhaps the most serious of all dangers. Beginning in 1835, and especially after Texas became a republic in 1836, there was a concerted effort on the part of many Texans to expel all free Negroes. Antebellum southern whites, including Texans, believed that free Negroes were a dangeous influence upon slaves.[65] "In the wake of this conviction there followed a train of manifestations and rationalization—unconscious, subconscious, and conscious—which reflected their [free Negroes] undesirability."[66] The Constitution of the Republic of Texas stated unequivocally: "No free person of African descent either in whole or in part, shall be permitted to reside permanently in the republic, without the consent of Congress''; and the manumission of slaves within the nation was forbidden without its consent.[67]

The whole affair almost became a comedy of errors. The Congress of Texas was deluged by petitions, signed by important and powerful whites, often members of Congress, to exempt certain free colored. On February 5, 1840, all free persons of color were ordered to leave unless Congress had made special provision for them. The 1840 ruling remained in effect, although it was not enforced with much diligence.[68]

Thomas J. Rusk, who had worked closely with Goyens during the Indian troubles of the 1830s, circulated a petition which supported Goyens. It was signed by fifty-four citizens of Nacogdoches, including Adolphus Sterne, Henry Raguet, Charles S. Taylor, and, of course, Rusk himself. The petition, dated September, 1840, at Nacogdoches, declared that Goyens "had conducted himself as an honest, industrious citizen and has accumulated considerable property in land, etc., and has been of great service to the country in our Indian difficulties."[69] Goyens's name also appeared a number of times on other petitions pertaining to the same problem during those years.[70] The injustice of the law was pointed out by such prominent leaders as Rusk and Houston, and consequently on December 12, 1840, Congress exempted from the provisions of the act all free Negroes who were resident in Texas prior to the Declaration of Independence.[71]

William Goyens's most important contribution to Texas was in the area of Indian affairs, and since the county in which he grew up was near the North Carolina Indian counties, he was familiar with Cherokee customs and language. Did Indians in Texas trust Goyens because he was part Indian and knew their customs and problems, or simply because he was not white? He could speak Cherokee at a level considerably above sign language.[72] Also, Goyens Hill was situated on the edge of Indian country to the northwest of Nacogdoches. Indians naturally stopped to use the clear springs at the foot of the hill and to talk with Goyens as a trusted friend and adviser. In addition, Goyens hauled freight between Natchitoches and Nacogdoches and at times did some trading, probably with the Indians.[73] The Indian pony acquired for Lundy indicates contact with them. As a

The Texas provisional government appointed Sam Houston and John Forbes to meet and treat with the Indians. There is no direct evidence that Goyens accompanied the Houston-Forbes expedition; but Rusk's letter, and Houston's dependence on Goyens, as well as the need for a trusted local guide, all point to his participation.[80] Houston and Forbes presented the proposed treaty to the senate of the Republic on December 20, 1836, but it ran into immediate opposition.[81] For several years the Houston-Forbes Treaty was argued in Congress, with the debate frequently acrimonious, and during these years Houston used Goyens to keep close contact with the Indians. On January 23, 1837, Houston wrote Dr. Robert A. Irion of Nacogdoches, "Give my respects to Mr. Guyons Agent, and tell him how much I rely upon him. Tell him to write me often."[82]

Houston also induced Chief Bowles, with some of his men, to visit hostile Indians in Central and North Texas to encourage them to keep the peace. Goyens, acting as Houston's agent, procured the various supplies and gifts carried by Bowles and his group. The total invoice, called the Goyens-Sparks Bill, came to $212.50 and included basic supplies for the trip and such trade goods and gifts as knives, blankets, tobacco, and tin cups.[83] Evidently Goyens did not make the entire trip with the expedition. His own activities must have kept him fully occupied, but he went at least part of the way with them. Whether William Goyens was an official Indian agent for the Texas government has been questioned, but the Houston letter from Columbia, dated January 24, 1837, to Jacob S. Snively states unequivocally, "I have appointed Goyens, to the Cherokees."[84]

President Houston continued to pressure Congress to pass the treaty, but to no avail. Chief Bowles and the Indians became even more desirous of its passage because there was a growing danger that their land claims might not be legalized. Bowles sent for Goyens and asked him to carry a message back to Houston. Complying with the request, Goyens, accompanied by Colonel Henry Millard, visited the Cherokee towns and made the following report:

Near Nacogdoches, May 10th 1837
Gen. Sam Houston
  Sir: During the week last past I was notified by Bowles of his return, and of his wish that I should attend a talk at his village

blacksmith and gunsmith, Goyens would have been useful to the Indians. If indeed he had Cherokee contacts from his North Carolina boyhood, it is more plausible and understandable why the Texas Indians trusted him.

Mexican documentation indicates that he was acting as an Indian interpreter as early as 1826, only six years after his arrival in Texas and long before he lived on the edge of Indian country.[74] When he moved to Goyens Hill sometime between 1832 and 1834, he did so without fear, even though his proximity to the Indian towns made life more dangerous. Negro participation in Indian affairs and border problems was not as uncommon as once thought; a number of black men, including Goyens, played leading roles in Indian affairs in Texas.[75]

The leader of the Texas Cherokees and their associated bands in the early 1820s was Chief Richard Fields. Mexican authorities dispatched Louis Porcela, Nathaniel Norris, and William Goyens to treat with Fields and his people during the summer of 1826; however, a letter from Fields to the alcalde in Nacogdoches dated August 26, 1826, refers to a number of earlier councils.[76]

Starting early in 1835, relations between Texas and Mexico began to grow more discordant day by day. People around Nacogdoches were understandably concerned over the position the Indians might assume. How loyal would they be to the Mexican government? Would they raid Anglo-American settlements if war broke out?[77] Goyens made a number of trips concerning these matters into Indian country during 1835. As a result Goyens became a friend and confidant of both Houston and Rusk.[78] General Rusk, the leading military figure in the Nacogdoches district, and Houston, sent a letter dated September 24, 1835, to Chief Bowles, the war chief successor to Fields, who had been executed by his own tribe in 1827, and to Big Mush, Cherokee civil chief, concerning past and present negotiations.

> Your talks have reached us by the hands of your friend William Goings . . . We have heard that you wish Mr. Goings to go with you and hear the Talk. We are willing that he should go because We believe him to be a man that will not tell a lie either for the White man or the Red man.[79]

on Saturday last. Pursuant to this invitation, together with colonel Millard, I arrived at Bowles' town . . . . The substance of
his speech in relation to his journey is as follows.

After his departure from his village he proceeded to the upper
waters of the Trinity where he found the Cados to whom he
made a speech; . . .

Bowles was a good deal chagrined at a report he heard from
some one on his arrival that the whites had talked of suspecting
him of an intention to form a league with the Indians against
Texas, . . .

When the council was about to break up Big Mush rose, and
in the most urgent manner requested that all that had
transpired in the council should be communicated verbatim,
without omitting anything, to general Houston. Thus far I have
endeavored to comply with the request faithfully, and hope it
may prove satisfactory.

> I have the honor to be with respect,
> Your obedient humble servant,
>   William Goyens[85]

President Houston was pleased with the work of Goyens and
Millard and hoped that the peaceful, sedentary Cherokees and their
associated bands would be more appreciated and accepted if they
helped quell the more warlike nomadic tribes to the north and west.
In a letter dated June 7, 1837, Houston wrote Rusk, instructing him
how to handle the situation and closing with this statement: "See
Goyens, and say that I will write very soon, and to do all in his power
to forward matters."[86]

A week later Houston again wrote Rusk on the Indian question.
Houston asked Rusk to have Goyens arrange a meeting for him with
the Indian leaders in Nacogdoches on June 30, but the meeting could
not be arranged.[87] Houston arrived in Nacogdoches to personally
direct operations in the field. On July 3, 1837, he sent a message to
Chief Bowles by Goyens, informing him he wished to meet with him
and other Indian leaders as soon as possible in Nacogdoches. A cover
letter sent to Goyens at his home on Goyens Hill said:

> Mr. William Goyens, Agent,
>   Sir, I send on the same sheet, a letter to my Brother Bowl, and

would be glad if you cou'd take it to him, and have it explained, and brought down with the other Chiefs. Let word be sent to the other Tribes; as directed. If you do not go, see that the letter goes directly to him. I will be happy to see you so soon as you can return. I will only have a short time to stay in this place. If you see Colonel Bean tell him that I am anxious to see him here. Give my compliments to your family.

Sam Houston[88]

Using Goyens in such an explosive situation strongly suggests that Houston relied on him as a trustworthy messenger and local guide. Certainly Houston would have little need for an interpreter since he had lived and worked with the Cherokees for a number of years. It is not at all unlikely that Houston met Goyens before the Revolution, when Houston was representing the United States govenment in its relations with the Cherokees in Texas, and recognized his ability.[89]

Houston and Goyens continued to correspond, and the good intentions of the Indians were repeated over and over to the senate. But Lamar supporters on the Standing Committee on Indian Affairs repudiated promises made by the Consultation Convention and finally rejected the treaty once and for all on December 16, 1837.[90] Then events began to conspire not only to defeat allocation of land to the friendly tribes but to increase pressure for their total expulsion from Texas soil. Evidence began to trickle in, some of it of dubious validity, that in fact a conspiracy did exist between the Indians of Texas and the Republic of Mexico. A number of Mexican agents were detected working among Texas tribes, including the Cherokees, encouraging them to rise and take the land they wanted.[91]

As the situation worsened, General Thomas J. Rusk was ordered to take command of field operations against the Indian-Mexican forces. Rusk continued to employ Goyens as an agent and guide, and in a letter to Houston dated August 14, 1838, he gave the following report:

> I have just heard from the spies I sent out this morning as an escort to Goyens who carried my letter to Bowles, a copy of which you have. They left Goyens at Laceys and he said he and Leonard Williams would go on to Bowles tonight.[92]

Rusk repeatedly sent messages (through Goyens, Colonel E. P. Bean and others), to the Cherokees, assuring them of his good intentions. Another letter from deep in Indian country, dated August 15, verified that Goyens had made contact with Chief Bowles. The letter went to great length to allay Indian fears of an attack. Rusk stated that the Texas army had no intention of harming Indian cornfields, women, or children. He accused Mexican agents of attempting to stir up trouble between whites and Indians. He continued, "Goyens and the agent are authorized to talk to you fully." In an attempt to get the Indians to peace talks, he promised, "Any of your men can come in perfect safety with Durst or Goyens to headquarters where I would be pleased to see any of you."[93] This message may not have been delivered by Goyens because a note of August 16 from Rusk to Houston stated that Goyens and others had returned without meeting Bowles.[94]

From that time on, the situation began to deteriorate very rapidly, especially after Mirabeau B. Lamar succeeded Houston as president of Texas in December, 1838. Lamar had little sympathy for Indians, especially after Bowles and other chiefs were linked more closely to Mexican intrigues, and decided to remove them by force, which was accomplished in the summer of 1839.[95]

William Goyens's career as an Indian agent came to an end with the removal of the Cherokees and their associated bands, but in all likelihood it ended when Houston left office and Lamar assumed the Presidency late in 1838.

In his declining years William Goyens lived much as he had lived during the years before the Texas Revolution. The social structure of Texas in the 1840s and 1850s was considerably less fluid for the free Negro, than the earlier times had been. How much this affected Goyens's personal feelings and life will never be known; however, he did not allow it to interfere with his business life. He continued to speculate in land; his last transaction was on January 17, 1856, when he sold two small tracts.[96] Frequent court appearances, usually represented by such distinguished attorneys as Thomas J. Rusk, Charles S. Taylor, and James S. Gillett, protected his financial interests. During September, 1853, his attorney, James S. Gillett of Austin, successfully sued the state for nonpayment of a debt dating back to the early days of the Republic.[97] Goyens operated his blacksmith-gunsmith shop until his death (shortly before, he had taken a local white youth as an apprentice), and he may have operated grist and sawmills as well.[98]

The exact date of Mary Goyens's death is not known, but she died sometime in February, 1856. William Goyens survived his wife by less than six months, his death occurring on June 20. He left an estate which included 12,423 acres of land. The total evaluation of his real and personal property came to $11,917.60.[99] By the standards of the time, he was wealthy. The executor of the estate, Henry C. Hancock, was unable to settle until late 1859 because of the many claims. Considering the business acumen Goyens had exhibited in life, it is highly unlikely that he would have left his business affairs in such disarray.[100]

Mary and William Goyens were buried in a small cemetery at the base of Goyens Hill, on what is called Moral Creek. Eighty years after his death, during preparations for celebrating the Texas Centennial, the state placed on his grave a granite monument commemorating his unique contributions to the state, the only Negro so honored.[101]

No one would postulate that the free Negroes' lot in the Old South was one of ease, plenty, and equality; but the life of William Goyens, and others like him, certainly provides ample evidence that free Negroes were not nearly so debased, exploited, or subservient as once thought.[102] Although many unscrupulous whites waited to take advantage of the sometimes illiterate and unprotected free Negro, there were just as many conscientious whites with high moral scruples who stepped forward in time of adversity to help and protect, as illustrated by the numerous petitions presented to the Republic of Texas and the state on behalf of Goyens and many other free Negroes.[103] Such outstanding individuals of early Texas history as Sam Houston, Thomas J. Rusk, Charles S. Taylor, Adolphus Sterne, Erasmo Seguin, and Henry Raguet frequently demonstrated their concern and friendship for Goyens.

At this time it would seem appropriate to ask certain basic questions and make some observations in regard to the free Negro in Texas as compared to the role he played in other areas. Why did free Negroes leave the United States and seek opportunity in the West and Southwest? It is safe to assume that the more lenient Spanish and French regimes attracted them. George R. Woolfolk, a well-known black scholar, has stated: "As conditions surrounding the existence of the Free Negro worsened North and South, he was persuaded that the West in general and the Spanish West in particular held the key to his freedom, dignity and security." He went on to say that the frontier "had attracted Negro slaves from the beginning, and the stories of their flight to these lands of freedom are legion."[104] Woolfolk in essence is arguing in support of the Turner safety valve theory. Free Negro migration to the West was simply part of the overall American movement westward, the constant seeking for fresh, fertile, and cheap land by those living in the East who were ambitious, unhappy, oppressed, and downtrodden, thus alleviating conditions of potential unrest, rebellion, and anarchy.[105]

Walter Prescott Webb felt that on the frontier the individual was weighed more for what he could accomplish or contribute to society than for his race, birth, wealth, and education. A substantial number of free Negroes in the West, including William Goyens, gained fame as Indian fighters, scouts, agents, traders, cowboys, and trappers. This holds true both before and after the Civil War.[106]

The upper South, which was the most developed part of the South, contained almost 86 percent of the free Negroes in the slave states in 1860. In fact, the states of Maryland, Virginia, and North Carolina accounted for 66 percent of the total. The free Negroes' position in these three states was modified by long occupation, public sentiment, economics, and outside moderating influences. Ira Berlin contended that the relative urbanization of these states, especially Maryland, explained the presence of so many free Negroes. This of course shows the contrast between the upper South, with Baltimore and other urban centers, where the free Negro could work and live in anonymity, and the more rural states such as Texas, where he found no such protection.[107]

A case in point would be the neighboring state of Louisiana, with the great urban complex of New Orleans. Under French and Spanish rule, and even after Anglo-American occupation, free Negroes were attracted to the state. French and Spanish colonial law, imposed from abroad, encouraged and protected Negro rights largely to offset "independence minded whites."[108] Many authors have also pointed out that Spanish and French attitudes toward the Negro were not as racially oriented as were those of Anglo-Americans. Also, both

France and Spain were frequently forced to depend upon free Negro militia units for protection against slave uprisings, Indians, the British, and often each other.[109] An important economic consideration would be that colonial Louisiana and other Gulf Coast areas did not develop a large white middle-class, and so the free Negro was able to enter, and frequently control, the skilled crafts and trades. Thus the free Negro was able to carve out for himself a special place in the economy.[110]

The free Negro population in Louisiana continued to grow by natural increase, frequent manumissions, and the large influx from the West Indies, especially Santo Domingo. Even after the area became part of the United States, the free Negro population continued to multiply, reaching its peak at 25,502 in 1840; then due to repressive laws passed about that time, it declined to 17,462 in 1850; but rose to 18,647 in 1860. During that last decade free Negroes in Texas declined from 397 to 355. About the only skilled crafts or trades open to the free Negro in Texas were blacksmithing and barbering. Opportunities in these areas were circumscribed by legal prohibitions to the free Negro residing in the Republic and later in the state.[111]

In conclusion, free Negroes lived and died in Texas much like their white counterparts. They had considerable freedom in the economic arena and seemed to enjoy almost complete mobility within the state, even though there were statutes which restricted their movements. It must be kept in mind that they lived in two worlds, one black and one white, but with no clear division. They possessed most of the liabilities of the enslaved black man, but none of his assets; and they had all of the liabilities of the white man, but possessed few of the rights and privileges. The title of one of the latest general works on the free Negro by Ira Berlin, *Slaves without Masters,* is indicative of the problem. The author describes the free Negro in the South as being ". . . balanced precariously between abject slavery, which they rejected, and full freedom, which was denied them."[112] William Goyens provides vivid evidence that despite the obstacles, some free Negroes in Texas survived, and even prospered to the degree of educating their children, holding slaves, and owning thousands of acres of land, and, like Goyens, made a strong imprint on Texas history.[113]

NOTES

1. U.S., Bureau of the Census, *Statistical View of the United States...being a Compendium of the Seventh Census* (Washington, D.C., 1854), 79.

2. During the 1840s and 1850s most slave states and some free states enacted laws severely restricting the free Negro. See Ira Berlin, *Slaves without Masters: The Free Negro in the Antebellum South* (New York, 1974), 182-216, and John Hope Franklin, *The Free Negro in North Carolina, 1790-1860* (Chapel Hill, N.C., 1943), 192-221.

3. U.S., Bureau of the Census, *Preliminary Report on the Eighth Census, 1860* (Washington, D.C., 1862), 131.

4. George R. Woolfolk, "Turner's Safety Valve and Free Negro Migration," *Journal of Negro History*, L. (July, 1965), 192.

A number of scholarly articles on the free Negro in Texas were written in the 1930s and 1940s by Harold Schoen and Andrew Forest Muir. Schoen's "The Free Negro in the Republic of Texas" is a series of articles published in the *Southwestern Historical Quarterly*: "Origins of the Free Negro in the Republic of Texas," XXXIX (Apr., 1936), 292-308; "The Free Negro and the Texas Revolution," XL (July, 1936), 26-34; "Manumissions," XL (Oct., 1936), 85-113; "Legal Status," XL (Jan., 1937), 169-199; "The Law in Practice," XL (Apr., 1937), 267-289; and "The Extent of Discrimination and Its Effects," XLI (July, 1937), 83-108. Schoen's series of articles will hereafter be cited as "Free Negro in the Republic of Texas," volume number and page numbers. Muir wrote "The Free Negro in Harris County, Texas," *Southwestern Historical Quarterly*, XLVI (Jan., 1943), 214-238; "The Free Negro in Fort Bend County, Texas," *Journal of Negro History*, XXXIII (Jan., 1948), 79-85; and "The Free Negro in Jefferson and Orange Counties, Texas," ibid., XXXV (Apr., 1950), 183-206.

In the years since that research was done, a number of new sources have become available or more readily available. Robert Bruce Blake, who worked extensively in manuscript materials relating to the Nacogdoches area, located much of the information pertaining to William Goyens. Blake compiled and transalted "The Robert Bruce Blake Research Collection" (typescript copies in seventy-five bound volumes of original documents and the translation of Spanish materials relating to Nacogdoches; Austin, 1958-1959). Copies (hereafter cited as Blake Collection) are located in the following three libraries: Archives, University of Texas, Austin, Texas; Special Collections (East Texas Collection), Ralph W. Steen Library, Stephen F. Austin State University, Nacogdoches, Texas; and Downtown Branch, Houston Public Library, Houston, Texas.

A master's thesis based largely on the Blake material and local folklore is Diane Elizabeth Prince's "William Goyens, Free Negro on the Texas Frontier" (M.A. thesis, Stephen F. Austin State University, 1963). More recently published is a rather brief, uncritical, and laudatory biography, by Daniel James Kubiak, *Monument to a Black Man* (San Antonio, 1972).

5. Benjamin Lundy, *The Life, Travels, and Opinions of Benjamin Lundy, Including His Journeys to Texas and Mexico; with a Sketch of Contemporary Events,*

and a Notice of the Revolution in Hayti (Philadelphia, 1847), 40-117.

6. United States, Seventh Census (1850), Schedule 1: Free Inhabitants, Nacogdoches County, Texas (Archives, University of Texas at Austin); The name has been variously spelled Goyen, Goyens, Goyan, Goyans, Goying, Goyings, Goin, Goins, Going, Goings, Goyn, Goyns, Gayan, Gayans, Guyn, Guyns, Guyan, Guyans, Guyon, and Guyons.

7. U.S., Bureau of the Census, *Heads of Families at the First Census of the United States, Taken in the Year 1790* (12 vols.; Washington, D.C., 1907-1908); Daughters of the American Revolution, North Carolina *Roster of Soldiers of North Carolina in the American Revolution* (Durham, N.C., 1932), 462, 576.

8. John M. Goings Petition from North Carolina, Mar. 1, 1852, Deed Records, Vol. F, 303-305, (Cherokee County Courthouse, Rusk, Texas).

9. Amelia W. Williams and Eugene C. Barker (eds.), *The Writings of Sam Houston, 1813-1816* (8 vols.; Austin, 1938-1943). Barker expressed the opinion that there was no doubt that Goyens had Indian blood, I, 37, 38.

10. Perhaps the major source of misconceptions and legends concerning William Goyens derives from an article done by H.C. Fuller, a well-known newspaper editor of Nacogdoches during the early twentieth century. Fuller interviewed people then still living who supposedly had direct or indirect contact with Goyens. R.B. Blake examined Fuller's original notes and the newspaper article or articles by Fuller. Most researchers since that time have made extensive use of Blake's quotes from Fuller, accepting this material as factual. The Blake Collection which is accurate in most respects—although Blake evidently made a mistake in his citation of the Galveston *Daily News* for December 8, 1904, because this researcher has been unable to locate the original article under that date, or any other logical transposition. It is worth noting that Blake early in his compilation accepted much of what Fuller related but later came to the conclusion that most of the material was unsubstantiated. Also, Blake came to feel quite strongly that William Goyens was born a free man in North Carolina, a quadroon, and came to Texas sometime about 1820. Blake Collection, L, 133-134.

11. Prince, "William Goyens," 4-5; Nacogdoches Archives, Aug. 16, 1826, (Archives Division, Texas State Library, Austin), xxx, 59-62. The Nacogdoches Archives, consisting of Spanish and Mexican official documents and records of all kinds for the Nacogdoches region, to 1836, were transferred from Nacogdoches to the office of the secretary of state in 1850, and from there to the State Archives in 1878. "These documents...have been transcribed and bound into eighty-nine volumes of approximately 250 pages each." Walter Prescott Webb, H. Bailey Carroll, and Eldon S. Branda (eds.), *Handbook of Texas* (3 vols. Austin, 1952, 1976), II, 257.

12. Nacogdoches Archives, July 5, 1824; Blake Collection, L, 98. Blake lists several court cases, one of which is dated Oct. 23, 1823; however, the original manuscript for this entry could not be located.

13. Blake Collection, X, 394. For alcalde Goyens campaigned and voted for E. Chirino, who lost to P. Torres.

14. Good examples of this would be the election of 1824, the various court cases in which he was involved, and his many land transactions. Lundy recorded his social

activities, and he seemed to be at liberty to do as he pleased, although he was thrown more into Mexican social events than Anglo-Texan.

15. Schoen argued that Goyens led a much freer life under Spanish and Mexican rule due to his mixed blood. Other researchers have stressed that in Latin America, where a three-caste system existed (black, colored, white), race was not nearly so important as was legal status, and any white dilution of Negro blood, was a step toward whiteness and acceptability. See Schoen, "Legal Status"; Frederick P. Bowser, "Colonial Spanish America," in *Neither Slave Nor Free: The Freedom of African Descent in the Slave Societies of the New World,* ed. David W. Cohen and Jack P. Greene (Baltimore, 1972), 21-58; David Brion Davis, "Slavery," in *The Comparative Approach to American History,* ed. C. Vann Woodward (New York, 1968) 121-134; and Carl N. Degler, "Slavery in Brazil and the United States: An Essay in Comparative History," *American Historical Review,* LXXV (Apr., 1970), 1025.

16. Census of 1828, Nacogdoches Archives. The name was spelled Guillermo Goen.

17. Census of 1829, ibid.

18. United States Seventh Census (1850), Schedule 1: Free Inhabitants, Nacogdoches Coutny.

19. Schoen, "Free Negro in the Republic of Texas," XLI, 98; Blake Collection, XXIV, 96-122. A number of the young white men living with Goyens through the years were probably apprentices to his blacksmithing operation. Anton Muller sued the Goyens estate for payment promised for living and working in the Goyens household for a stipulated length of time, and won.

20. Virdian Alice Barham, "A History of Nacogdoches, Texas" (M.A. thesis, George Peabody College, 1926), 59-60; Prince, "William Goyens," 19; Kubiak, *Monument to a Black Man,* 36-41.

21. Blake Collection, XXIV, 211-217.

22. United States Seventh Census (1850), Schedule 1: Free Inhabitants, Nacogdoches County; Blake Collection, L, 123.

23. Sam Houston to Goyens, July 3, 1837, in Charles Adams Gulick, Jr. (ed.) *The Papers of Mirabeau Buonaparte Lamar* (6 vols.; Austin, 1921), I, 559; Blake Collection, XXIV, 320-321; Lundy, *Life, Travels, and Opinions,* 116.

24. Census Records, 1828-1835, Nacogdoches Archives; Blake Collection, XXIII, 20-25; Texas (Republic) District Court Records, Nacogdoches, Texas, Apr. 12, 1839, *William Goyens v. Nacogdoches County Land Commissioners.* Goyens declared he had resided in Texas since 1820, was married, and therefore entitled to land under Spanish, Mexican, and Anglo-Texan law.

25. United States Seventh Census, (1850), Schedule 1: Free Inhabitants, Nacogdoches County; Blake Collection, XXIV, 320-321.

26. Prince, "William Goyens," 20.

27. Blake Collection, XXIV, 285-288.

28. Lundy, *Life, Travels, and Opinions,* 116.

29. Ibid., 117; Barham, "History of Nacogdoches," 60; Blake Collection, L, 138.

30. William Fairfax Gray, *From Virginia to Texas, 1835-1836; The Diary of Col-*

onel William Fairfax Gray (Houston, 1909), 91-93; Lundy, *Life, Travels, and Opinions*, 117.

31. H. P. N. Gammel (comp.) *The Laws of Texas, 1822-1897 (10 vols. Austin, 1898), I, 1294-1295; United States Seventh Census (1850), Schedule 1; Free Inhabitants, Nacogdoches County*, ibid., *Eighth Census...(1860),...*

32. Muir, "Free Negro in Jefferson and Orange Counties," 198.

33. *United States Seventh Census (1850), Schedule 1: Free Inhabitants, Nacogdoches County;* ibid., Eighth Census...(1860),...Schoen, "Free Negro in the Republic of Texas," XL, 190-191; Muir, "Free Negro in Jefferson and Orange Counties," 197.

34. Webb, Carroll, and Branda (eds.), *The Handbook of Texas*, I, 713; Schoen, "Free Negro in the Republic of Texas," XLI, 101.

35. *Telegraph and Texas Register* (Houston), June 13, 1837.

36. Kubiak, *Monument to a Black Man*, 26-36.

37. Goyens's signed statement as an arbitrator in a legal action, June 15, 1827 (2023/452 Nov., 1826-June, 1827), Nacogdoches Archives; Petition from blacksmiths of Nacogdoches, Dec. 20, 1841 (one of twenty-eight who signed was Wm. Goyens), Memorial No. 14, 2-9/125 OFB 69-14, (Archives Division, Texas State Library, Austin); Deed signed by William Goyens, Oct. 13, 1841, Henry Raguet Papers (Archives, University of Texas at Austin).

38. Schoen, "Free Negro in the Republic of Texas," XL, 105-106.

39. Nacogdoches County Tax Roll, 1840 (Archives, Stephen F. Austin State University, Nacogdoches). The manuscript returns appear in a more readable form in Gifford E. White (ed.), *The 1840 Census of the Republic of Texas* (Austin, 1966), 125.

40. United States Seventh Census (1850), Nacogdoches County; Nacogdoches County Tax Rolls, 1840, 1842, 1846, and 1847.

41. Prince, "William Goyens," 76.

42. Berlin, *Slaves without Masters*, 277-278.

43. Blake Collection, XI, 170-178.

44. Ibid., II, 239.

45. Harriet Smither (ed.), "Diary of Adolphus Sterne," *Southwestern Historical Quarterly*, XXXII (Oct., 1928), 179.

46. Census of 1830, Nacogdoches Archives; Blake Collection, XXIII, 9.

47. Smither (ed.), "Diary of Adolphus Sterne," 166.

48. Schoen, "Free Negro in the Republic of Texas," XLI, 98; Webb, Carroll, and Branda (eds.), *Handbook of Texas*, I, 713.

49. Deed to 1,000·acres called the Mill Tract from Wm. Goyens to Henry Raguet dated Dec. 13, 1841, Raguet Papers.

50. Blake Collection, XXIII; Schoen, "Free Negro in the Republic of Texas," XLI, 100.

51. Blake Collection, XXIII, 6.

52. Ibid., 7-8; Robert Bruce Blake, "Locations of the Early Spanish Missions and Presidio in Nacogdoches County," *Southwestern Historical Quarterly*, XLI (Jan., 1938), 217-219.

53. Lundy, *Life, Travels, and Opinions,* 116.

54. Blake, "Location of Early Spanish Missions," 219; Blake Collection, L, 134-135.

55. Deed to Mill Tract, Raguet Papers.

56. Texas, Legislature, Senate, *Journal of the Senate of the State of Texas, Fourth Legislature* (Austin, 1852), 340-341.

57. Ibid., 340: Senate Bill dated May 21, 1838, recognizing William Goyens as a participant in the Texas Revolution in 1836, in Texas (Republic), Congress, House, *Journal of the House of Representatives of the Republic of Texas: Second Congress—Adjourned Session* (Houston, 1838), 173.

58. Blake Collection, XXIII, 20-25. Goyens on April 12, 1839, filed suit in *Goyens* v. *Republic of Texas* against the Land Commissioners of Nacogdoches County in District Court, but received an unfavorable decision on May 7, 1841. Goyens declared in his suit that he was "a resident citizen of said county, with a wife, children, & other family. That he emigrated to the Republic of Coahuila & Texas in the year A.D. one thousand eight hundred & twenty; that he has continued an actual resident citizen ever since. That he was married during the year 1823."

59. Thomas Lloyd Miller, *Bounty and Donation Land Grants of Texas, 1835-1888* (Austin, 1967). Why William Goyens was rejected despite the support of such luminaries as Thomas J. Rusk, Charles S. Taylor, Henry Reguet, Bennett Blake, and Sam Houston is not clear. An educated guess would be that he was already a man of wealth, and this would be a way of "putting him in his place." Also, many people of the period did not believe free Negroes should or could own land.

60. Nacogdoches County Tax Rolls, 1840, 1842, 1846; White (ed.), 1840 Census, 125; Blake Collection, XXIV, 211-216.

61. Earl W. Fornell, "The Abduction of Free Negroes and Slaves in Texas," *Southwestern Historical Quarterly,* LX (Jan., 1957), 369-380.

62. Document stating that Goyens had arrived in Nacogdoches in 1820, dated Aug. 16, 1826, Nacogdoches Archives.

63. The documents relating to this episode in William Goyens's life are at best confused, making it difficult to ascertain exactly what transpired. The man or men appear under such various names as Bailey, Baily, Bele, English, Lorca, Yngles, and York.

64. These stories, found in the writings of H. C. Fuller, Robert B. Blake, Virdian Barham, Diane Prince, and Daniel Kubiak, are based upon documents which at best can be described as vague, esoteric, and conflicting. See Blake Collection, XI, 170-178, L, 136-137; and Oct. 25, 1826, Nacogdoches Archives.

65. Most southern states had laws similar to the eventual Texas statute. During the Texas Revolution there were moves to bar free Negroes because it was feared that they would assist Mexico or encourage slave insurrection.

66. Franklin, *Free Negro in North Carolina,* [vii]. Denmark Vesey and Nat Turner did much to condition the thinking of people in the antebellum South.

67. Gammel (comp.), *Laws of Texas,* I, 872, 1079.

68. Ibid., II, 325-326.

69. Original Petition of William Goyens by Thomas J. Rusk, dated Sept., 1840,

Nacogdoches Archives.

70. Texas (Republic), Congress, Senate, *Journal of the Senate of the Republic of Texas: Second Congress—Adjourned Session* (Houston, 1838), 90, 98-99, 173; Texas (Republic), Congress, House, *Journal of the House of Representatives of the Republic of Texas: Fifth Congress—First Session, 1840-1841* (Austin, 1841), 54; Texas Congressional Papers, 2-8/4 (Old File Box 11), Files 984-1021, May 23, 1838 (Archives Division, Texas State Library, Austin).

71. Gammel (comp), *Laws of Texas,* II, 549-550.

72. Texas, *Journal of the Senate...:Fourth Legislature,* 340, 341; Goyens to Lamar, Sept. 19, 1835, including speeches of Chief Bowles and others, Lamar, *Papers,* I, 238.

73. Williams and Barker (eds.), *Writings of Sam Houston,* II, 38; Nacogdoches Archives; Dorman H. Winfrey and James M. Day (eds.), *Texas Indian Papers, 1825-1843* (4 vols.; Austin, 1959), I, 19-20.

74. Chief Richard Fields to Alcalde in Nacogdoches, Aug. 26, 1826. ''The three persons whom you sent to me, Luis Procela, William Gaines [Goyens], Nathaniel Norris, will bear testimony to the disposition evinced by my men and those of the nations on whose assistance I can rely so soon as they are established here.''; Nacogdoches Archives.

75. Kenneth W. Porter, ''Negroes and Indians on the Texas Frontier, 1831-1876,'' *Journal of Negro History,* XLI (July, 1956), 185-214 (Oct., 1956), 285-310.

76. W. W. Newcomb, Jr., *The Indians of Texas: From Prehistoric to Modern Times* (Austin, 1961), 343-348; Nacogdoches Archives.

77. All of the following works cover various aspects of the Cherokee problem and make some mention of William Goyens. Mary Whatley Clarke, *Chief Bowles and the Texas Cherokees,* The Civilization of the American Indian Series, Vol. 113, (Norman, 1971); Ernest William Winkler, ''The Cherokee Indians in Texas,'' *Southwestern Historical Quarterly,* VII (Oct., 1903), 97-99; Marilyn McAdams Sibley, ''The Texas Cherokee War of 1839,'' *East Texas Historical Journal,* III (Mar. 1965), 19-21; Dorman H. Winfrey, ''Chief Bowles of the Texas Cherokees,'' *Chronicles of Oklahoma,* XXXII (Spring, 1954), 33-35.

78. Mary Whatley Clarke, *Thomas J. Rusk: Soldier, Statesman, Jurist* (Austin, 1971), 112-115.

79. Rusk to Chief Bowles, Sept. 24, 1835, Thomas J. Rusk Papers (Crocket Collection, Stephen F. Austin State University, Nacogdoches).

80. Texas (Republic), Congress, Senate, *Journal of the Senate of the Republic of Texas: Seventh Congress* (Austin, 1842), 499; Gammel (comp.), *Laws of Texas,* I, 546, 1001-1002; Winfrey and Day (eds.), *Texas Indian Papers,* I, 20; Schoen, ''Free Negro in the Republic of Texas,'' XL, 173.

81. Winfrey and Day (eds.), *Texas Indian Papers,* I, 10-17.

82. Houston to Dr. Robert A. Irion, Jan. 23, 1837, in Williams and Barker (eds.), *Writings of Sam Houston,* II, 36.

83. Winfrey and Day (eds.), *Texas Indian Papers,* I, 19-20.

84. Houston to Jacob S. Snively, Jan. 24, 1837, in Williams and Barker (eds.),

Writings of Sam Houston, II, 38.

85. *Telegraph and Texas Register* (Houston), June 13, 1837.

86. Houston to Rusk, June 7, 1837, in Williams and Barker (eds.), *Writings of Sam Houston,* II, 114-115.

87. Houston to Rusk, June 16, 1837, ibid., 123-124.

88. Houston to Goyens and Chief Bowles, July 3, 1837, ibid., 131-132.

89. Llerena B. Friend, *Sam Houston: The Great Designer* (Austin, 1954), 30-66; Marquis James, *The Raven: A Biography of Sam Houston* (Indianapolis, 1929), 125-136, 223, 309; M. K. Wisehart, *Sam Houston, American Giant* (Washington, D.C., 1962), 209-210; Williams and Barker (eds.), *Writings of Sam Houston.* Houston wrote to Chief Bowles in personal terms; evidently they were acquainted before either came to Texas.

90. Winfrey and Day (eds.), *Texas Indian Papers,* I, 22-28.

91. Joseph Milton Nance, *After San Jacinto: The Texas-Mexican Frontier 1836-1841,* (Austin, 1963), 118-120, 136-137; Clarke, *Thomas J. Rusk,* 114-115.

92. Letter from Rusk to Chief Bowles, dated August 13, 1838, apprises the Cherokees that William Goyens is bringing dispatches. On the following day, Rusk wrote Houston in regard to the problems he was having with Indian negotiations. Thomas Jefferson Rusk Papers (typescript; Archives, University of Texas at Austin).

93. Rusk to Colonel Bowles, Aug. 15, 1838, Rusk Papers (Austin University).

94. Rusk to Houston, Aug. 16, 1838. "Wright, Lewis, and Goings the latter of whom I sent along with Lewis and Wright have returned without seeing the Indians." Rusk Papers (U.T.).

95. George Louis Crocket, *Two Centuries in East Texas: A History of San Augustine County and Surrounding Territory From 1685 to the Present Time,* (Dallas, 1932), 189-193.

96. Blake Collection, XXIII, 133-136.

97. William Goyans Military Claim against the Republic of Texas, Audited Military Claims, 2-12/345 (Archives Division, Texas State Library, Austin).

98. Blake Collection, XXIV, 96-122, 211-217.

99. Ibid., XXIV, 200, 225-238.

100. Ibid., XXIII, 142-163, XXIV, 18-200, 285-288.

101. Robert Bruce Blake, *Historic Nacogdoches, Texas* (Nacogdoches, 1939), 21. Goyens was buried beside his wife in a cemetery about two miles from his home. The cemetery has been variously described as a Mexican or Indian burial ground. It is situated on a slight ridge in the bottom land of Moral Creek. A short distance away one can still detect the remains of the millrace for the Goyens mill operations. The usual cemetery features were obliterated years ago by sawmill operations, farming, and inundation by the creek. In 1936 the state of Texas placed a monument on the site commemorating the life of Goyens; unfortunately, the inscription contains a number of factual errors. It reads: "William ('Bill') Goyens, Born a Slave In South Carolina, 1794, Escaped to Texas in 1821, Rendered Valuable Assistance, To the Army of Texas, 1836; Interpreter for the Houston-Forbes Treaty With the Cherokees, 1836; Acquired Wealth And Was Noted For His Charity; Died at his Home on

Goyens' Hill, 1836. His Skin was Black, His Heart True Blue. Erected By the State of Texas, 1936.''

102. Theodore Brantner Wilson, *The Black Codes of the South* Southern Historical Publications No. 6, (Ala., 1965), 13-41; Berlin, *Slaves without Masters,* 343-346.

103. The Archives Division of the Texas State Library contain hundreds of examples of whites who gave protection to certain free Negroes; and the legislative journals of the Republic of Texas and the state reflect similar attitudes.

104. Woolfolk, ''Turner's Safety Valve and Free Negro Migration,'' 188.

105. Ibid., 189-195; See Frederick Jackson Turner, ''The Significance of the Frontier in American History,'' (Chicago, 1893), reprinted in his *The Frontier in American History* (New York, 1920).

106. Walter Prescott Webb, *The Great Frontier* (Boston, 1952); Kenneth Wiggins Porter, *The Negro on the American Frontier* (New York, 1971); Porter, ''Negroes and Indians on the Texas Frontier.''

107. U.S. Bureau of the Census, *Preliminary Report on the Eighth Census, 1860;* Berlin, *Slaves without Masters,* 54-56, 173-174.

108. Berlin, *Slaves without Masters,* 111.

109. Herbert E. Sterkx, *The Free Negro in Ante-Bellum Louisiana* (Rutherford, 1972), 63-90.

110. Laura Foner, ''The Free People of Color in Louisiana and St. Domingue: A Comparative Portrait of Two Three-Caste Societies,'' *Journal of Social History,* III (Summer, 1970), 406-430.

111. United States Sixth Census (1840), Schedule 1: Free Inhabitants, Texas, Louisiana; ibid., Seventh Census...(1850)...; Eighth Census...(1860)...

112. Berlin, *Slaves without Masters,* xiv.

113. United States Eighth Census (1860), Schedule 1: Free Inhabitants, Texas.

Matthew Gaines. Courtesy Lois Smith.

III

MATT GAINES: Reconstruction Politician

Ann Patton Malone

When emancipation came for black people in Texas and the South at the end of the Civil War, it did not bring with it political participation. Leadership positions for blacks came first in new churches and schools. Opportunities to vote and to become political leaders came only in 1867, when Congress took control of Reconstruction and opened the way for black political involvement. The Republican party organized in every southern state and initially won control of most state and local governmental positions. A majority of Republican leaders continued to be white, but blacks held a number of positions in each state. Because the black population percentage in Texas fell below those of other states in the Deep South, the black political leaders also remained fewer in number. Their collective careers may be explored in J. Mason Brewer, *Negro Legislators of Texas* (Dallas, 1935; reprint ed., Austin, 1970).

Among this group the ranking positions as state senators went to George T. Ruby and Matt Gaines. Each of them represented one of the general backgrounds which produced the black political leaders of Reconstruction. Ruby had been born a free man, had acquired an education before the Civil War, and had been a newspaper reporter. After the war he served as an agent of the Freedmen's Bureau in Louisiana and Texas, where he established schools. His state senate district contained a large black minority along with a white majority; thus he sought to balance or unify their interests and to represent both groups. His career may be followed in Randall B. Woods, "George T.

Ruby: A Black Militant in the White Business Community,"
Red River Valley Historical Review, I (Autumn, 1974), 269-280.

Matt Gaines, a former slave who had educated himself, attained leadership through his role as a black minister. His district with a large black majority allowed him to act more clearly as a spokesman for Texas freedmen.

For general accounts of black leaders during Reconstruction, see Lerone Bennett, Jr., *Black Power U.S.A.: The Human Side of Reconstruction, 1867-1877* (Chicago, 1967); Robert Cruden, *The Negro in Reconstruction* (Englewood Cliffs, N.J., 1969); W. E. B. DuBois, *Black Reconstruction in America* (New York, 1935; reprint ed., New York, 1969); and E.L. Thornbrough (ed.), *Black Reconstructionists* (Englewood Cliffs, N.J., 1972).

                                                    The Editors

---

After the Radical Republican era in Texas had been ushered in by mass mobilization of the black vote, a black leader in 1870 enthusiastically proclaimed the victory a "great revolution."[1] Another asserted that "the old state of affairs [has] died out" and that the Radical ascendancy marked the dawning of a "new day" of justice and of opportunity for his long-oppressed people.[2] These two men—the first blacks elected to the Texas senate—represented the high expectations that Texas blacks had under the new regime. Among the most often mentioned benefits that they hoped to achieve were meaningful participation in government, educational opportunities, and justice before the law. However, by 1874 the Radical experiment had prematurely ended, and a period of conservative retrenchment had begun. The so-called revolution of 1870 was aborted, and the "new day" had closed with black dreams largely unfulfilled. The hope, purpose, and the tragedy of those years are in many ways epitomized in the career and life of one of those black senators who greeted the new era with such faith and eagerness, Matthew Gaines. A former slave in Louisiana and Texas, by 1870, Gaines had made a rapid rise to the Texas state senate, where he proved to be the antithesis of the lackadaisical, deferential, and uninformed black legislator of Reconstruction mythology. In his brief senatorial career,

Gaines assumed dual roles: guardian of black interests and critic of contemporary politics. Both roles will be explored in this essay. His mass appeal among Texas blacks may not have been equaled by any black politician since. However, his political career was ended in 1874, when he was denied his seat in the Fourteenth Legislature. After sporadic attempts at civil rights agitation in the rural area of his old district, Gaines resumed his earlier role as a preacher and died in poverty and obscurity in 1900, remembered only by his friends and relatives in the small town of Giddings, about twenty miles from the predominately black village of Burton, where he had appeared around 1866 as an idealistic young man ready to bring that "new day" to his people.[3]

Gaines spent approximately the first two decades of his life in slavery. He was born about 1840 to a slave mother on a small plantation in Pineville, Louisiana, just across the Red River from Alexandria in Rapides Parish.[4] The plantation—an estate, actually—was owned by Madame Candida Grandi Despallier, a Spanish-speaking woman born in Texas and married to a French/Creole, Martin G. Despallier.[5] Their sons, both of whom served in the Texas Revolution [Charles G. Despallier, the younger son, died at the Alamo], were known to have spoken with heavy French accents.[6] Gaines's descendants have always claimed that he could speak several languages, and it is quite possible that on this small plantation orders and conversations did take place in three languages: English, French, and Spanish.[7] Surely the story that Gaines could speak seven languages is apocryphal, but it must have been a wonder, indeed, to the semi-literate black folk of the Giddings area to have one among them who could speak phrases in two foreign tongues.

Gaines's childhood history was intimately tied to that of the Despallier family. Gaines used the surname "Despallier" on his first marriage certificate, indicating that in 1867 he considered it his real or legal name, although he usually went by Gaines.[8] In the 1850 census of Rapides Parish—the first census on which the Despallier name appears in that parish—the white household consisted only of Madame C. G. Despallier, age sixty-three, and her heir, age eight, who is erroneously listed as her son.[9] The child was her grandson, Blas Philippe Despallier, II, whose parents had died of smallpox a short time earlier. The Despallier slave household consisted only of one female slave, age thirty-nine, and six children ranging in age from five to sixteen.[10] Matthew is probably the ten-year-old male listed, since the other two males were ages five and sixteen.

Gaines's paternity is unknown. His father may have been sold away from the Despallier family before the census was conducted—perhaps at the death of Martin Despallier—or he may have been a slave from a neighboring plantation. There is also the possibility that the slave children were fathered by Madame Despallier's son, Blas Philippe Despallier, a Nachitoches journalist who frequently visited his mother's Pineville estate and who appears to have lived there several years prior to his death about 1849. His son, as has been noted, continued to live with his grandmother after his parents' deaths.

After Madame Despallier's demise in the middle 1850s (probably 1855 or 1856), the grandson inherited a large estate, including thousands of acres in Texas which had been received as bounty lands for his father's and uncle's services in the Texas Revolution.[11] The Texas lands were sold off by his executors, and the Pineville estate was also finally sold in 1866, apparently to settle the young man's gambling debts.[12] Shortly thereafter, the only remaining white Despallier left the area; no further trace of him can be found in local records.

This young Despallier may have been the boy to whom Matthew Gaines referred many years later. Gaines told his own son that he had learned to read by candlelight, crouched down among the stalks in the corn patch in the evening, from books smuggled to him by a little white boy on the place near his own age.[13]

Whether or not the child was Gaines's half brother will never be determined; only circumstantial evidence exists. The only substantiated photograph of Gaines shows him to be thin-lipped and fine-featured, but also distinctly negroid in appearance. The photograph is badly faded, and it is difficult to judge from it the hue of his complexion. His sons and daughters recalled him as "fair." One of Gaines's sons and his granddaughter recalled that Gaines's second wife, Mrs. Elizabeth Harrison Gaines, had said that he had brothers and sisters in Louisiana who were "nearly white."[14]

Gaines and his family were sold shortly after Madame Despallier's death (the master, Martin G. Despallier, had died before the 1850 census was taken). Unfortunately, all official local records regarding the estate settlement were destroyed in the 1864 courthouse fire, and no mention was uncovered of an auction or estate sale in extant Alexandria, Rapides Parish, or Shreveport newspapers. Gaines did, however, provide some information about his adult years in bondage in an 1870 *Daily State Journal* article, obviously based on an interview.

Gaines related that he was sold as part of the Despallier estate to a trader en route to the New Orleans market. There he was auctioned, bought by a Louisiana man (Gaines did not give his name), and was subsequently hired out as a laborer on a steamboat. In a few months, with the aid of a forged pass provided by an unnamed white man, he was able to make his first escape from slavery, crossing the several hundred miles of rural Louisiana plantation country to Camden, Arkansas. Inexplicably, Gaines left Camden after six months and returned to New Orleans, where he was discovered and returned to his master. In 1859 he was sold again; this time to a trader bound for Texas. The Texas planter who bought him was Christopher Columbus Hearne, one of the wealthiest and most respected cotton planters on the Brazos. Gaines worked on one of the Hearne plantations in Robertson County until 1863, when he made another escape attempt. This time his goal was Mexico. Again, he got through the plantation country somehow and made it as far west as abandoned Fort McKavett in Menard County. He was caught by a company of Rangers, who were using old Camp San Saba as a base for their frontier operations, and sent back as far as Fredericksburg, under guard. He stayed in that area for the remainder of the Civil War; no attempt seems to have been made to return him to Robertson County. Although ostensibly still a slave and under arrest, Gaines had considerable freedom of movement and worked as a blacksmith and a sheepherder. After the war he migrated back to the familiar Brazos bottomland, settling eventually in the community of Burton in western Washington County.[15]

Except for this general outline, Gaines was uncharacteristically silent on the details of his life in slavery. He bitterly assailed the institution, in general terms, both at home and in the pulpit, but he said little that could be recalled by his sons about his personal experiences. As a legislator, he rarely referred to his former status, but the few statements he did make reveal the intensity of his feelings.

One example is the following excerpt from an 1871 speech:

> When I study the laws of 1856 and 7, I can't be a
> Democrat. I can remember when old Master gave me 500 lashes
> and said he only raised the ashes on me, and next time he would
> reach the clean dirt. And when they could brand me with the
> letter C, and the Democrats made these laws, and would not
> open the school house door to us and we had to ask leave to
> marry and get a pass to go a half a mile, and if it was not spelt
> out all grammerly [*sic*] the patrollers would whip you for that.[16]

Other statements indicate that he was a field slave rather than a house
servant or skilled craftsman.[17] One additional story of Gaines's experiences in bondage has survived, one which suggests that his
preaching predated Reconstruction. He often told his wife and
children, much to their amusement, of disguising himself as a
woman—replete with dress and sunbonnet—so that he could drive a
buckboard to nearby plantations to preach, without being stopped by
the patrollers.[18] He was able to carry out his ruse because, according
to several accounts, he was a very small man—slender and scarcely
over five feet in height.[19] Perhaps it was because of the oratorical skill
that he gained as a slave preacher and the prestige which the black
community customarily accorded its lay ministers that Gaines was
able to quickly build up a following in Washington County.

In 1867 Gaines married for the first time, under a license issued
to Matt C. Despallier and Fanny Sutton. Like the minister who married them, Gaines functioned in the Burton area as an effective but
untrained lay preacher of the Baptist church. Although this union
with Fanny Sutton was short-lived and they were living apart by 1869,
he was as shocked and surprised as the man who performed their marriage ceremony when the visiting bishop told the lay preachers that all
baptisms and marriages they had performed before ordination were
invalid and would have to be repeated. After the bishop's visit,
Gaines and most of the blacks in Burton considered his marriage to
Fanny Sutton Gaines null and void.[20] When he married a second
time, in 1870 to Elizabeth Harrison, Gaines guilelessly applied for
and was issued a license in nearby Fayette County, without having
been officially divorced—a set of circumstances which would later
result in a very damaging bigamy trial.

In 1869, however, Gaines's political star was just beginning to rise. The first official mention of him as a political activist appeared in the Houston *Union* in 1869. A Brenham correspondent reported that "[Edmund] Davis will carry the county easy. We have Matt. Gaines on the war path, and he is doing good work."[21] No mention was made of Gaines's own candidacy for the state senate in this or intervening issues, but three months later the same paper reported that the Radical faction of the Republican party had easily carried Washington County and that Matthew Gaines had been elected to the senate by a two to one margin over his closest contender.[22] The contender was also a black, G. O. Watrous. Gaines's election over Watrous is an early indication of his appeal to black voters in the area, for Watrous was well known, having represented Washington County in the Constitutional Convention of 1868-1869.[23]

Gaines's election to the state senate occurred in one of the most chaotic political periods in the state's history. In 1869 four distinct groups were struggling for political ascendancy: the Independent Conservatives, the Democrats, the Moderate Republicans, and the Radical Republicans. In addition, internecine quarrels constantly raged within each of these factions. When the Twelfth Legislature convened in January, 1870, the Independent Conservatives and the Democrats were already beginning to combine forces in a fusion movement to "redeem" the state. The Republicans had a majority, but the Radicals could not depend upon the moderate and conservative wings of their party to support many of their most vital programs.[24] In the senate there was almost a balance between the Republicans, on the one hand, and the Democrats and Independent Conservatives, on the other. Therefore, when Moderate Republicans opposed the Radicals on an issue, the balance was broken in favor of the Conservative-Democratic coalition. In the House the Republican majority was about ten votes.[25] Gaines was elected to a body which, for three years, was a constant scene of bitter partisan and factional strife.

In 1870 Gaines was one of two black senators and eleven representatives seated in the Twelfth Legislature; Texas had one of the smallest percentages of Negroes elected to legislatures of reconstructed states.[26] The other black state senator was George T. Ruby. Both Gaines and Ruby were effective, but their backgrounds and careers were very dissimilar. Gaines, as noted earlier, was a self-taught former slave. Ruby had been a northern, urban, free black before the war; he was a light-skinned mulatto born in New York City in 1841 and reared and educated in Maine. Before coming South in 1864 to serve as a traveling agent and principal in the schools of the Louisiana Freedman's Bureau, he served as a correspondent in Haiti for James Redpath's Boston-based immigrationist journal *Pine and Palm*. He came to Texas in 1866, settling in Galveston, and was subsequently elected from the predominatly white Galveston district to the Constitutional Convention of 1868-1869, where he became a staunch supporter of Edmund J. Davis's Radical faction, a loyalty from which he never swerved. In 1869 he was elected to the senate, where his educated manner and personal qualities of tact and diplomacy won him the respect of his party colleagues and many political opponents as well.[27]

Eleven black representatives also served: Mitchell Kendall, Henry Moore, Richard Allen, Goldstein Dupree, John Mitchell, Silas J. (Giles) Cotton, Sheppard Mullens, B. F. Williams, R. Williams, J. J. Hamilton, and David Medlock.[28] All identified themselves as Radicals and voted accordingly. Perhaps the most able was Richard Allen, representing the Fourteenth District. Allen was brought as a slave from Virginia to Texas a decade before the war. A skilled builder and designer, Allen and his master settled in Harris County; after emancipation he became a successful bridge contractor and minor public official. Allen was one of the original Davis faction who bolted the regular Republican Convention in 1869.[29] Another of the bolting Radicals who became a state representative was Sheppard Mullens, also a delegate to the 1868-1869 Constitutional Convention. He was one of the most promising of the black representatives but died in office and was not replaced.[30] B. F. Williams, originally a Virginia slave, came the closest of all thirteen black legislators to being elected to a major office in the Twelfth Legislature. He was nominated for Speaker of the House and placed third in a field of eight. Williams, too, had some political experience, as a delegate to the Constitutional Covention and as a participant in the Davis rump convention.[31]

Not enough reliable research has been done on all the individual black legislators of Texas to provide the necessary information for a composite biography. However, from available data on six of the legislators, it appears that Gaines is fairly typical in his background. Gaines, Allen, Moore, and B. F. Williams were all Southern-born former slaves, although Moore purchased his freedom before coming to Texas. Only Gaines, of the four, migrated to Texas from a southern state after the war. Ruby and Kendall were both northern-born (Kendall was born in Illinois) and both came to Texas after 1865. Ruby was the only member of the group known to have received a formal education. Occupationally, they were diverse. Two were skilled workers—Allen had been a slave engineer and Kendall, a free blacksmith. Moore's slave occupation is unknown, but he was regarded as one of his master's "choice men" and probably either occupied a managerial position or was a skilled worker. Both Williams and Gaines appear to have been field slaves. Gaines was the only black legislator in Texas known to have been a slave preacher.[32]

Because Gaines's background was not notably different from that of several of his fellow black solons, his divergent actions and attitudes seem the more extraordinary. Unlike most of his black colleagues in the legislature who performed their duties quietly and rather subserviently, Gaines made it clear in his first year in office that he would not be a passive legislator and acquiescent party man. He early viewed himself as a spokesman for the black masses, becoming an active participant in debate and a constant inquirer into the motives of his fellow senators. He developed a critical, emotional, and apocalyptic style in politics. He soon gained powerful enemies in the senate, while attracting a vocal and loyal following among his black constituents.

An early indication of Gaines's interests and style as a legislator was provided by his actions in a contested election case in the senate in May, 1870, when Radical M. Peterson challenged the seat of conservative Democrat E. L. Dohoney.[33] Gaines used the rather insignificant case as a vehicle , first, to challenge the credibility of influential Moderate Republican Webster Flanagan and, second, to raise the issue of black voter intimidation. On the day that the hearing was scheduled, Webb Flanagan moved for a postponement because of the absence, allegedly due to illness, of a Democratic senator, M. H. Bowers. Gaines, in objecting to the delay, claimed that the case had been pending for weeks and that there would "always be another sick Democrat" to indefinitely postpone the proceedings.[34] By his inferences that Flanagan's motion was inspired by political sympathy for Democrat Dohoney, Gaines was, in effect, challenging the legitimacy of Flanagan's republicanism. Flanagan, whose family's wealth and power were well-known, was indignant. He accused Gaines of "exhibiting the craven" in daring to question his motives, adding that he had been a Republican before the Negro senator had known "there was such a party."[35] Undaunted, Gaines used the same case to make an impassioned denunciation of black voter intimidation during the 1869 election. He described such an incident in Doheney's Lamar County district and told of similar incidents in his own district where "colored men [were told] that if they voted for Davis . . . and Gaines . . . they would have to go to Davis for employment and Gaines for protection."[36] The speech evolved into a general indictment of Democrats throughout the state who had practiced fraud, harassment, and violence against black voters; he condemned as well the Conservative and Moderate Republicans who, he believed, had sanctioned the persecution of his people. The speech, typical of Gaines's developing oratorical style, ended on a militant note, as he reminded his party colleagues that they were elected by Negroes who were in some cases killed as a result of their voting. To these Republicans who now showed little interest in the protection of the Negro voter, he gave warning: "I will remember [you] in the days to come."[37] The caustic remarks were followed by cheers and applause from the gallery of the senate chamber.

Gaines was not simply dealing in political invective or capitalizing on a dramatic issue in his remarks; voter intimidation was a critical problem for Texas blacks throughout the Reconstruction era. Black voters were threatened, injured, and even killed during the 1869 election campaign, and the harassment continued unchecked until the state was "redeemed" in the fall elections of 1873.[38] Without federal assistance and with a legislature divided on the issue, Governor Davis's efforts to prevent unfair voting practices were basically limited to the support of rather innocuous election laws, the use of handpicked Republican registrars, and the employment of a peacekeeping force of special policemen at polling places. In the eastern portion of the state, however, the Conservative-Democrat coalition had gained sufficient control by fall, 1871, to violate the governor's directive and appoint their own white, Democratic special policemen to oversee elections.[39] Throughout the state, from 1869 on, a wide range of techniques of intimidation, from subtle psychological and economic pressures to violence, was used to influence or prevent black voting. The extent and variety of such techniques can be seen in the scores of letters and affidavits of Texas freedmen which are enclosed with the election returns, 1870-1874, in the Texas State Library.[40] Statements made under oath before county clerks are vivid evidence of the difficulties encountered by black voters even when the administration proved sympathetic.

Concern for the safety of Texas freedmen was also evident in Gaines's vigorous support of strong militia and police laws in 1870. Governor Davis, concerned about the rising crime rate and the inadequacies of local law enforcement, recommended the organization of two racially integrated forces: a general militia to be called up in periods of "extreme emergencies" and a mobile and semiautonomous state police force to deal with individual lawbreakers.[41] Gaines championed both the militia and the police bills. In the senate debates of early summer, 1870, he engaged in constant dialogue with Democratic, Conservative, and Moderate Republican opponents of the bills. One of the most dramatic exchanges of the session took place between Gaines and Moderate Republican B. J. Pridgen on July 17. Speaking on behalf of the stronger House version of the militia bill, Gaines claimed that racism, not centralization, was at the root of conservative opposition. He said, "It is not so much the idea of placing . . . great power in the hands of the executive, but it is the idea of gentlemen of my color being armed" that is so repugnant. In ironic rebuttal to critics of the bill who appealed to the romantic image of the fallen South in their arguments, Gaines said,

> the dead spirits of those who were massacred at Fort Pillow will also rise if this bill does not pass . . . [for] this is a new day . . . the old corruption of the Confederacy was buried at the surrender of General Lee.[42]

Pridgen responded by ridiculing Gaines's "theatrical mode" and "earnest gesticulations," suggesting that Gaines in his ignorance had "revealed [the militia bill's] hideous proportions and monstrous design."[43] Gaines had clearly added another powerful enemy among the ranks of the Moderate and Conservative members of his party.

Gaines's concern was not limited to his black constituency. Like so many Negro legislators of the Radical period, he demonstrated an interest in bills promoting the general welfare. In his first year as senator, for example, he spoke out strongly in favor of frontier defense, although few blacks inhabited the southern and western portions of the state. The occasion was the debate on the frontier defense bill to which an amendment was sought by the conservatives which would reduce the salaries of the frontier forces by half and probably render them inoperative. He voted against the amendment with the following remarks:

> I am astonished to think that this Legislature has been here for such a period of time without passing any laws that will protect the people on the frontiers . . . I know the price of the lives of the people of the West. I feel the interest of the people of Texas. Let me tell Republicans that they will have to wake up out of their drowsy sleep . . . and speedily legislate for the benefit of the people at large in this state.[44]

By the end of 1870, the freshmen senator from Washington County had attracted considerable attention. His critical approach to men and issues had antagonized many of his senate colleagues, but he was not yet considered a serious political threat. In his first year, he had confined most of his activities to the senate, and he had acted primarily as a critic rather than as an initiator of action. In 1871, however, he became embroiled in controversy after controversy as he moved into the wider circle of state politics and began to emerge as a black leader.

In the spring of 1871, Gaines gained statewide notoriety as an advocate of black immigration to Texas. The desirability of increased immigration was recognized by almost all classes in the state, and the Radical administration, seizing upon a unifying issue, had recommended the creation of a Bureau of Immigration. What they had in mind, of course, was white immigration, and a bill was proposed in 1871 creating such an agency and providing for agents in the northern United States, western Europe, and the British Isles to encourage immigration to the state.[45] Gaines considered the bill discriminatory since no agents were to be stationed in areas of the world inhabited primarily by dark-skinned peoples. To point up its prejudicial nature, he offered on April 11, 1871, an amendment which would provide an agent to encourage immigration to Texas from Africa.[46] The amendment was voted down by an eighteen-to-four vote, with Gaines's only black colleague, G. T. Ruby, voting against.[47] In May, Gaines introduced another bill—one designed to encourage immigration to the state from the southern United States and aimed at the mobile freedman population. Apparently, it never got out of committee.[48] Old fears of black domination came to the surface as the conservative Texas populace reacted to the proposals with predictable shock. Major newspapers aggravated these fears by tying Gaines's support of African and American black immigration to a controversy in which he had been involved with the German-American faction in his Third Congressional District.

Gaines's conflict with the German faction antedated his amendment by several months. In a February, 1871, speech, he had chided local German-Americans for not utilizing their considerable ethnic strength through bloc voting, as had the blacks. He was reported to have said that because of black bloc voting, "the Republican Party was a Black man's party; and that the white members of the Radical party would not elect a flea."[49]

Gaines denied that he had made the statement, but the Brenham *Banner* claimed that "at least fifty of our German citizens" could attest that it was accurately reported.[50] By July the large newspapers had picked up the issue. The Houston *Times* claimed that in a July speech in Brenham Gaines had become "very abusive of the Germans, declaring that it was a sin to have power and not to use it."[51] The Dallas *Herald* reported that Gaines, in the same speech, "pledged himself to initiate an immigration from Africa that will neutralize the German power." The article equated his criticism of the German-Americans for not using their political potential with a general ethnic prejudice:

> The [anti-German] sentiment is not a new one, and all reading Germans must have observed the jealousy and suspicion with which they are regarded by the colored people of the state.[52]

By August the press had become virulent in its condemnation of Gaines. One editor called him "an ignorant and arrogant ass" and

"an uneducated cornfield Negro who accidentally got into a prominent State office"; "respectable" Germans were advised to ignore
him.[53] Another paper urged "every German citizen to vote against
any and every body who has anything to do with Matt Gaines."[54] The
motives behind such news items appeared to be, first, to discourage
German-Americans from voting with the Radical faction of the party
and, second, to discourage them from voting for black candidates.

Gaines's motives for stirring up the controversy in the first place
probably had little to do with anti-German prejudice. At this point
he had a rather naive and exaggerated conception of the potential influence of mass voting by sizable minorities. He thought that black
voting coupled with another large minority such as the German-
Americans would provide the Radicals with a power base secure
enough to offset the growing strength of the conservative coalition.
He also thought that such a combination might be able to exert
pressure on the Radical leadership in regard to policy-making and offices.

Second, Gaines was undoubtedly disappointed, as were many
blacks, that so many German-Americans, who had been courageously
against slavery and opposed to secession—and often were pro-
Unionist during the conflict—now seemed to turn their backs on the
political and social aspirations of the blacks. Probably a typical attitude of a white, Moderate Republican German-American was that
of Galveston editor Ferdinand Flake, who said in 1871 that although
he supported Negro suffrage, he disapproved of the Negro's efforts to
"offensively intrude himself into the white man's house, the white
man's carriage, the white man's social enjoyment" and the white
man's offices.[55]

Another controversial issue in which Gaines figured in 1871 was
that of public education for all races. The state constitution of 1869
had recommended free public schools for all Texas children; it was
the task of the Twelfth Legislature to overcome not only the prejudice
against Negro education but also the prejudice against compulsory
education of any kind—and to pass the implementing legislation.[56]
An inoperable free school bill had been passed in 1870, but the first
strong school bill was introduced by the Radicals in February, 1871.[57]
Before its final passage, the legislative chambers rang with debate,
much of it centering around the questions of Negro education and in-

tegrated classrooms; Matthew Gaines was one of the most active defenders of both.

Like so many freedmen, Gaines had great respect for education, viewing it as a key to the progress of his race. It is therefore not surprising that he would react strongly to attempts by conservative legislators to curtail educational benefits for blacks. During the 1871 school debates, he had a memorable exchange with two conservative colleagues, one a powerful Democrat, J. E. Dillard, and the other, an old Republican foe, Webb Flanagan.[58] After hearing for days their harangue on the evils of integrated classrooms, Gaines told them that if they objected to whites sitting next to blacks, they should resign their posts and go home, adding that he did not particularly enjoy fraternizing with them, either.[59]

Not all Republicans were as bold as Gaines, and the comprehensive free public school bill which passed was silent on the subject of integration.[60] With Radical sanction the bill was locally interpreted as providing for separate free schools for black and white children.[61] Segregated public education never satisfied Gaines, and in the summer of 1871 he criticized the Radical measure in a frank statement which also hinted at the most deep-rooted of all southern taboos—miscegenation.

> They talk about separating them. It can't be done. They are of all shades of color, and there is no dividing line, and my children have the right to sit by the best man's daughter in the land. [A]nd if they ain't together in the day, they will run together at night.[62]

He also urged parents to make a test case, saying ''send your children to any of the free schools you want to; go and attend yourselves, and see who puts them out; let me know who tries it.''[63] If such a test case was made, no mention of it appeared in the Republican press. Despite his reservations he supported the free school program which, by fall of 1872, had over two thousand schools in operation with an enrollment of 55 percent of the scholastic population; many children of poor whites as well as blacks were attending school for the first time. The program achieved this limited but heartening success despite many obstacles: the difficulty of finding qualified teachers, public suspicion of compulsory education, hostility of the propertied classes toward the 1 percent school tax, and racial prejudice which led to the burning of Negro schools and the intimidation of teachers of black children.[64]

Gaines continued to be concerned about the integration of transportation facilities as well, and in September, 1871, he introduced an equal accommodations bill.[65] It did not pass, but like his African immigration amendment, it demonstrated his perception as a social and political critic.

In the late summer of 1871, he reached the peak of his political career. Democrats in his home district had begun planning strategy to quiet him through using the courts, and he had developed formidable enemies among the leadership of the Conservative Republicans. Now he would also antagonize the Radical hierarchy, and by late fall all the major political factions had turned against him, fearful of his influence among Texas blacks, his political ambitions, his growing militancy, and his political independence. The issue which would complete the estrangement between Gaines and the state's political power structure was that of black officeholding.

The paucity of blacks in major offices remains a controversial aspect of the Radicals' record in Texas and in most of the other reconstructed states; the charges of tokenism and opportunism—in different terminology—were leveled as often against the Radical Republicans as they would be against their political counterparts nearly a century later. Not a single major state office or congressional post was held by a Negro during the Davis administration, although many local offices—both appointive and elective—were filled with blacks.

One of the most important of the elective offices held by a black was that of the district clerkship of Galveston. Johnson Reed, the candidate of the Loyal Union League, won over candidates sponsored by the local bar association and the Knights of the White Camellia, both whites, of course, after a bitterly racist campaign. On the last day of the election, as Reed began to pull ahead, Galveston papers assumed a hysterical tone; two items appearing separately in the *Tri-Weekly News* are fairly representative of media response to black candidates:

> In a few hours . . . the fate of our county will be sealed, either with an intelligent citizen or with a carpet-bag ignorant negro

filling the most important office we have.

The reputation of Galveston county is at stake. The first city of Texas must not be cursed with this prowling vagabond from Oberlin . . . . It would . . . justly exposed us to the ridicule . . . of the whole state.[66]

Other elective offices held by blacks during the Radical administration include those of sheriffs, justices of the peace, and at least one inspector of hides and animals.[67] Black officeholders were often resented. The white citizens of Fort Bend County eventually accommodated themselves to black sheriff Walter Burton, an unusually capable man who was later elected to the Texas senate, but at first there was determined opposition to him. Threats and general lawlessness prompted him to request the governor to declare martial law in his county in 1871. Likewise, in 1872 a mob attack on the Negro inspector of hides and animals, Edward Hee, was brought to the governor's attention.[68]

More numerous than elective offices held by Negroes were the appointive posts, at least on the local level. Probably the most influential appointment was that of supervisor of education for the Seventh District (Waco), a post held by Thomas Ford, whose appointment the *Semi-Weekly Examiner* called "an insult to the people of the whole state."[69] Several blacks were appointed as county registrars, many having similar experiences to those of the Reverend Mr. Monroe Wilson, who performed his official duties during the critical October election of 1871. Fear for his life prompted him to resign shortly thereafter.[70] Davis appointed several black justices of the peace, such as John de Bruhl in Galveston County, and minor municipal offices such as city aldermen and commissioners were often filled with Negroes in the Black Belt counties.[71]

Despite these appointments, many blacks were disappointed with the limited political role allowed them. Although there is little concrete evidence of widespread disenchantment among Texas blacks, a small group of politically ambitious black men were highly critical of the Radical hierarchy's dispensation of offices and influence. The leader of these advocates for more and better offices for qualified blacks was Senator Matthew Gaines.

The controversy over black officeholding climaxed in the summer of 1871 during the campaign for the Republican congressional nomination in the Third District. Two Radicals were already engaged in bitter competition for the nomination when the picture was further complicated by announcements of two black candidates: a respected minister, Israel Campbell, and a Galveston justice of the peace and editor, Richard Nelson.[72] Nelson, who was Gaines's choice, conducted a vigorous campaign based on black solidarity. Both blacks were sent as delegates to the Houston nominating convention to continue their efforts. The Radicals, however, were determined to elect their incumbent congressman, William T. Clark, and the convention was a farce. According to a preconceived strategy, the Davis Radicals denied admittance to some twenty to thirty legitimate delegates known to favor the nomination of another white candidate, Louis Stevenson, or a black contender.[73] A rival meeting was held nearby where Israel Campbell withdrew in favor of Stevenson.[74] Gaines stayed with the main body, still hoping to win support for a black candidate. But in the regular meeting, which came to be known as the Clark Padlock Convention, Nelson's sponsors were not recognized, and his name was not put into nomination. Party regulars gave George T. Ruby the honor of a token nomination (which he predictably and modestly declined), but the gesture was made only after Clark had been renominated in glowing terms. In a surprise move from the convention floor, black delegate Fred Lumpkin interrupted the proceedings and nominated Representative Richard Allen, whose candidacy Gaines fully endorsed.[75] When the resulting vote overwhelmingly favored Clark, Lumpkin and Gaines denounced the convention for its arbitrary proceedings and its failure to nominate a black candidate.[76]

In the weeks following the Padlock Convention, Gaines publicly condemned Radical leaders for spurning potential black candidates. Two days after the meeting, he urged blacks in his district to ignore the party's white nominee and follow him in supporting a black man of their choice, saying "now is the time to try their faith and see what they will do. My people say a colored man and so do I."[77] A week later he appeared at a mass meeting of blacks which had been advertised as a Clark ratification meeting. Washington County party officials had arranged for several speakers to make addresses in Clark's behalf, and since Gaines's endorsement was especially sought, he was scheduled to make a major speech. With his usual dramatic flair, Gaines came late, and his tumultuous reception by an estimated three thousand blacks completely drowned out the Clark speaker, who reluctantly relinquished the platform. Gaines thanked the crowd for coming to the festivities in his honor, and instead of endorsing Clark, he delivered a thundering attack on Democrats and Radicals alike as exploiters of the black people, pledging to organize black strength to "prevent any more bought up and packed conventions." "We are entitled to the candidate," he shouted. "Shall we turn the mill forever and somebody else eat the meal?"[78] His mass appeal was apparent in his reception; his growing militancy was equally obvious in such excerpts from his speech as the following:

> I have heard that the Democrats have threatened to kill me. They may kill me but I pray that if they do that you who are present today will take seven fold vengeance for me. The Democrats seem to want to fight . . . . There is no better time than this. We will arm our old women with axes and hoes and our young men with double barrel guns and clean them up as easy as we outvoted them in the last election.[79]

Such remarks, delivered in Gaines's emotional manner to a surging crowd of several thousand freedmen, must have sent cold shivers up the spines of every Democrat within hearing distance.

The rebellious actions of Gaines and the Galveston officeholder politicians during and following the Houston convention brought no less a person than Governor Edmund Davis to Washington and Galveston counties in mid-August. According to news accounts of the Galveston appearance, the governor failed to salve the wounds inflicted at Houston. When Davis spoke of Clark as the legitimate Republican nominee, he was interrupted by loud cries of protest from the crowded Negro gallery. When he asked the body to vote for Clark, Frank Webb, a black editor, answered with a resoundingly audible "No!" Ruby, who accompanied Davis on the political canvass and was acting as sergeant at arms, ordered Webb's immediate arrest, but Davis, obviously shaken, told him to leave the defiant blacks alone.[80] Still, the faction of the black community with which Davis had lost favor must have been relatively small because he was warmly received by blacks even in Brenham, the heart of Gaines's district. While Democratic hecklers prevented Davis from finishing his speech there, throngs of Negroes of all ages gathered at the railroad station to see him depart, cheering and holding up their children to get a glimpse of the governor of the state.[81]

Unappeased by the governor's mission and angered by indictments of his motives in the Radical press, Gaines made the most inflammatory speech of his career just prior to the October election. Speaking before the senate, he accused the Radical elite of being "as dishonest as they are powerful" and "of using their official positions to enslave the . . . blacks through their ignorance of politics and their faith in the Republican Party." He said that Davis and his "corrupt ring" had "set themselves up as the BIG GODS of the negroes" and they expected "worship, offices, money and power . . . while deep . . . in their hearts they despise us." He charged Davis and other Radical leaders with destroying the party and claimed that because he was true to himself and his constituents and "refused to accept the Governor as God, he was to be read out of the party."[82] It was true that since the Houston meeting the Davis faction had begun to regard Gaines as a political liability, but after this scathing attack on the floor of the senate, the break was complete. After October, Gaines was a permanent exile from his party.

Another blow to his prestige came two months later when, on December 9, 1871, he was indicted on a charge of bigamy by the grand jury at La Grange. He was released on one-thousand-dollar bail, and his case was set for the following May.[83] He was able to postpone his trial by filing repeated petitions to have his case transferred to a federal court; the basis of his petition was that his civil rights as guaranteed by the Civil Rights Act of 1866 were being denied. The district judge was not convinced that Gaines could not receive "full and equal protection" in a state court, however, and the petition was denied.[84] While under indictment he remained politically active, completing his term in the Twelfth Legislature and serving in the brief Thirteenth Legislature.[85]

His case finally came to trial on July 15, 1873. The jury, composed of eleven whites and one black, heard testimony that marriage licenses had been issued to Matt G. Despallier and Fanny Sutton in 1867 and to Matt Gaines and Elizabeth Harrison in 1870, without a divorce having taken place.[86] The defense called several witnesses, including the minister who performed the original ceremony, who testified that the first marriage was thought to have been illegally performed. The jury found Gaines guilty, and he was sentenced to one year of hard labor in the state penitentiary.[87] While awaiting the outcome of his appeal, however, he was held in the Fayette County jail.[88] Gaines's conviction was triumphantly reported in local newspapers. The Brenham *Banner* exulted "that the late so-called Negro senator from Washington County . . . is now enjoying the hospitalities of the Sheriff of Fayette County, where he is detained as a convict."[89] The *Fayette County New Era* reported that Gaines's senate career was over and that the next seat the senator would occupy would be in the Huntsville prison.[90] Gaines's popularity with his old constituency did not diminsh while he was in jail awaiting appeal, for on July 19, the Austin *Statesman* reported that it was rumored that the "irresponsible, rip-snorting Matt. Gaines" was being talked about as a possible candidate for governor.[91]

On November 24, 1873, the Texas Supreme Court reversed the findings of the district court and reprimanded the judge for denying Gaines's petition for transfer to a federal court.[92] Although the Texas Supreme Court's decision is a matter of public record, Gaines continued to be referred to as a convicted felon who had somehow evaded serving his sentence.[93]

Four months after the decision, Gaines was reelected to the senate of the Thirteenth Legislature over a white Democratic candidate, Seth Shepard. One of the few black legislators of the Radical period to be returned in that election,[94] Gaines was given the certificate of election, but his seat was challenged by Shepard, who contended that Gaines was a convicted felon and ineligible for the office.[95] Gaines was neither represented by counsel nor given an opportunity to testify before the senate committee on privileges and elections, the chairman of which was one of his old political enemies, J. E. Dillard.[96] On March 25 the chairman reported that Gaines was ineligible and recommended that Shepard be seated as the eligible candidate receiving the highest number of votes.[97] The senate accepted the recommendation and seated Shepard.[98] The full report of the committee is not in the State Archives and presumably was destroyed. With his seat denied and without the political connections to fight the decision, Matthew Gaines's career was over.[99] And with the Bourbon Democrats in full control of the state machinery after 1874, further political aspirations for a black politician as militant as he were hopeless.

Gaines was only in his early thirties when he was ousted from the senate, but in the next twenty-six years he virtually dropped from public knowledge. Local newspapers rarely reported his activities. A few items appeared in the 1870s, such as in 1875, when he was arrested for making civil rights speeches in Giddings. The Brenham *Banner* said that Gaines was attempting to organize local blacks into a secret society "for the purpose of making as much trouble as possible between them and the white people." The same paper continued, "Matt's little black hide is stretched tight over a bundle of nefarious meanness, and he will not fail to avail himself of such a splendid opportunity as the Civil Rights bill offers for getting his black bretheren into trouble."[100] And in 1878 the *Banner* reported that Gaines was urging local blacks to support only black candidates for office and to ignore political affiliations.[101]

Except for such occasional comments picked up by the local paper, Gaines's political activities were ended, without even the shaky vehicle of the Republican party to sustain him. After 1875 his life can be described as that of the prototypal rural black minister who shared the isolation and poverty of his congregation and attempted to keep up its spirit during the dark years of increased segregation in the last quarter of the nineteenth century. The several members of his congregation who survived in 1970 remembered him as a wizened little man looking older than his middle years, who habitually wore a black suit and black skull cap. He taught the youngsters' Sunday School, and former pupils remembered that he had constantly reminded them of their worth and dignity as a people. Mrs. Ida Wade said that he told them that although they had to work as white men's servants, they were really only the servants of God. She said, "Old man Gaines made no exceptions when he spoke about people's rights."[102]

But it was at the annual Juneteenth (June 19, 1865, was the date that General Granger read the Emancipation Proclamation in Texas) celebrations that Gaines exhibited a spark of his old fire. According to Mrs. Alice White Wornley, the celebrations—all-day picnic affairs—were held in the next county, on the Brazos River bottom, far from the eyes of curious whites. Here, the Reverend Mr. Gaines would hold forth for hours on political as well as religious themes, always ending with the assurance that, in the eyes of God, black men and women were as good and well loved as any white, exhorting them to hold up their heads with pride, even in troubled times.[103] Here, in the rich and sleepy bottomlands which in many respects closely resembled the geographic area of his birth, Gaines's oratory still exerted a certain magic; as a charismatic black preacher rather than as a political figure, he may have entered the folklore of the Giddings area. One story is told of how Gaines got the nickname "waterduck."

It seems that Gaines had a local reputation for his prophetic abilities as well as for an ability to bring rain through the power of his prayer and preaching. During a debilitating drought, white farmers in the Giddings area promised to build Gaines a permanent church if he could "preach down the rain." The proposal was especially attractive to Gaines, for while he preached at several little churches in the area, at Giddings he preached only from an arbor in his yard. Soon after, cooling rains drenched the Giddings farmlands, and he did eventually receive a small white frame church (a Baptist church called Saint Paul's Chapel) courtesy of local white farmers. From that time on, Gaines was teasingly called the "waterduck" by his congregation.[104]

The Gaines family was large and close. The two children of his first marriage, Matthew, Jr., and Margaret, maintained contact with their half brothers and sisters long after their father's death. Gaines's children of his second marriage, that to the patient, good-natured Elizabeth Harrison Gaines included six boys (John, Leandra, Levater, Aaron, Robert, and Nathaniel) and two girls (Minnie and Ella; the latter died as a young girl). Robert, seven when his father died, remembered that his father often took the younger children with him when he traveled around the area preaching. He also has a vivid memory of the public hanging of a black man, Oscar Hennigan, in Giddings. The boy attended the hanging with Gaines, who led onlookers in a prayer for the man's soul. Robert said that of all the children, his brother John, who had also been a minister, was most like the father, intelligent and "not afraid to speak out." Neither Robert nor Leandra could recall that their parents owned any property to speak of, and a neighbor said that Gaines "lived in a shack like the rest of us." The last twenty-six years of Gaines's life was the poor, rural, hardworking existence of the great majority of his people at the turn of the century.[105]

Gaines died on June 11, 1900; it was said that two months before he had predicted his own death. According to his son Leandra, who was thirteen at the time, Gaines died of an abscessed liver. A long procession of mourners, riding horses or mules or walking, followed the wagon which carried his body to the colored section of the town cemetery, a few miles east of Giddings. Matthew Gaines was buried there in an unmarked grave.[106] At his death he had few possessions. One, his collection of old, leather-bound law books inscribed with his name, survived another generation but were eventually lost or destroyed, according to his granddaughter who handled them with awe as a young girl. Today, only three items once belonging to Gaines remain in the family: a faint photograph, a set of cuff links, and a small gold tie pin engraved with his initials and the date of his senate term.[107]

Most Texans today—black or white—have never heard of Matthew Gaines; probably a majority of the state's historians have not, either, for even more than other black legislators, he has been omitted from the general histories. How do you gauge the importance of such a man? In terms of the power and influence he wielded in his party and within the legislature, his career was insignificant. He was never a nationally known figure comparable to Hiram Revels or John Lynch of Mississippi, Robert Smalls of South Carolina, P. B. S. Pinchback of Louisiana, or even Norris Wright Cuney of Texas, a few years later.[108] In fact, there is little evidence that he was ever known outside the confines of Texas politics. He succeeded in forcing few concessions from the state powers, and in the halls of the senate, he had no important backers, not even his fellow black senator. But in writing the history of the common people, one cannot use the usual gauges of accomplishment—power, riches, or the creation of great and lasting deeds. One has to consider not only how far a person went but how far he came. In understanding a man such as Gaines, one has to realize that his vision was as important as his achievement. In another time, another place, his ideas may have taken root; his tactics may have worked. He tried to bring about a "new day" for Texas and his people. That he failed is unimportant in measuring the man.

In terms of his vision, his proposals, his criticisms, Gaines—in retrospect—can be viewed as one of the most farsighted of Reconstruction legislators. At a time when many able black lawmakers were magnanimously proposing resolutions for the relief of their former masters, he was arguing for a strong, mobile state police with black members to prevent voter intimidation and general lawlessness. At a time when most other black legislators were satisfied with a statewide, free, but segregated system of public schools, he cried out against the hypocrisy of separate and equal and demanded the right for his children to sit next to white children in the free schools of the state. He urged blacks in his district to mobilize their voting strength and to obtain as much political independence as possible in order to influence both issues and the choice of candidates; at that time most black legislators were loyal party men who accepted the white Radicals' guidance in matters of issues and candidates. He saw in 1871 the possibilities of black power and the error of segregation; he deplored bigotry, whether in formulation of immigration policies or in the manning of law enforcement bodies; he rejected paternalism in government whether it came from Democrats or Radical Republicans. He was honest—as were most of his fellow black legislators—but he cared less than most of them for image and respectability; his "honesty" was highly vocal and often embarrassing for his colleagues.

Despite his omission from published histories, Matthew Gaines is not entirely forgotten: read the debates of the Twelfth Legislature and the man and the era will come rushing back to life. Read his words, and you will almost be able to see the intense young black, noticeable in the sea of white faces on the floor of the Texas senate, thundering out his challenges and issuing his scathing criticisms.

NOTES

1. G. T. Ruby in *State Journal Appendix Containing Official Report of the Debates and Proceedings of the Twelfth Legislature of the State of Texas* (Austin, 1870), 91 (hereafter cited as *Debates of the Twelfth Legislature*).

2. Matthew Gaines, *Debates of the Twelfth Legislature*, 83.

3. Ludwell H. Johnson, *Red River Campaign: Politics and Cotton in the Civil War* (Baltimore, 1958), 269-273; *State of Texas* v. *Matthew Gaines*, Statement of Facts, Testimony of M. G. Turner, July 24, 1873, M6816 (hereafter cited as *State* v.

Gaines). District court records pertaining to Gaines's trial were transferred to the Texas Supreme Court, Austin, Texas.

Almost all public documents dealing with local slaves, such as probated wills, sales records, transfers of land and property titles, were destroyed when Alexandria, Louisiana (Gaines's birthplace), seat of Rapides Parish, was burned by Federal forces in 1864. The story of Gaines's early years is still incomplete, but some of it was pieced together from myriad sources: field trips, interviews, trial testimony, slave censuses, and family lore and legend, among others. As a result my respect for orally transmitted history grew. In numerous instances members of Gaines's family or friends provided bits of information which I was later able to substantiate from documentary evidence unavailable to the informants.

4. *Gaines* v. *State* (607), Affidavit of Matthew Gaines, Dec. 16, 1872, in *Cases Argued and Decided in the Supreme Court of the State of Texas,* XXXIX (St. Louis, 1875, 1882), 529 (hereafter cited as *Gaines* v. *State*—Supreme Court). Also see J. Mason Brewer, *Negro Legislators of Texas and Their Descendants: A History of the Negro in Texas Politics from Reconstruction to Disfranchisement* (Dallas, 1935); J. Mason Brewer to A. P. M., Feb. 16, 1970, telephone interview. Although Brewer thought that 1841 was the probable date of Gaines's birth and an 1870 *Daily State Journal* (Austin) article (July 15) gives 1842, the correct year appears to be 1840, based on information concerning the only slave family owned by the Despalliers in 1850. United States Seventh Census (1850), Schedule 2: Slave Inhabitants, Orleans to West Feliciana, Louisiana.

5. B. M. Despallier to Louis Lamot, No. 1, May 18, 1813, Index and Conveyances Book A-M, Book 3, 1, and B. P. Despallier and Carindite Chabrus, July 18, 1827, Book 17, 171, both located in the Parish Clerk's Office (Rapides Parish Courthouse, Alexandria, Louisiana).

6. Charles G. Despallier is listed as or e of the men who died at the Alamo in A. Garland Adair and M. H. Crockett, Sr. (eds.), *Heroes of the Alamo: Accounts and Documents of William B. Travis, James Bowie, James B. Bonham and David Crockett, and Their Texas Memorials* (New York, 1956), 70; Amelia W. Williams, "A Critical Study of the Siege of the Alamo and Its Defenders," *Southwestern Historical Quarterly,* XXXVII (April, 1934), 254-255; Testimony of Justin Costanie in regard to Charles Despallier, Memorial 83, July 27, 1856, File Box 22, Rapides Parish Clerk's Office. Costanie was the attorney who administered the estate of Charles Despallier. He also traveled with Blas P. Despallier in January, 1836, and noted that "in my conversations…he told me they were creole French—from their dialect I judged them to be Canadian French."

7. Brewer, *Negro Legislators,* 51; Lois Smith (granddaughter of Matthew Gaines) to A. P. M., May 1, 1974, interview.

8. Transcripts of the marriage license are contained in Statement of Facts, July 24, 1873, *State* v. *Gaines.*

9. United States Seventh Census (1850), Schedule 1: Free Inhabitants, Rapides Parish, 189.

10. Ibid., Schedule 2: Slave Inhabitants.

11. Testimony of Justin Costanie, Memorial 83, 1-2, Blas P. Despallier to Jean

David, Sale Book A, Sept. 8, 1866, 267, Parish Clerk's Office (Rapides Parish Courthouse, Alexandria).

12. Despallier to David, Sale Book A, Sept. 8, 1866, 267, Parish Clerk's Office (Rapides Courthouse, Alexandria).

13. Robert Gaines (son of Matthew Gaines) to A. P. M., Apr. 27, 1970, interview.

14. Ibid.,; Lois Smith to A. P. M., May 1, 1974, interview.

15. Leandra Gaines (son of Matthew Gaines) to A. P. M., Feb. 10, 1970, interview; *Daily State Journal* (Austin), July 15, 1870; J. W. Baker, *A History of Robertson County, Texas* (Waco, 1970), 240, 252-253; Ralph Wooster, "Wealthy Texans, 1860," *Southwestern Historical Quarterly*, LXXI (Oct., 1967), 178; Estate of C.C. Hearne, Deceased, 1867, Probate Records (Robertson County Courthouse, Franklin, Texas); Walter Prescott Webb, H. Bailey Carroll, and Eldon Stephen Branda (eds.), *The Handbook of Texas* (3 vols.; Austin, 1952, 1976), I, 628. The ranger unit which found Gaines was probably attached to Company K, commanded by W. G. O'Brien, stationed at Camp San Saba. Some of their papers can be found in the Reports of the Adjutant General's Department 1863 (Archives Division, Texas State Library, Austin, Texas).

16. Speech, Matthew Gaines, Aug. 10, 1871, as quoted in the Brenham *Banner,* Aug. 15, 1871.

17. One of several references that Gaines made to having been a field slave can be found in the *Debates of the Twelfth Legislature*, 82.

18. Lois Smith (as told to her by her mother, Mrs. M. S. Maxwell, and her grandmother, Elizabeth Harrison Gaines) to A. P. M., May 1, 1974, interview.

19. Stafford Wornley remembered Gaines as a "small man, about 125 pounds, short and slender," and Ida Wade described him as a "very small man, little over five feet and very thin." Stafford Wornley to A. P. M., Jan. 29, 1970, interview; Ida Wade to A. P. M., Jan. 29, 1970, interview.

20. *State* v. *Gaines*, Statement of Facts, Testimony of M. G. Turner, Joshua Miles, Washington Wade, and Adam Sutton.

21. Houston *Union*, Sept. 7, 1869.

22. Ibid., Dec. 9, 1869.

23. Houston *Tri-Weekly Union*, Dec. 9, 1869; Texas, *Reconstruction Convention Journal, 1868-1869*, 2nd Sess. (Austin, 1870), 534; Brewer, *Negro Legislators*, 24.

24. The political affiliation of members of the Twelfth Legislature can be determined by consulting the following sources: Tommy Yett et al., *Members of the Legislature of the State of Texas from 1846 to 1939* (Austin, 1939), 57-68; *Texas Alamanac for 1870 and Emigrant's Guide to Texas* (Galveston, 1870) 197; Dallas *Herald,* Jan. 15, 1870; *Proceedings of the Democratic State Convention, January 23-26, 1871* (Austin, 1871), 2-10; James Alex Baggett, "Origins of Early Texas Republican Party Leadership," *Journal of Southern History*, XL (Aug., 1974), 441-454, passim. The legislative journals of the period are indispensable for factional identification of individual members.

25. *Texas Alamac*, 1870, 197.

26. John Hope Franklin, *Reconstruction After the Civil War,* The Chicago History of American Civilization (Chicago, 1961), 133-138; Kenneth M. Stampp, *The Era of Reconstruction, 1865-1877* (New York, 1965), 167-168.

27. Houston *Union,* July 30, 1870; Paul A. Casdorph, *A History of the Republican Party in Texas, 1865-1965* (Austin, 1965), 5-6. While Ruby served as a legislator, he also edited a black newspaper, the Galveston *Standard.* After he failed to be reelected to the Texas senate, he returned to New Orleans, where he was clerk to the surveyor of the port of New Orleans from 1875 through 1876. In 1877 and 1878 he was a gauger for the Internal Revenue Department, and from 1879 through 1882, he again edited a black newspaper, the New Orleans *Observer.* He does not appear in the city directories of New Orleans after 1882. Galveston *Standard,* Oct. 14, 1872; *Soard's New Orleans City Directory for 1875* (New Orleans, 1875), 596; *Soard's New Orleans City Directory for 1876,* p. 586; *Soard's New Orleans City Directory for 1877,* p. 558; *Soard's New Orleans City Directory for 1878,* p. 591; *Soard's New Orleans City Directory for 1878,* p. 591; *Soard's New Orleans City Directory for 1879,* p. 576; *Soard's New Orleans City Directory for 1880,* p. 642; *Soard's New Orleans City Directory for 1881, p. 631; Soard's New Orleans City Directory for 1882,* p. 606. For an account of Ruby's career in Texas, see Randall B. Woods, "George T. Ruby: A Black Militant in the White Business Community," *Red River Valley Historical Review,* I (Autumn, 1974), 269-280. For a discussion of the important role that Ruby played in the Louisiana branch of the Kansas Exodus movement of 1878-1880, see William Ivy Hair, *Bourbonism and Agrarian Protest: Louisiana Politics, 1877-1900* (Baton Rouge, 1969), 84, 89-92.

28. Register of State and County Officers, Election Register No. 264, 1870-1874, pp. 2-5, 14-17, V/74 (Archives Division, Texas State Library, Austin); Brewer, *Negro Legislators,* 52-53; Texas Almanac, 1870, p. 197. Another source which can be helpful if used with caution is Yett et al., *Members of the Legislature.* An important source is the Secretary of State's file of Bonds and Oaths of Elected and Appointed Officials (Archives Division, Texas State Library, Austin). Richard Williams and David Medlock are generally omitted from published lists, but both were elected and seated, although Medlock appears not to have served his full term. Medlock's oath is file 2-9/858, RG 307; Richard Williams, 2-9/907, RG 307. Some information on Medlock is also found in Walter F. Cotton's *History of Negroes of Limestone County from 1860 to 1939* (Mexia, 1939), 25.

29. Richard Allen, a Virginia-born slave, was owned by J. J. Cain of Harris County. The Houston *Union,* July 6, 1870, states that "the finest and most elegant mansion that graces our city—[that of] Mayor J. R. Morris—was the handiwork of the Hon. Richard Allen while he was a slave; not the mere mechanism only, but the design, the draft, and all." Although Brewer, *Negro Legislators,* 53, describes Allen as an escaped slave, Allen himself said in a speech in 1871 that he had been emancipated "when the rest...were by order of Gen. Granger." Allen was a bridge builder after emancipation and a controversial supervisor of registration in the Fourteenth District in 1868. Dallad *Herald,* Feb. 8, 15, 1868. For his post-Reconstruction career, see Lawrence D. Rice, *The Negro in Texas, 1874-1900* (Baton Rouge, 1971), 38, 57-58, 201, 202; Casdorph, *Republican Party in Texas,* 39, 47, 48, 66, 251-252.

30. Sheppard Mullens had been a delegate to the Reconstruction Convention representing Bell, McLennan, and Falls counties. He was elected to fill a vacancy and is often left off lists of delegates. He was a member of the influential "Special Committee on the Condition of the State" in that body and was subsequently elected to the Twelfth Legislature. *Reconstruction Convention Journal*, 2nd Sess., 535; Dallas *Herald*, Nov. 28, 1868; Yett et al., *Members of the Legislature*, 63, 66; *Texas Almanac*, 1870, 197.

31. An interesting story about Williams's generosity to his master is found in Houston *Union*, July 6, 1870. Williams, too, was a delegate to the Reconstruction Convention and served on the Executive Committee. He was elected to the Twelfth Legislature from the Twenty-fifth District (Lavaca and Colorado counties) and was elected again in 1878. He was a delegate to the Nashville Negro Convention of May, 1879, but probably did not support Allen and the Kansas migration plan. Austin *Republican*, July 21, 1868; Rice, *Negro in Texas*, 92, 200.

32. Although none of the black politicians in Texas were born in the state, the majority were southerners who had migrated (often as slaves) in the 1850s. Only Ruby, Mitchell Kendall, and Johnson Reed (the district clerk of Galveston) are known to have been northern-born. At least half the black officeholders were former slaves, literate but lacking formal education. Few were field slaves. Most had been artisans, slave or free, practicing such occupations as shoemaker, wheelwright, engineer, and blacksmith. Several Texas black politicos were editors during the Radical period, including Richard Nelson, Frank Webb, Johnson Reed, and G. T. Ruby. In addition to Gaines, C. W. Bryant, and Israel Campbell were ministers. Only Gaines gave his occupation as "laborer." The Texas black reconstructionists were young. All except sixty-year-old Stephen Curtis (a delegate to the 1868-1869 Constitutional Convention) were in their mid or late twenties in 1870.

In other states, a similar pattern existed: most were southern-born; at least half were former slaves, often having been slave artisans and having received some education. In most states there was an influential minority among the black politicos who were northern-born, well educated, who came South after the war, and who were somewhat zealous in their Radical Republican "cause." See peter Kolchin, *First Freedom: The Responses of Alabama's Blacks to Emancipation and Reconstruction*, Contributions in American History, No. 20 (Westport, Conn., 1972), 166-167; Joel Williamson, *After Slavery: The Negro in South Carolina During Reconstruction, 1861-1867* (Chapel Hill, N.C., 1965), 376-377. Harrel T. Budd, "The Negro in Politics in Texas, 1867-1898" (M.A. thesis, University of Texas at Austin, 1925), 18, 19; Slave Narrative of Jerry Moore, son of a slave mother, Amy Van Zandt Moore, and former slave, Henry Moore (Harrison County), WPA Slave Narratives of Texas (Archives, University of Texas at Austin).

33. Debates of the Twelfth Legislature, 22, 23, 27.

34. Ibid., 22.

35. Ibid., 23. Webster Flanagan was the son of Lieutenant Governor and Senator James Winwright Flanagan. Both men were Moderate Republicans, but Webster Flanagan's voting record was generally more conservative than that of his father. Webb, Carroll, and Branda (eds.), *Handbook of Texas*, I, 608-609.

36. *Debates of the Twelfth Legislature*, 27.

37. Ibid.

38. For statistics, see the following: Texas, *Reconstruction Convention Journal*, 1st Sess., 193-194, 500-505, 2nd Sess., 107-109; *Debates of the Twelfth Legislature*, 91-94. For accounts of individual incidents see affidavits filed with the Election Returns, 1867, 1870, Registers of Elected and Appointed State and County Officials, Secretary of State's Papers (Archives Division, Texas State Library, Austin).

39. Texas, Legislature, *General Laws of the Twelfth Legislature* (Austin, 1871), 1st Sess., 72; W. H. Tracy to E. J. Davis, Oct. 8, 1871, A. R. Parsons to James P. Newcomb, Sept., 1871, Election Returns, Secretary of State's Papers.

40. In an 1871 sampling of these affidavits, one can find several examples of voter intimidation by threats and violence. See Affidavit, George Wilson, Sept. 25, 1871, Affidavit, James Taylor, Apr. 18, 1870, Affidavit, E. M. Mitchell, Dec. 2, 1871, Affidavit, James Coleman, Oct. 4, 1871, Election Returns, 1870-1874, Secretary of State's Papers.

41. Texas, Legislature, Senate, *Journal of the Senate of the State of Texas: Twelfth Legislature—First Session* (Austin, 1870), 14.

42. *Debates of the Twelfth Legislature*, 82.

43. Ibid., 83.

44. Ibid., 39.

45. Texas, *Journal of the Senate...: Twelfth Legislature—First Session* (Austin, 1872), 603.

46. *Senate Journal*, 1871, p. 725.

47. Ibid., 785-786.

48. Ibid., 967.

49. Brenham *Banner*, Feb. 28, 1871.

50. Ibid.

51. Houston *Times*, as quoted in the Dallas *Herald*, July 15, 1871.

52. Dallas *Herald*, July 15, 1871.

53. *Flake's Daily Bulletin*, July 11, 1871, Aug. 1, 1871.

54. Brenham *Banner*, Aug. 4, 1871.

55. *Flake's Daily Bulletin*, editorial, Dec. 4, 1869, Ferdinand Flake, who emigrated from Germany to the interior of Texas in the 1840s, became a Unionist journalist and businessman in the 1850s in the Galveston area. He was the editor and publisher of the popular *Flake's Bulletin* until his death in 1872. Webb, Carroll, and Branda (eds.), *Handbook of Texas*, I, 608.

56. *Texas Constitution*, 1869, Article IX.

57. Texas, Legislature, House, *Journal of the House of Representatives of the State of Texas: Twelfth Legislature—First Session* (Austin, 1870), 317, 803; Ibid., Second Session, 82; Texas, Legislature, Senate, *Journal of the Senate of the State of Texas: Twelfth Legislature—First Session* (Austin, 1870), 609, 1049; Texas, *Annual Report of the Superintendent of Public Instruction, 1871* (Austin, 1872), 36; H. P. N. Gammel (comp.), *The Laws of Texas, 1822-1897* (10 vols.; Austin, 1898), VI, 292; Frederick Eby, *The Development of Education in Texas* (New York, 1925), 157.

58. *Daily State Journal* (Austin), Mar. 30, 1871. J. E. Dillard, a senator from the

Third District (Cherokee and Houston counties), was also a power in the state Democratic organization. *Proceedings of the Democratic State Convention, January 23-26, 1871,* 3-10.

59. *Daily State Journal* (Austin), Mar. 30, 1871.

60. Gammel (comp.), *Laws of Texas,* VI, 959-961.

61. Brenham *Banner,* Sept. 1, 1871; *Daily State Journal* (Austin), Dec. 19, 1871.

62. Brenham *Banner,* Aug. 15, 1871.

63. Ibid.

64. Texas, *Report of the Superintendent of Public Instruction, 1871,* pp. 50-51; Texas, Report of the Superintendent of Public Instruction, 1872 (Austin, 1873), 5.

65. Dallas *Herald,* Sept. 23, 1871.

66. Galveston *Tri-Weekly News,* Dec. 3, 1869.

67. *Texas Almanac,* 1870, "Lists of Sheriffs and District Clerks," 198; Rice, *Negro in Texas,* 93-94; Pauline Yelderman, "The Jaybird Democratic Association of Fort Bend County" (M.A. thesis, University of Texas at Austin, 1938), 13-20; Election Register of Elected and Appointed Officials, 1870-1874, Series 10, Secretary of State's Papers.

68. Secretary of State James P. Newcomb's report to the senate on Lawlessness, in *Debates of the Twelfth Legislature,* 92; W. M. Burton to Governor E. J. Davis, Feb. 7, 1871, Calendar of Military Correspondence (Archives Division, Texas State Library, Austin); Justice of the Peace J. S. Rogers to Davis, Aug. 13, 1872, Texas State Police Letters, Archives Division, Texas State Library, Austin. Though Hee is referred to as an appointee in this letter, the post became elective, according to the Election Register and various ballots found in Election Returns, Secretary of State's Papers.

69. *Texas Almanac for 1873 and Emigrant's Guide to Texas* (Galveston, 1873), 25; Waco *Semi-Weekly Examiner,* Dec. 5, 1871.

70. Ed T. Randle to Davis, Oct. 6, 1871, Election Returns, Secretary of State's Papers.

71. Election Register, 1870-1874, Secretary of State's Papers; Rice, *Negro in Texas,* 93-94; *Flake's Daily Bulletin,* Aug. 9, 1871; Galveston *Daily Civilian,* Dec. 10, 1869; Galveston *Tri-Weekly News,* Dec. 8, 1869.

72. *Blake's Daily Bulletin,* July 5, Aug. 6, 1871; Budd, "Negro in Politics in Texas," 50. Nelson edited the Galveston *Spectator,* was justice of the peace in precinct one in 1870, and was an active seeker of offices for blacks as late as 1884. Brenham *Banner,* May 27, 1878; Election Register, 1870-1874, p. 258, Secretary of State's Papers; Rice, *Negro in Texas,* 38, 39.

73. *Flake's Daily Bulletin,* Aug. 3, 1871.

74. Ibid., Aug. 6, 1871.

75. Ibid., Aug. 3, 1871.

76. Ibid.

77. Brenham *Banner,* Aug. 4, 1871.

78. In contrast to Gaines's ability to draw crowds of blacks numbering in the thousands, Ruby's appearance at Brenham in November, 1873, reportedly attracted

only about 250 Negroes. The Brenham *Banner* approved of his more respectable demeanor, making an obvious comparison to Gaines's flamboyant political style: "Ruby is a bright light in the Republican ranks, talks well, does not pound the desk much nor does he 'claw the air' to any great extent." Brenham *Banner*, Nov. 20, 1873.

79. Brenham *Banner*, Aug. 15, 1871.

80. *Flake's Daily Bulletin*, Aug. 18, 1871.

81. Brenham *Banner*, Aug. 18, 1871.

82. Ibid., Sept. 26, 1871.

83. *State* v. *Gaines*, Criminal Docket of District Court, 1872, Fayette County, Texas; *State* v. *Gaines*, Indictment, Nov., 1872, p. 1, District Court, Fayette County.

84. *State* v. *Gaines*, Motion to Remove Cause to Federal Court, p. 5, District Court, Fayette County.

85. Gaines had drawn a six-year term in the senate. Dallas *Herald*, May 14, 1870.

86. *State* v. *Gaines*, Motion for a New Trial and Motion in Arrest of Judgment, July 17, 1873, Statement of Facts, Exhibits 1 and 2, July 24, 1873, District Court, Fayette County.

87. *State* v. *Gaines*, Statement of Facts, Testimony of M. G. Turner, Joshua Miles, et al., July 24, 1873, *State* v. *Gaines*, Criminal Docket, District Court, summer term, 1873, case no. 1522; *Fayette County New Era* (La Grange), July 18, 1873.

88. *State* v. *Gaines*, Order of the Court, July 15, July 23, 1873.

89. Brenham *Banner*, Aug. 2, 1873.

90. *Fayette County New Era* (La Grange), July 15, 1873.

91. Austin *Statesman*, as quoted in the Brenham *Banner*, July 19, 1873.

92. *Gaines* v. *State* (606)—Supreme Court, M6816 (1873).

93. As late as 1875 such comments as the following were being made in the conservative press: "Matt belongs...in the state penitentiary. He is under conviction for felony, and a sentence to hard labor...stands of record against him. (W)hy (is) so notorious a convict...allowed to run at large?" Brenham *Banner*, Apr. 23, 1875.

94. Dallas *Herald*, Mar. 21, 1874.

95. "Memorial of Seth Shepard," in Texas, Legislature, Senate, *Journal of the Senate of the State of Texas: Fourteenth Legislature—First Session* (Austin, 1874), 567-570.

96. Ibid., 645; Dallas *Herald*, Mar. 28, 1874.

97. Dallas *Herald*, Mar. 28, 1874.

98. Ibid.

99. Gaines unsuccessfully attempted to get the Republican State Convention of 1876 to pass a resolution condemning the actions of the Fourteenth Legislature in denying him his seat. Rice, *Negro in Texas*, 102.

100. Brenham *Banner*, Apr. 23, 30, 1875.

101. Ibid., May 27, July 12, Aug. 23, Nov. 8, 1878, quoted in Rice, *Negro in Texas*, 58.

102. Ida Wade to A. P. M., Feb. 3, 1970, interview; Alice White Wornley to A.

P. M., Jan. 23, 1970, interview; Stafford Wornley to A. P. M., Jan. 29, 1970, interview.

103. Alice White Wornley to A. P. M., Jan. 29, 1970, interview.

104. Ibid.

105. Interviews, Robert Gaines, Leandra Gaines, Stafford Wornley, Alice White Wornley, Ida Wade, dates previously cited.

106. Ibid.

107. Lois Smith to A. P. M., May 1, 1974, interview. The photograph is in the possession of Lois Smith. The cuff links and tie pin are in the possession of another of Gaines's granddaughters, Willie K. McDowell.

108. For brief biographies of leading black officeholders, see Vernon Lane Wharton, *The Negro in Mississippi, 1865-1890* (Chapel Hill, N.C., 1947; Harper Torchback Edition, 1965), 157-180. George Brown Tindall, *South Carolina Negroes, 1877-1900* (Baton Rouge, 1952, reprint, 1966) 54-67; Williamson, *After Slavery;* Joe Martin Richardson, *The Negro in the Reconstruction of Florida, 1865-1870,* Florida State University Studies No. 46 (Tallahassee, 1965); Okon Edet Uya, *From Slavery to Public Service: Robert Smalls, 1839-1915* (Oxford, 1971); James Haskins, *Pinckney Benton Stewart Pinchback* (New York, 1973); Kolchin, *First Freedom;* Maud Cuney Hare, *Norris Wright Cuney: A Tribune of the Black People* (1913; facsimile ed., Austin, 1968); Brewer, *Negro Legislators.* Most of the black officeholders who achieved prominence during Reconstruction came from more privileged backgrounds than Gaines (some were former slaves but had been favored by their masters and often received at least some formal education), held more temperate views, and were less independent in their party affiliation.

William M. McDonald. Courtesy Barker Texas History
Center, University of Texas, Austin.

IV

WILLIAM M. McDONALD: Business and Fraternal Leader

Bruce A. Glasrud

Black leaders in Texas and the South at the dawning of the twentieth century found themselves in a difficult transitional period. In the late nineteenth century, even after Reconstruction, some black politicians had exercised considerable influence in the Republican party, while others achieved significant roles in the Populist party. Norris Wright Cuney established himself as the leader of Texas Republicans and served as the state's national committeeman for the party from 1886 to 1896. President Benjamin Harrison appointed Cuney federal customs collector at Galveston, the key patronage position in Texas. Among Texas Populists, John B. Rayner won acclaim as an eloquent stump orator and organizer of black Populist clubs in the 1890s. He also served on the state executive committee of the party. For their careers, see Maud Cuney Hare, *Norris Wright Cuney: A Tribune of the Black People* (New York, 1913; reprint ed., Austin, 1968), and Jack Abramowitz, "John B. Rayner—A Grass Roots Leader," *Journal of Negro History,* XXXVI (Apr., 1951), 160-193.

At the turn of the century, however, the Democrats pushed through a variety of disfranchisement measures, such as the poll tax and the white primary, to eliminate challenges to Democratic dominance in southern politics. Lily-White Republicans also sought to reduce black influence in their party. Faced with the loss of leadership opportunities in politics, a younger generation of black politicans, such as William M. McDonald, struggled to retain their political role. Yet those who could successfully turn their abilities to fraternal and business realms found greater chances for continued guidance of black community endeavors in the twentieth century.

Blacks had been active in these fields since Prince Hall founded a Masonic chapter at Boston in 1787 and James Forten became a wealthy sail manufacturer in Philadelphia during the early nineteenth century. Cuney had furthered the tradition in Texas as a labor contractor in Galveston and as Grand Master of the black Masons in Texas. McDonald represented a new generation and style, however, for he struck a new balance between roles when related fraternal and business activities replaced politics as the primary path to prominence and leadership.

For a general account of black leadership in this period, see August Meier, *Negro Thought in America, 1880-1915* (Ann Arbor, 1963).

The Editors

"America has produced no greater man than William Madison McDonald" concluded McDonald's major biographer in 1925. That author, William Oliver Bundy, further declared that McDonald's

> integrity has never been questioned. His honesty is above suspicion. His judgment is sought by all classes. His love of justice and fair play is recognized by all. He stands today as the leading Negro, in many respects, upon the Western Hemisphere.

Not all observers agreed with this highly laudatory view of McDonald. One commentator asserted that "McDonald used his political prestige by exploiting the Negro for his economic gain." A recent writer called him "an educated but abrasive, quarrelsome Negro." Another, an acquaintance of McDonald's, more cautiously related that "many Negroes . . . felt that McDonald was an opportunist."[1]

Despite such comments, surprisingly little, either of a scholarly, or of a popular, nature has been written about this black Texan, perhaps because of the dearth of personal papers and correspondence and because of the caution of potential writers. The existing studies lack a critical eye. The extremely eulogistic biography written by his friend and associate, William Oliver Bundy, twenty-five years before McDonald's death, portrays McDonald as he would wish to be remembered. And an article entitled "From Poverty to Banker," which borrowed heavily and favorably from Bundy, was published by *Negro Achievements* in 1951-1952.[2] McDonald also was referred to as one of "The Ten Richest Negroes in America" in a 1949 article in *Ebony;* the following year a posthumous article in the same magazine declared that "Death Comes to the World's Richest Negro."[3] For other sources, the prospective biographer of McDonald must search for descriptions and comments from secondary studies which mention, but do not linger on, McDonald, and from newspapers, especially the black press of the state, although McDonald's activities were carried quite extensively in the white press as well. But this man who dominated black Texas for so many years was not included in even one of the seven editions of *Who's Who in Colored America.*[4] In retrospect, however, it seems clear that his contribution and influence was far greater than that of some of his Texas contemporaries who were included in one or more editions of *Who's Who.*

McDonald's voice and authority permeated most black activities in the Lone Star state. He was a powerful force in many black organizations, particularly the fraternal groups which he used as a base for both political advancement and economic advantage. As Grand Secretary, he was the real voice of the Prince Hall Free and Accepted Masons of Texas, one of the oldest and most important of black fraternal orders in the United States. McDonald commanded the Black and Tan faction of the Republican party for over thirty years, and, at times during that period, the entire Republican party in Texas. The personal objectives he sought were wealth and power, coequal branches of the same tree; but he also sought to advance the interests of the black race in Texas.

Undoubtedly, McDonald's physical attributes aided his rise to wealth and power. The adulatory Bundy described him as looking something like an Indian chieftain, "six feet tall, slender, wiry, and of brown complexion" with a prominent brow, a Roman nose, and sparkling eyes. Other writers noted that "McDonald was tall, robust, . . . smoked cigars constantly, . . . wore Texas-style hats and bow ties," and "was always immaculately, yet plainly, dressed." In a less favorable portrait, a comtemporary described McDonald as a "tall, gaunt, colored man with thin hawk-like features, a tufted crop of jet-black hair, and a narrow head, mounted on a scrawny neck."[5] This thin neck was the source of McDonald's nickname, "Gooseneck Bill," which derived from a report from the Republican national convention of 1896 in the Dallas *Morning News* that a black at the convention "has an Irish name, but is a kind of goosenecked Negro."[6]

McDonald also was a polished speaker. Contemporary writers extolled his oratorical skills: the Fort Worth *Star-Telegram* called him "a finished orator," the Dallas *Express* announced in 1924 that he had delivered a "burning message to businessmen" at Dallas, and perhaps Bundy only slightly exaggerated when he stated that "nature has blessed him with all the elements of the great orator."[7]

McDonald was born on June 22, 1866, in Kaufman County, Texas, to parents who had been slaves. His mother, Flora Scott, whose father was a Choctaw Indian, was born in Alabama and died when McDonald was only five years old. His father, George McDonald, who at one time had been purchased by the notorious slave trader, Nathan Bedford Forrest, was born in Tennessee. He eventually labored as a blacksmith, a farmer, and a teamster in order to support his family. McDonald's background gave him advantages, particularly educational, which were often not available to his black contemporaries. In 1872 McDonald began attending a small segregated school which ran for about three months a year. During his school years he worked for Z. T. Adams, a white Kaufman County lawyer and cattleman, who gave McDonald additional tutoring and encouragement in law and business matters, help that was eventually to be of substantial commercial benefit to McDonald. He received his high school diploma from a Kaufman County school in 1884 at the age of eighteen. A good student, perhaps as the Houston *Informer* suggested years later, "the most brilliant student, white or black, in the schools in Kaufman County," he graduated at the top of his high school class.[8]

A number of sources indicate that McDonald, after graduation from high school, traveled to Nashville, Tennessee, where he attended Roger Williams University, now part of Fisk University. Because of his perseverance, intelligence, and friendship with Z. T. Adams, McDonald was encouraged and supported by money from white residents in Kaufman during his years at Roger Williams University. There McDonald prepared for either the law or the ministry. Since Z. T. Adams early encouraged McDonald in the law, it seems likely that he might have continued his interest, especially since Adams helped finance his college education. However, he later reported that his father wished him to study for the ministry. Despite his efforts at Roger Williams University, he did not graduate, apparently because he became involved in a threatened student strike in 1887, the year he would have graduated. He was probably suspended and his diploma withheld.[9]

Following his graduation from high school in 1884 and during the years when he apparently attended the Tennessee college, McDonald engaged in various activities before finding his métier in black capitalism. He taught for a year at the Flat Rock Public School in Kaufman County, but the meager salary soon sent him to Fort Worth in search of more remunerative employment. He accepted a position as a clerk with D. Schwartz and Company, where he remained until the business concern went broke in 1887. The following year his abilities as an organizer and promoter were called into play when he became president of the Texas Colored State Fair Association, which he had helped organize the previous year. The first fair was held in 1887 at Fort Worth; the following year, at Marshall. Both were well-attended ventures. Despite the crowds, the fairs apparently were financially unsuccessful. McDonald resigned his post in 1889, and losing its guiding hand, the fair shortly became more local in nature. After resigning, he accepted employment as a teacher and the principal at the black high school in Forney, where he remained for six years.[10]

The first of McDonald's several marriages was contracted during the time he was affiliated with the Colored State Fair Association. He and Alice Gibson married in 1888, but in about a year his wife became ill and apparently died, since McDonald married again in 1896, this time to Helen Ezell. Two years later McDonald's only child was born. The son, named for his father, died in 1918 while attending Howard University; that death was a cruel blow to McDonald.[11]

McDonald's second wife died in 1926 after thirty years of marriage. Although some years later the lonely McDonald asserted that "I have no kinfolk," he reportedly married again three more times.

In 1937 he married his fifth wife, a recent graduate of Wiley College,
Mae Pearl Grayson, to whom he was married at his death in 1950. An
intelligent, quiet person, she was described as "an olive brown beauty with thick, lovely hair and light hazel eyes, stately figure and quiet
mannerisms." His last three wives were considerably younger than
McDonald, prompting comments such as that of the Houston *Informer,* that he "is sixty or more, but likes young wives."[12]

Also, reported one observer, "wealth became an obsession to
him," and McDonald eventually acquired considerable financial
holdings.[13] He used the essential ingredients available to him to acquire and maintain wealth and power—a solid base of individual and
organizational support from his extensive social and fraternal associations. McDonald received substantial financial backing, and
developed an understanding of how to use influence, perseverance,
an image of prestige, and a willingness to develop diversified ap-
proaches and techniques. McDonald succinctly asserted in a 1925
speech at Houston that "successful men must hold three very essential qualities: financial, mental and physical ability." In terms of
political power, his basic limitation was his inability to dominate
whites, although he used them. As a result he "lost his power [in the
Republican party] which he later spent a fortune trying to regain."[14]

His early emergence as an influential Texan arose from his use of
and support from the secret societies of black fraternal and
benevolent associations. These organizations furnished security,
friendship, and unity to members. They helped develop a tradition
of organized charity, self-help, and self-reliance. They provided a
place for community gatherings and social intermingling and for
political and economic advancement. They were responsible for training members for leadership roles in the black community and for
enabling individual blacks to develop efficient technical and business
skills. Help for the black community as a whole came in the form of
effective and trained leaders, increased economic efficiency, active
state and local political involvement, and struggles for civil rights.
Specifically, the black community was aided by establishing insurance
systems, charity funds, old age and orphans' homes, credit unions,
banks, printing presses, and scholarship funds. The failure of Texas
whites to be concerned with black life, the relatively small size of the
black middle class, and a dearth of other agencies for black involve-

ment meant that fraternal and benevolent associations bore a much larger share of support for the black community than was the case in the white society. As an editorial in the black Dallas *Express* pointed out:

> fraternities in Texas are the bed-rock of our success. . . . They represent our greatest accumulation of cooperative wealth. They have brought together in a compact organization more individuals of the virile sort than any other of our organizations, the church included.[15]

Few other avenues for political, economic, and social activity, with the exception of churches, were open to blacks.

For McDonald, as for a few other black Texans, membership, and ultimately leadership, in the fraternities brought advantages. He developed his political and economic skills; he became well known as a black leader; and he gained the voting support of his fraternal brothers (and later sisters) for the Black and Tan wing of the Republican party (or for any independent political maneuvers for which McDonald needed backing). The fraternities gave financial aid when he decided to open a bank in Fort Worth, and as a leader in the societies, he was called upon to speak both in and out of the state, further enhancing his own prestige and gathering supporters for his own causes. At times McDonald apparently used fraternal funds to pay poll taxes for blacks who could not afford to pay their own. As Arthur H. Lewis asserted, "using every possible means, even if it meant depleting the treasury of some local lodge, he saw to it that poll taxes were paid and that members of his race voted." McDonald's active participation in the lodges of Texas led him to become "one of the leading fraternalists of the race."[16]

McDonald's first venture into the realm of the secret orders began in 1882, when he joined the Seven Stars of Consolidation of America, an order which had been formed in 1881 on the principles of Wisdom, Love, and Truth. Leaders of the Seven Stars encouraged McDonald to be an active member because they needed "a clever bookkeeper and a man who could encourage others to join." McDonald apparently succeeded. By 1885 he was a delegate to the Grand Lodge meeting at Shreveport, Louisiana, and the same year he became Lecturer for the state of Texas—no small achievement, since by 1889 the order claimed a national membership of ten thousand. That year members of the Seven Stars elected McDonald to the position of Supreme Grand Chief.[17] Although his wife's illness later that year prevented his candidacy for reelection, he had enjoyed the prestige, money, and travel which came with leadership in a fraternal order. And among blacks he had gained statewide recognition.

Although McDonald's initial activities in the secret societies were with the Seven Stars, in 1886 he joined three older, larger, and more prominent bodies, fraternities with which he remained affiliated for the duration of his life: the Knights of Pythias, the Odd Fellows, and the Prince Hall Free and Accepted Masons. Even though McDonald apparently never held statewide office in the first two organizations, he was a leading member who frequently addressed local, state, and even national gatherings of those fraternities. These appearances enhanced both his reputation and his following in the two societies. More important, financial support from those organizations enabled him to start a Fort Worth bank which provided a solid foundation for his financial empire.[18]

It was, however, McDonald's position of leadership in the Prince Hall Free and Accepted Masons upon which his support and influence was founded. The Texas Masons for blacks originally started in San Antonio in 1871, spread to six cities by 1875, and then moved rapidly throughout the entire state. By the early 1920s membership numbered about thirty thousand.[19] The Masons, as did other fraternal orders, grew because it furnished its members with insurance and death benefits. In addition to being a social and benevolent organization, after 1907, when Texas blacks were essentially politically disfranchised, the Masons, as well as other lodges, offered limited political activities to its members through selection and election of local, state, and national officers. The lodge was also used as a civic gathering place. Eventually the Masons moved their activities into other fields. In 1901 in Dallas they launched the New Century Cotton Mills, which by 1903 produced three thousand pounds of yarn daily. In 1912 the Masons supported McDonald's efforts to erect a bank, and they later entered the publishing field. Their operation of a printing press was attacked by C. F. Richardson, editor of the Houston *Informer,* because its rates were so low that it took business from the established printing companies. The Texas Masons published *The Masonic Quarterly*, which helped spread the Masonic message to Texas blacks.[20]

McDonald's rise in the Masonic lodge was meteoric, and he remained the dominant force in that organization for most of his life. The Masons began paying him a small salary in 1890, probably for recruiting purposes. He helped organize the Heroines of Jericho in 1892 and for about half a century was the leader of the Heroines, with the official title of Hero. In 1899 after thirteen years of membership and nine years of travel and service, the Masons selected him as their Right Worshipful Grand Secretary, a position he retained for nearly fifty years. The job of secretary was vital to the organization; as Bundy remarked, "this office is the most important in the order." In 1929, the Grand Lodge of Texas held an elaborate celebration honoring McDonald's long tenure of thirty years as Grand Secretary of the Masons. The principal speaker, Roscoe Conkling Simmons of Chicago, declared that "no history of America is complete without Texas, and no history of Texas is complete without McDonald, who is known wherever Texas is known."[21]

McDonald's position as secretary of the Masonic lodge is illustrative of the way he wielded power. He was "not the titular head of the Texas Masons," the Grandmaster, but from his post as secretary he exercised contol over the entire organization. William A. Muraskin referred to him as the "kingpin," "the absolute ruler of Texas black Masonry." Because of his position, admirers and detractors called him the kingmaker, since others, commonly believed to be selected by McDonald, held the titled offices while he ruled the Masons and made the decisions. As Carter Wesley, the influential black editor of the Houston *Informer* and the Dallas *Express*, asserted, "he chose not to be Grandmaster but to select and to run the Grandmasters of the Masons over the years." McDonald recognized the extent of his power and in 1949, a year before his death, ruefully pointed out that "I don't run . . . the Texas Negro Masonic Grand Lodge like I used to."[22] Not only was McDonald able to dominate the Masons because of his controlling post, but he was physically proximate to the Grand Lodge which enabled him to keep close tabs on its activities. In 1906, probably due to pressure from McDonald, the Masons agreed to hold all subsequent annual meetings in Fort Worth and to build a Masonic temple in the city in which McDonald's residence was located. The Masons built the temple, and a drug store and a bank which McDonald eventually established held space in the Masons' building.[23]

Running a well-established fraternal order such as the Masons was not always an easy task. From his position as secretary, McDonald controlled the finances of the organization. He needed to be careful to see that the order was financially secure and to prevent any potential mishandling of funds. He also strove to keep members satisfied, to enroll new ones, and to pay insurance benefits when necessary. McDonald received both direct and indirect financial aid from the Masons for his services. He was a paid official of the lodge; in a 1929 report he contended that he had grossed only $21,700 during the thirty years in which he had been secretary, an average of $723.33 per year.[24] He received financial aid, however, from the Masons to help finance his bank in 1912, and Masons were encouraged to use the bank as well as other McDonald enterprises.

The greatest difficulty McDonald faced while Grand Secretary of the order arose from the emergence of a plethora of other black Masonic groups in Texas. They challenged the McDonald order, especially over the question of which was the official, established fraternity and which the newcomer. These rival groups, such as the Free and Accepted Ancient York Masons, the Ancient Free and Accepted Scottish Rite Masons, and the United Most Worshipful King Solomon Grand Lodge, were also a threat to the financial and numerical security of the Free and Accepted Masons with which McDonald was associated. McDonald refuted the usurpers by pointing out the history of Texas Masonry among blacks, by tracing the roots of his order to Prince Hall (the founder of black Masonic orders in the United States), and by showing the wealthy status of the Free and Accepted Masons, particularly the value of their insurance and death benefits. He referred to the leaders of the other organizations as "the bootleg peddlers and grafters of these clandestine, so-called local, Masonic Lodges." On another occasion McDonald noted a rival fraternalist's "colossal deception, cheek, ignorance, and effrontery."[25] Despite competition, criticism, and varying other difficulties, the Prince Hall Free and Accepted Masons grew numerically and financially, due in no little part to its secretary.

The Masons and other fraternal orders were not the only

organizations which received McDonald's membership and encouragement. He realized that to grasp and retain power, he needed a wide-ranging base of influence. Although not a deeply religious man, he attended a Baptist church. Also, he served as chief justice of the Sanhedrin Court, a Fort Worth society which met on Saturdays to debate issues, listen to speeches, and review the behavior of members. Organized by McDonald, this court "controls the actions of the colored citizens in and about Fort Worth."[26] Among many other ventures, in 1931 he supported the Negro Civic and Economic League of Texas. He was one of a few black Texans who issued a call in 1934 for a meeting "which will result in a statewide movement for the civic betterment of the Race," and in 1936 he served on a committee to celebrate "a century of Negro progress at Fort Worth."[27]

"From fraternal activities...[McDonald] slid into politics"; it was as a politician that he achieved his greatest fame.[28] From his partisan involvement, McDonald secured power, national and local prestige, and a solid financial base. His successes stem in part from his background and training, his character strengths, and his personal skills. McDonald skillfully used the support and influence that he gained from his work with the fraternal orders, and—probably of even greater significance, as The Dallas *Morning News* reported years later—the "political sagacity and the friendship of Colonel E. H. R. Green . . . made him a dominating figure in Texas."[29]

McDonald launched his political career when he joined the Republican party of Kaufman County in 1890. His initial advancement was rapid, and within two years he became chairman of the Kaufman County Republicans. That same year he was a delegate to the state Republican convention. He soon became the second most important black politician in the state, next in line to Norris Wright Cuney, the brilliant and influential leader of the Texas Republicans. The Texas Republican party of the 1890s that McDonald entered had split into two factions: the Lily-Whites and the Black and Tans. The Black and Tan faction, composed mainly of black members of the party, held the majority. The leader of the Black and Tans, until his death in 1897, was Norris Wright Cuney.[30] The Lily-Whites, as the white Republicans became known, sought a solitary goal: the elimination of blacks from leadership ranks of the Republican party and, ultimately, removal of blacks from the party.

After the death of Cuney in 1897, the leadership of the Black
and Tans passed to McDonald and his white ally, E. H. R. Green. In
1896 McDonald had met and joined forces with Green, a New York
millionaire who had moved to Texas to become president of the Texas
Midland Railroad, which was owned by his mother, the very wealthy
Hetty Green. McDonald and Green entered into a mutually
agreeable and profitable alliance. Green wanted to enter state politics
and needed the help of an astute politician, and McDonald needed
financial support for his political and financial activities. Green gave
McDonald a salary of $575.00 per month, ostensibly to act as secretary
but in reality to help Green become the dominant political figure in
Texas. The alliance of Green and McDonald lasted from 1896 to
1909, and as one writer claimed, for a few years "this pair, with
Green as titular party chairman and McDonald as his chief advisor
and dispenser of patronage, ran the Texas Republican party."[31]

Ironically, just when McDonald assumed command of the Black
and Tans, they were dispossessed of the leadership of the Texas
Republican party, not necessarily through any fault of McDonald's
and despite substantial effort on his part to prevent the Lily-White
takeover. Actually, Cuney and the Black and Tans had been defeated
in 1896, perhaps partially because of a split between McDonald and
Cuney; and neither Cuney while he lived, nor McDonald later, was
able to wrest control back to the Black and Tans. In comparing the
qualities of Cuney and McDonald, newspaper editor Carter Wesley,
reported that "[Norris] Wright Cuney was the personification of individual, rugged leadership, and of dominance in politics as an individual, Gooseneck Bill was the personification of the Warwick or
the Kingmaker, who was pushing Joe Green to the top in politics."[32]

As political kingmaker, McDonald operated within the party in a
manner similar to the way in which he directed the fraternal orders.
He never held, nor appeared to seek, either of the two major offices at
his party's disposal in Texas. Instead he helped Green pursue office.
Some writers have asserted that McDonald was offered a number of
patronage positions but that he refused them because he did not
desire to hold office. This would fit with his general demeanor, but
none of the alleged offers are substantiated by the evidence.
McDonald held the status he wanted—he was known as the most important black politician in the state. As Steve D. Gulley stated, albeit

in an uncomplimentary tone, "to do anything in the political affairs of Texas one had to follow the formula laid down by McDonald."[33]

One symbol of power which McDonald did seek was to be a delegate to the national conventions of the Republican party. Although he attended all the Republican conventions from 1896 to 1928, he was officially seated as a delegate only in 1904, 1912, and 1916. At the other sessions, he and the Black and Tans unsuccessfully challenged the Lily-Whites for official recognition. Nonetheless, as a result of McDonald's political participation, particularly his role as kingmaker, he became "the political sage of Texas, . . . one of the most astute and resourceful political leaders in America."[34]

McDonald's political promise was quickly proved as he and Green initially retained partial control of the state Republican party. In 1896 and again in 1898, McDonald helped elect Green chairman of the state executive committee, one of the two most important state Republican posts. Perhaps the initial successes of McDonald and Green were due in part to the solid party organization developed by Cuney, but certainly Green's money and McDonald's astuteness contributed. But continued political control rested on a large black voter turnout, patronage distribution, and national party support. Suffrage restrictions reduced the black vote in the early twentieth century, and with the reduction of the black vote went a lessening of the influence of the Black and Tans within the state Republican party. And in 1900 the Lily-Whites, led by Cecil A. Lyon, a close friend of Theodore Roosevelt, wrested the post of state chairman from Green and with that went control of the party from McDonald and the Black and Tans. Although continually challenged by the Black and Tans, led by the McDonald-Green coalition, Lyon and the Lily-Whites retained their dominance until the tumultuous election of 1912.[35] But McDonald and the Black and Tans could not be disregarded by the Lily-Whites; McDonald was an official delegate to the 1904 National Republican Convention, and he traveled to Washington, D.C., to confer with Republican advisers about patronage distribution in Texas.[36]

The election of 1912 returned the Black and Tans to political prominence in the Republican party of Texas for a few years. The national split between Theodore Roosevelt and William Howard Taft played a major role in the state party lineup. At the national conven-

tion the Taft steamroller commanded the meeting and seated
McDonald and other Taft delegates rather than Cecil Lyon and the
Lily-Whites, who supported Roosevelt.[37] Thus, after twelve years the
hegemony in Texas of Cecil Lyon and the Lily-Whites was broken,
but McDonald's victory was short-lived. Leadership of the state party
did not pass to blacks but to whites who previously had been Taft
boosters. But for a few years McDonald and the Black and Tans
helped determine state party nominees and participated fully in the
party processes. McDonald held considerable influence in the party
and attended the 1916 national convention where he served on the
Committee on Permanent Organization, but the emergence of the
Black and Tans brought little additional personal power since the national administration shifted to the Democrats, which meant that
Texas Democrats, not Republicans, would be distributing
patronage.[38]

The 1920s witnessed the final removal of the Black and Tans,
and with them McDonald, from a position of influence in Republican
party politics. Naturally, many potential candidates vied for the
Republican presidential nomination in 1920 since that party was virtually assured of victory; McDonald and the Black and Tans threw
their support to General Leonard Wood, clearly the candidate most
favorable to blacks. Rival Texas delegations were sent by the Lily-
Whites and the Black and Tans to the national convention; the Lily-
Whites were seated and retained control of the state party. Warren G.
Harding captured the Republican nomination, leading McDonald to
warn that "if Harding is elected President of the United States
Negroes in Texas will get no post offices, no internal revenue jobs,
and no representatives in Washington." He declared that "he would
probably go fishing on election day."[39]

Although McDonald dismissed his defeat in 1920 by asserting
that "its all in the great game of politics . . . . One cannot always be
on the winning side," it was McDonald's misfortune to be on the
wrong side, probably inevitable since he was a black in Texas. Failure
in 1920 drastically altered McDonald and the Black and Tan's influence in Republican party politics. No longer would his voice be
heeded. As R. B. Creager, the white Republican leader, later announced, the Republicans stood "unquestionably for white leadership."[40]

McDonald's behavior in the election of 1920 clearly illustrated another key political trait of his—his independence, his willingness to forsake the Republican party when he deemed it necessary and expedient. He had shown this political characteristic earlier in his career. When the Republicans and Populists adopted a policy of fusion in 1896, McDoanld opposed them and actively campaigned for the Democratic gubernatorial candidate, Charles A. Culberson. In 1905 a thoroughly disillusioned McDonald declared that "I am not in politics any longer—not the kind of Republican politics we have in Texas . . . . I am looking to the Democrats of Texas."[41] But his choice for the Democratic party's gubernatorial nomination lost, and McDonald returned to the Republican party in 1906.

His independence was further accentuated during the 1920s. When the Lily-Whites ran a particularly racist nominee for the governorship in 1920, McDonald and the Black and Tans ran their own candidate, a tactic they had sometimes used in the early twentieth century. That McDonald and the Black and Tans had little other alternative is evidenced by comments of the white Republicans. In the 1920 campaign the Lily-White gubernatorial nominee, John G. Culberson, referred to black political activists, such as McDonald, as "odorous beasts with charcoal complexions." In 1924 McDonald backed Democrat Miriam "Ma" Ferguson for governor, rather than the Republican candidate. McDonald's support of Ferguson led the Republican candidate, Dr. George C. Butte, a recipient of the Ku Klux Klan vote, to claim that "for every vote that Gooseneck Bill delivers to Ferguson I will get the vote of ten thousand of the finest and best democrats who ever cast a ballot in Texas."[42]

For McDonald an even more drastic change took place during the presidential elections of 1924 and 1928, when for the first time on the national level he switched allegiance from the Republicans, first to the Progressives, and then to the Democrats. In 1924 McDonald refused to "support the [Republican] party as now led and managed" and decided to back the nominee of the Progressive party, Robert M. La Follette.[43] As did many other prominent black leaders throughout the nation in 1928, McDonald actively campaigned for Democrat Al Smith rather than Republican Herbert Hoover. McDonald was "opposed to the way the Republican party has been led, used and directed for the past eight years." He further stated that he had "a right to enter my protest, as I am a Republican.''[44] But the efforts of McDonald and other black leaders were largely futile; both the Republicans (with their Lily-White policy) and the Democrats (with their statewide white primary) actively discouraged black political participation on the state level.

By the middle 1920s McDonald decided to leave the political arena. Bundy reported in 1925 that "he was retired from politics now." In the campaign of 1926 "he decided to let the younger men 'carry on' in the political arena." But by December, 1927, he entered the fray once more and urged Republicans to "clean up house"; in 1928 he continued his involvement, in most respects for the last time, when he campaigned for Smith.[45] Generally, during the last twenty years of his life, McDonald was not actively engaged in politics. Partly this was due to age (he was sixty-four in 1930), partly to the fact that he had grown tired of politics, but primarily because there really was not a place for him, or for other blacks, in the political structure of Texas.

Having switched to the Democratic presidential nominee in 1928, McDonald continued his allegiance in 1932 and again in 1936 by voting for Franklin D. Roosevelt. In fact, he boasted that he had been responsible for bringing blacks to the Democratic side. But he apparently tired of the New Deal, described New Deal measures as "cranky tomfoolery," and in 1940 delivered a speech at Houston urging black support for Republican Wendell Wilkie, in order once more to create a viable two-party system in the state. In 1944 and 1948 McDonald apparently supported Republican Thomas E. Dewey for president.[46] However, with the exception of his speech in 1940, he took little part in the political process after 1928.

Political participation proved beneficial to McDonald. He acquired prestige, influence, and power from his partisan role. By dominating the Black and Tan faction of the Republican party, he not only influenced Texas political decisions but had a national impact as well. As early as 1896 Matt Quay, the Pennsylvania Republican political boss, summoned McDonald to the national capital to enlist his support for Thomas B. Reed's bid for the presidency. During Theodore Roosevelt's administration, as previously mentioned, McDonald traveled to Washington to discuss patronage. In World War I he was one of the "big guns" used by the government to enlist support among Texas blacks for the war effort. When black Republicans, finding themselves increasingly outside the national leadership ranks of the Republican party, organized the Republican Lincoln League, McDonald acted as state chairman. In 1928 leading black politicians started the National Negro Voters League in Chicago, and McDonald was elected treasurer of the organization. National news publications, such as the white New York *Times* and the black Kansas City *Call,* covered his activities. Certainly McDonald was "known wherever Texas is known."[47]

Participating in politics was also financially lucrative for McDonald. His association with Green brought him a salary of $575 per month for a number of years. Such a sum enabled him to establish his financial independence. Perhaps McDonald also received money from the sale of patronage. Critics charged him with such behavior, and in a 1936 tax trial he reportedly announced that he had earned over $300,000 by selling patronage to the highest bidder.[48] But it is difficult to believe that he could have sold as much patronage as he supposedly claimed, given the circumstances of the years when he was a political power. According to one author, "His chief concern was to see how much he could make this position pay in dividends." On occasion he also was criticized by a few blacks who were unable to buy these offices because they could not outbid the whites. Nonetheless, the Fort Worth *Star-Telegram,* in a 1920 article, may have best explained his anomalous position: "His enemies charge that his participation in politics is mercenary at the base but his negro supporters believe him to be devoted to the best interest of his race."[49] As a political and fraternal leader, McDonald did seek rewards for his race as well as for himself.

In many respects, as Carter Wesley has pointed out, "the collapse of Negro dominance in politics generally coincided with the death of Wright Cuney. But for Gooseneck Bill it was the beginning of the fruition of his power and leadership in other fields of life." During the succeeding years, "he was accumulating property shrewdly, carefully, and quietly." And successfully, since by the mid-1930s McDonald's financial worth approached $500,000 and at his death in 1950 he retained a substantial estate.[50] Compared to his black contemporaries, and most of his white ones as well, McDonald amassed a large fortune.

The substantial sums derived from political remuneration added to McDonald's wealth, but other factors played a part in his financial achievements. Two white leaders helped him: Z. T. Adams early drilled him in financial matters; and later, as Richard Bardolph remarked, "his tutelage under [E. H. R.] Green enabled him to dabble with great success in banking and real estate." McDonald also developed an almost single-minded drive for money; as one commentator declared, "wealth was an obsession for him." There was method to his obsession; he "saw that one of the best ways to overcome the Southern prejudice against his race was the power of money." As Carter Wesley and others depicted, he possessed other attributes of the successful businessman; he was shrewd, careful, and "cautiously conservative."[51] McDonald acquired money from salaries, from property investments, from farming, from business operations, and from controlling a bank. He also had access to large sums of money from the fraternal orders.

McDonald's early employment laid a basis for his later financial gains. Even before graduating from high school, he worked as a houseboy, on a cattle ranch, and in the law offices of Z. T. Adams. By 1895 he had taught school for seven years and had worked as a clerk in a Fort Worth business for an additional two years. Beginning in 1890, he also received a salary from the Masons, and in 1896, one from E. H. R. Green. This steady income permitted an independence and risk taking in financial affairs unusual for an aspiring black capitalist. While president of the Colored State Fair Association in 1888, he undoubtedly received financial compensation from it. McDonald astutely utilized more than one source of salary in his efforts to acquire money during the latter nineteenth century. During these years "he conducted a lucrative loan shark business on the side," and he began to acquire property.[52]

Property meant land. To begin with, McDonald "farmed on shares and by skimping saved enough to buy a farm of his own" in Kaufman County.[53] He used sharecroppers to work it and with the profits he gradually bought more land. Early in the twentieth century, he acquired land in Fort Worth which he developed into a substantial residential section for blacks. Still later he bought real estate in Dallas, in Oklahoma, and as far away as Chicago. Not only did McDonald prosper as a landowner, receive salaries, obtain money from politics, and lend to other blacks at a high rate of interest, he also operated independent businesses. In Fort Worth he ran a drug store, was a real estate agent and, according to Paul Lewinson, owned a newspaper.[54] Even more important, in 1912 McDonald became a banker.

In 1911 he convinced some black fraternal orders—the Knights of Pythias, the Heroines of Jericho, the Ancient Order of Pilgrims, the Odd Fellows, and the Masons—to help him establish a bank by purchasing shares in it. The shares sold for eleven dollars, and McDonald opened the Fraternal Bank and Trust Company in 1912. Although he was the controlling stockholder, McDonald's penchant for remaining out of titular positions is apparent in his role at the bank. From 1912 to 1924 the president was Tom Mason, not McDonald. Instead, McDonald ran the bank from the post of cashier. However, with Mason's death in 1924, McDonald became president, a title he held until 1948, when he was named president emeritus.[55]

McDonald's guidance kept the bank afloat during the years when many other banks established for blacks were going bankrupt. It was not always an easy task. Shortly after the bank opened, McDonald was besieged with requests from officers of some of the shareholding lodges for preferential treatment. They "demanded unreasonable personal loans," and when McDonald refused to grant these special favors, the officers convinced their orders to withdraw support from McDonald's bank. But the bank was solidly established. Eventually only the Masons and the Heroines continued to support the bank, and it became essentially "a clearing house for funds of Negro Masons in Texas, New Mexico, Arizona, Utah, and Nevada."[56] In 1930 McDonald sold his controlling interest to the Masons; he had been trying to persuade them to purchase his interest during the previous four years. The bank survived the Depression years, but in a somewhat changed form: after the Banking Act of 1933, the bank in 1935 became a private bank which would not loan depositors' money.[57] Even after selling his majority interest, McDonald remained closely aligned with the bank until his death in 1950.

McDonald attained the pinnacle of his financial achievements in the 1930s. In 1930, although he retained one hundred shares, he transferred controlling interest in the Fraternal Bank and Trust Company to the Free and Accepted Masons for the sum of $220,000, to be paid over a ten-year period. He still received a salary of $1,200 per year for acting as president of the bank, and the Masons paid him at least $1,500 a year for his duties as their secretary. He derived income from land he owned in Kaufman and Tarrant counties, Oklahoma, and Chicago. McDonald also invested in government bonds; according to a story in the Kansas City *Call*, he owned $105,000 worth of bonds in 1940. Reports circulated that McDonald was a millionaire, one of the wealthiest blacks in the United States. For example, at his death an article in *Ebony* stated that McDonald was "the world's richest Negro." He was not, but the size of his estate probably ranged from one-third to one-half a million dollars at its height. He definitely was one of the richest black men in the Southwest.[58]

However, for a number of reasons, McDonald's estate had dwindled to approximately $100,000 by the time of his death. The Depression, which affected the financial well-being of nearly everyone, hurt McDonald despite his diversification. Some of his tenants were unable to pay rent. Also, the value of property declined during the years of the Depression, and since McDonald owned considerable property, his net worth went down. Financially, McDonald retired during the last years of his life, not adding to his holdings. He lived well in an elaborate house ostensibly modeled after the plantation home where his father was a slave. He hired servants to help care for the house as well as his personal needs. McDonald owned expensive cars and liked to wear diamond rings and other accoutrements of wealth. He spent funds for philanthropy as did other businessmen later in their lives. A further drain on his estate were two brief marriages and divorces during the 1930s, from which his young wives may have derived substantial benefit in settlements. His illness during the last years of his life also depleted his financial reserves. Even so, McDonald left a valuable estate to his wife when he died on July 4, 1950.[59]

Perhaps it was fitting that William Madison McDonald's life should end on the Fourth of July, since he rose to heights attained by few other black southerners during the first half of the twentieth century, literally, as one observer declared, "from poverty to banker."[60] Although a black man in white Texas, his life fulfilled the promises set forth by the Declaration of Independence. Not only did McDonald's successes epitomize the American Dream, but he believed in those promises and ideals and accepted the basic tenets of capitalism. Although he was apparently neither a close friend nor a disciple of Booker T. Washington, the prominent southern black leader, some of McDonald's expressed views appeared reminiscent of the Tuskegee leader's philosophy. In a 1919 speech at Shreveport, McDonald pointed out his devotion to self-help when he said that "we must do all of these things ourselves." He then continued:

> If you want a beautiful home, go build it. If you want concrete sidewalks, go have them put down . . . . Do you wish to have Negro clerks in grocery stores? Go and establish such stores. Do you wish to have negro bank clerks and cashiers? Go and establish you a bank . . . . Do you wish to have Negroes manage great business concerns and great enterprises? Go and establish them. Treat these as we have the church and lodge—stand by them, support them and feel that you are honored when you support and maintain business enterprises managed and controlled by Negroes for the benefit of our race.[61]

His beliefs, reflecting his status as a successful black businessman and politician, sometimes failed to acknowledge the advantages he possessed for his quests and the obstacles placed in the path of the black majority. At the same time, though, he called for blacks to work together, to support each other, to pursue a policy of self-help—essentially to acquire what has been referred to as Green Power.

McDonald's devotion to self-help and racial solidarity was derived from his experience as a fraternalist, a politician, and a financier. McDonald was no outspoken advocate of race pride and confrontation as was the northern leader, W. E. B. DuBois, nor was he a devotee of public accommodation as was Washington. Rather, an independent and successful politician and businessman, his racial views appeared somewhere between the two. August Meier, in *Negro Thought in America, 1880-1915,* declared that "politicians . . . in overt expression . . . were, on the whole, the most conservative of the elite group during the age of Washington." But, Meier also showed, the conservative politicians were those indebted to Booker T. Washington;

other politicians, such as Judson Lyons of Georgia and George H. White of North Carolina, were not nearly so conservative.[62] William Madison McDonald's attitudes and directives were similar to those of Lyons and White; he was not a follower of Washington and was able and willing to speak out strongly on a variety of issues.

McDonald's personal goals—wealth and power—dominated his life and seemed at times to overshadow his racial goals. But he believed that if one succeeded in a world of white power that individual attainment would also bring racial strength, that for a black to be successful he must operate within a segregated society but have contact with whites. His early years were devoted to personal aggrandizement. He later became something of a philanthropist, seemingly less concerned with the acquisition of wealth and power, no doubt because he had accomplished his goals. The intriguing aspect of McDonald is that his quest for personal advancement (often supported by, if not at the expense of, fellow blacks) pushed forward the black cause in Texas. He fought for political rights. He spoke out against mob rule, referring to a Fort Worth mob as "deliberate, cruel, insane, unreasonable and revengeful." "In McDonald's opinion," Melvin James Banks argued, the "vicious circle of suppression and denunciation could be broken only by a solid, determined Negro movement that would expose Texas and southern behavior before the court of national and world opinion."[63] McDonald argued for black economic enterprises. He aided black cultural growth, and he called upon whites for equitable justice.

His own racial program McDonald termed "uplift and justice." In a speech given to the bishops of the African Methodist Episcopal church, he stated that

> we are often confronted with the theory of Bishop Turner, deportation, or of that school of theorists who advocate assimilation, or of the Rev. Dixon class, who preaches annihilation.... Over against that trinity of impossibilities, deportation, assimilation or annihilation, let me offer the simple plan of uplift and justice. Let the superior adopt the policy of uplift by encouraging and teaching the inferior the great lessons of our life's problems.... Let the superior demonstrate its superiority by the manner in which it applies justice to the inferior.[64]

But for the majority of blacks, whites gave little justice and produced little encouragement for uplift.

McDonald's path to accomplishment was both similar to and different from that of his black Texas contemporaries who also achieved distinction. As did other black leaders, he participated actively in the fraternal orders; he taught school and indicated an interest in education. He engaged in business, and he argued for a philosophy of self-help among blacks. But he was also a very independent person, one who preferred to operate as a kingmaker rather than hold the titular offices. He operated effectively with whites, using their assets to advance his own interests. And given the social conditions of Texas, he was more successful than most. In politics, no black Texan has outranked him in the twentieth century. Very few were wealthier. In the fraternities, although he had his counterparts in the Pythians and other societies, he controlled one group totally, and he wielded decision-making influence in other organizations. McDonald sought and gained personal wealth and power, and as a black leader in white Texas, he strove for racial advancement.

NOTES

1. William Oliver Bundy, *Life of William Madison McDonald, Ph.D.* (Fort Worth, 1925), 331, 333; Steve D. Gulley, "M. M. Rodgers, the Politician, 1877-1909" (M.A. thesis, Prairie View Agricultural and Mechanical College, 1955), 36; Thomas Robert Cripps, "The Lily White Republicans: The Negro, the Party, and the South in the Progressive Era" (Ph.D. diss., University of Maryland, 1967), 176; A. Maceo Johnson to L. B. M., June 17, 1958, interview, in Leonard Brewster Murphy, "A History of Negro Segregation Practices in Texas, 1865-1958" (M.A. thesis, Southern Methodist University, 1958), 264.

2. "From Poverty to Banker: Life Story of William Madison (Gooseneck Bill) McDonald," *Negro Achievements*, V (Dec., 1951), 3-4, 29-31, VI (Jan., 1952), 5, 45-47. Other accounts include "Fabulous Bill McDonald," *The Christian Science Monitor*, Dec. 3, 1949, magazine section, 20; Richard Bardolph, *The Negro Vanguard* (New York, 1959), 200-201; A. W. Jackson, *A Sure Foundation and a Sketch of Negro Life in Texas* (Houston, 1940), 120-121; Effie Kaye Adams, *Tall Black Texans: Men of Courage, A Relevant Reading Worktext with Comprehension Vocabulary and Study Skills Exercises* (Dubuque, 1972), 151-152; and Walter Prescott Webb, H. Bailey Carroll, and Eldon Stephen Branda (eds.), *The Handbook of Texas* (3 vols.; Austin, 1952, 1976), III, 556.

3. "The Ten Richest Negroes in America," *Ebony*, IV (Apr., 1949), 13-18; "Death Comes to the World's Richest Negro," *Ebony*, V (Oct., 1950), 66-68, 70. The extremely inflated evaluations of McDonald's wealth in these articles led E.

Franklin Frazier to use them as examples of the uncritical reporting of the black press. Frazier caustically remarked that "as in the case of many other wealthy Negroes, when this Negro multimillionaire died, only $100,000 remained of his reputed $3,000,000 fortune." E. Franklin Frazier, *Black Bourgeoisie: The Rise of a New Middle Class in the United States* (New York, 1957), 155.

4. *Who's Who in Colored America: A Biographical Dictionary of Notable Living Persons of African Descent in America* (7 vols.; New York, 1927-1950). His death was reported in Jessie Parkhurst Guzman (ed.), *Negro Yearbook*, 1952, (New York, 1952), 382.

5. Bundy, *McDonald*, 281, 332; "Death Comes to the World's Richest Negro," 66; Adams, *Tall Black Texans*, 152; Arthur H. Lewis, *The Day They Shook the Plum Tree* (New York, 1963), 81.

6. Bundy, *McDonald*, 112-113; Houston *Informer*, Oct. 31, Nov. 7, 1925; Dallas *Morning News*, Sept. 18, 1949; Lewis, *Day They Shook the Plum Tree*, 81.

7. Dallas *Morning News*, Sept. 18, 1949; Houston *Informer*, Oct. 31, Nov. 7, 1925, July 15, 1950; Dallas *Express*, Apr. 19, 1924, July 15, 1950; Fort Worth *Star-Telegram*, quoted in Texas Writers' Project, *Fort Worth and Tarrant County, Texas* (Fort Worth, 1941), 19870; Bundy, *McDonald*, 263-282.

8. Bundy, *McDonald*, 1-15; Fort Worth *Star-Telegram*, July 6, 1950; Lewis, *Day They Shook the Plum Tree*, 81-82; McDonald to W. L. Dixon, Mar. 14, 1911, in Bundy, *McDoanld*, 202; Houston *Informer*, July 8, 1950.

9. Dallas *Morning News*, Sept. 14, 1949; Kansas City *Call*, Feb. 2, 1940; Lewis, *Day They Shook the Plum Tree*, 82; Douglass Geraldyne Perry, "Black Populism: The Negro in the People's Party in Texas" (M.A. thesis, Prairie View University, 1945), 29; William ("Gooseneck Bill") McDonald Folder, Arthur H. Lewis Notes (Free Library of Philadelphia). A copy of the materials from the McDonald folder in the Lewis Notes are in the possession of the author, courtesy of Arthur H. Lewis and Frances H. Ritchey. Information on the 1887 student strike at Roger Williams University can be found in James M. McPherson, "White Liberals and Black Power in Negro Education, 1865-1915," *American Historical Review*, LXXV (June, 1970), 1371.

10. Bundy, *McDonald*, 15, 20-24, 33, 81-90; Adams, *Tall Black Texans*, 151; Lewis, *Day They Shook the Plum Tree*, 82; Lawrence D. Rice, *The Negro in Texas, 1874-1900* (Baton Rouge, 1971), 197.

11. Bundy, *McDonald*, 91-98; Dallas *Express*, June 5, 1926; "From Poverty to Banker," VI, 47; Murphy, "Negro Segregation Practices in Texas," 90; Fort Worth *Star-Telegram*, July 6, 1950; Lady George Munchus-Forde, "History of the Negro in Fort Worth—Syllabus for a High School Course" (M.A. thesis, Fisk University, 1941), 140.

12. Dallas *Express*, May 29, June 5, 1926, July 8, 15, 1950; Texas Writers' Project, *Fort Worth*, 22458; *Vivienne McDonald* v. *W. M. McDonald*, divorce granted in District Court, Seventeenth Judicial District, Tarrant County, Texas (certified copy in author's files); Jackson, *Sure Foundation*, 564-565; Adams, *Tall Black Texans*, 152; Houston *Informer*, June 5, 1926, June 29, 1929, Apr. 18, Oct. 10, 1936, July 8, 15, 1950.

13. Texas Writers' Project, *Fort Worth*, 22457.

14. Houston *Informer*, Nov. 14, 1925; Texas Writers' Project, *Fort Worth*, 22458.

15. Charles W. Ferguson, *Fifty Million Brothers: A Panorama of American Lodges and Clubs* (New York, 1937), 184-202; William A. Muraskin, "The Social Foundations of the Black Community: The Fraternities, the California Masons as a Test Case," *Midcontinent American Studies Journal*, XI (Fall, 1970), 12-35; idem, *Middle-Class Blacks in a White Society: Prince Hall Freemasonry in America* (Berkeley, 1975); Harold Van Buren Voorhis, *Negro Masonry in the United States* (New York, 1940); William H. Crimshaw, *Official History of Freemasonry among the Colored People in North America* (New York, 1969).

16. Lewis, *Day They Shook the Plum Tree*, 83; Houston *Informer*, Oct. 31, 1925.

17. Bundy, *McDonald*, 17-20, 23-24.

18. Ibid., 37-39, 65, 78; Houston *Informer*, Aug. 7, 1926, Aug. 6, 1927, Aug. 11, 1928, May 4, 1929; Texas Writers' Project, *Fort Worth*, 22456.

19. Houston *Informer*, Aug. 18, 1928, June 29, 1929; Bundy, *McDonald*, 37, 101; Rice, *Negro in Texas*, 269; Dallas *Express*, July 23, 1921.

20. Bundy, *McDonald*, 101; Dallas *Morning News*, Aug. 3, 1901, Feb. 1, 1903; Houston *Informer*, Aug. 18, 1928; Rice, *Negro in Texas*, 195.

21. Bundy, *McDonald*, 37-38; Lewis, *Day They Shook the Plum Tree*, 83; Texas Writers' Project, *Fort Worth*, 21664; Neil Gary Sapper, "A Survey of the History of the Black People of Texas, 1930-1954" (Ph.D. diss., Texas Tech University, 1972), 510; Houston *Informer*, Nov. 14, 1925, June 29, 1929.

22. Bundy, *McDonald*, 38-39; Muraskin, *Middle-Class Blacks*, 170, 225; Houston *Informer*, June 29, 1929, July 15, 1950; Dallas *Express*, July 15, 1950; Fort Worth *Press*, July 5, 1950; Dallas *Morning News*, Sept. 18, 1949.

23. Bundy, *McDonald*, 38-39; Houston *Informer*, June 29, 1929.

24. Ibid.

25. Houston *Informer*, Dec. 12, 1925, Oct. 16, Nov. 27, Dec. 18, 25, 1926, June 16, 1928, June 8, 22, 29, 1929.

26. Bundy, *McDonald*, 100, 215-216, 233-234; Kansas City *Call*, Feb. 2, 1940; Perry, "Black Populsim," 29; "From Poverty to Banker," *Negro Achievements*, V, 29.

27. Bundy, *McDonald*, 235; Houston *Informer*, Jan. 19, 1931, Nov. 24, 1934; June 6, 1936; Dallas *Express*, Nov. 17, 1934.

28. Lewis, *Day They Shook the Plum Tree*, 83. The background of black political participation in Texas can be found in the relevant chapters of Rice, *Negro in Texas;* Bruce Alden Glasrud, "Black Texans, 1900-1930: A History" (Ph.D. diss., Texas Tech University, 1969); and Sapper, "Black People of Texas." Rice, Glasrud, and Sapper wrote dissertations under the direction of Lawrence L. Graves, Professor of History at Texas Tech University. See also Alwyn Barr, *Black Texans: A History of Negroes in Texas, 1528-1971* (Austin, 1973); Lamar L. Kirven, "A Century of Warfare: Black Texans" (Ph.D. diss., Indiana University, 1974); and William Joseph

Brophy, "The Black Texan, 1900-1950: A Quantitative History" (Ph.D. diss., Vanderbilt University, 1974).

29. Rice, *Negro in Texas*, 50-51; Dallas *Morning News*, July 6, 1950.

30. Houston *Informer*, July 8, 1950; Bundy, *McDonald*, 104-106, 111-112; William M. Ellison, Jr., "Negro Suffrage in Texas and Its Exercise" (M.A. thesis, Colorado State College of Education, 1943), 56-57; William ("Gooseneck Bill") McDonald Folder, Lewis Notes. Studies of Cuney include Paul Douglas Casdorph, "Norris Wright Cuney and Texas Republican Politics, 1883-1896," *Southwestern Historical Quarterly*, LXVIII (Apr., 1965), 455-464; Virginia Neal Hinze, "Norris Wright Cuney" (M.A. thesis, Rice University, 1965); Maud Cuney Hare, *Norris Wright Cuney: A Tribune of the Black People* (New York, 1913); and Carter G. Woodson, "The Cuney Family," *Negro History Bulletin*, XI (Mar. 5, 1948), 123-125, 143.

31. Lewis, *Day They Shook the Plum Tree*, 85-91; Bundy, *McDonald*, 143; Texas Writers' Project, *Fort Worth*, 20692-20693, 22458; Oliver Knight, *Fort Worth: Outpost on the Trinity* (Norman, 1953), 148; Paul Casdorph, *A History of the Republican Party in Texas, 1865-1965* (Austin, 1965), 70-71; Dallas *Morning News*, Sept. 18, 1949, July 6, 1950; Estate of E. H. R. Green, in William ("Gooseneck Bill") McDonald Folder, Lewis Notes; Murphy, "Negro Segregation Practics in Texas," 89.

32. Dallas *Express*, July 15, 1950.

33. For an example, see Bundy, *McDonald*, 143-144; Gulley, "M. M. Rodgers," 36.

34. Casdorph, *Republican Party in Texas*, 252-259; Houston *Informer*, Mar. 13, 1920.

35. Bundy, *McDonald*, 113-126; Lewis, *Day They Shook the Plum Tree*, 85-91; Casdorph, *Republican Party in Texas*, 70-72; Alwyn Barr, *Reconstruction to Reform: Texas Politics, 1876-1906* (Austin, 1971), 186-190; Dallas *Morning News*, July 10, 1950; Henry Lee Moon, *Balance of Power: The Negro Vote* (Garden City, N.Y., 1948), 106.

36. Casdorph, *Republican Party in Texas*, 252-259; Dallas *Morning News*, Jan. 28, 1903.

37. San Antonio *Express*, Aug. 15, 1912; Gulley, "M.M. Rodgers," 56-58; Casdorph, *Republican Party in Texas*, 98-108; Glasrud, "Black Texans," 60-63; William F. Nowlin, *The Negro in American National Politics* (New York, 1931), 53-55.

38. San Antonio *Express*, Aug. 12, 1914; Dallas *Morning News*, Aug. 3, 1916; Casdorph, *Republican Party in Texas*, 108-117, 256; Glasrud, "Black Texans," 63-65; Ernest Winkler (ed.), *Platforms of Political Parties in Texas*, Bulletin of the University of Texas, September 20, 1916: No. 53 (Austin, 1916), 616-617.

39. Houston *Informer*, Mar. 13, 1920; Austin *Statesman*, May 26, 1920; Dallas *Morning News*, Aug. 11, 1920, Sept. 18, 1949; Casdorph, *Republican Party in Texas*, 118-124; *Christian Science Monitor*, Dec. 3, 1949; Fort Worth *Star-Telegram*, June 9, 17, 1920.

40. *Christian Science Monitor,* Dec. 3, 1949; Houston *Informer,* May 26, 1928.

41. Dallas *Morning News,* Oct. 2, 1896; Rice, *Negro in Texas,* 83-84; Barr, *Reconstruction to Reform,* 170; Perry, "Black Populism," 29; Roscoe C. Martin, *The People's Party in Texas: A Study in Third Party Politics,* The University of Texas Bulletin No. 3308; February 22, 1933, Bureau of Research in the Social Sciences Study No. 4 (Austin, 1933), 243-245.

42. Glasrud, "Black Texans," 77-78; Dallas *Express,* Sept. 18, 1920, May 29, 1926; Houston *Informer,* Nov. 21, 1925, Apr. 21, 1928.

43. Dallas *Express,* Aug. 16, Sept. 6, 27, Oct. 11, 25, Nov. 1, 1924; William ("Gooseneck Bill") McDonald Folder, Lewis Notes.

44. Dallas *Morning News,* July 17, 1928; New York *Times,* July 17, 1928; Houston *Informer,* Aug. 25, Sept. 22, Nov. 3, 1928; Casdorph, *Republican Party in Texas,* 122; John Hope Franklin, *From Slavery to Freedom: A History of Negro Americans* (3rd ed.; New York, 1969), 524; Sister Frances Jerome Woods, "Negro Suffrage under the Texas Direct Primary System" (M.A. thesis, Catholic University of America, 1945), 54; Paul Lewinson, *Race, Class, and Party: A History of Negro Suffrage and White Politics in the South* (New York, 1932), 158-173; McDonald to J. R. Hawkins, in Houston *Informer,* Sept. 22, 1928. See also, "An Open Letter from Wm. M. 'Goose-Neck Bill' McDonald to Hon. J. R. Hawkins," *Fraternal Review,* VII (Oct., 1928), 4-5.

45. Bundy, *McDonald,* 144; Houston *Informer,* Aug. 7, 1926, Dec. 24, 1927, Aug. 25, 1928; Dallas *Morning News,* July 17, 1928; New York *Times,* July 17, 1928.

46. Houston *Informer,* Oct. 19, 1940; Dallas *Morning News,* Sept. 18, 1949; Sapper, "Black People of Texas," 114-115; Murphy, "Negro Segregation Practices in Texas," 88-90; Perry, "Black Populism," 29; Fort Worth *Press,* July 5, 1950; William ("Gooseneck Bill") McDonald Folder, Lewis Notes.

47. Bundy, *McDonald,* 113-114, 249-253; Lewis, *Day They Shook the Plum Tree,* 86-87; Dallas *Morning News,* Jan. 28, 1903; Munchus-Forde, "History of the Negro in Fort Worth," 121; New York *Times,* July 17, 1928; Kansas City *Call,* Feb. 2, 1940; Houston *Informer,* Feb. 7, 1920, Oct. 31, Nov. 7, 1925, Sept. 8, 1928, June 29, 1929.

48. Lewis, *Day They Shook the Plum Tree,* 90; Fort Worth *Press,* July 5, 1950; Texas Writers' Project, *Fort Worth,* 20693, 22458; Woods, "Negro Suffrage under the Texas Direct Primary System," 53-54. The case involved the estate of E. H. R. Green, who died on June 8, 1936. The United States Supreme Court eventually settled the matter of Green's residence in *Texas* v. *Florida,* 306 U.S. 398 (1939). See also information in William ("Gooseneck Bill") McDonald Folder, Lewis Notes, and Truman O'Quinn, "Texas, Taxes, and Where Did Colonel Green Live?" *Texas Bar Journal,* XXIV (Sept. 22, 1961), 827-828, 884, 886-893.

49. Woods, "Negro Suffrage under the Texas Direct Primary System," 53-54; Fort Worth *Star-Telegram,* cited in Texas Writers' Project, *Fort Worth,* 19870. See also Gulley, "M. M. Rodgers," 36.

50. Dallas *Express,* July 15, 1950; Texas Writers' Project, *Fort Worth,* 22455; Kansas City *Call,* Feb. 2, 1940; Fort Worth *Star-Telegram,* July 12, 1950.

51. Bundy, *McDonald*, 13-14, 103, 209-211; "From Poverty to Banker," *Negro Achievements*, VI, 5, 45-47; Houston *Informer*, July 8, 1950; Kansas City *Call*, Feb. 2, 1940; Bardolph, *Negro Vanguard*, 201; Dallas *Express*, July 15, 1950; Texas Writers' Project, *Fort Worth*, 20692, 22455, 22459; "Death Comes to the World's Richest Negro," 68.

52. Bundy, *McDonald*, 13-15, 20-24, 81-90, 126; Houston *Informer*, July 8, 1950; Adams, *Tall Black Texans*, 151; Lewis, *Day They Shook the Plum Tree*, 82; William ("Gooseneck Bill") McDonald Folder, Lewis Notes; Texas Writers' Project, *Fort Worth*, 21907-21908, 22457.

53. Texas Writers' Project, *Fort Worth*, 20692.

54. Fort Worth *Star-Telegram*, July 12, 1950; Kansas City *Call*, Feb. 2, 1940; Texas Writers' Project, *Fort Worth*, 20692, 21907-21908, 22457-22458; Bundy, *McDonald*, 39; Lewinson, *Race, Class, and Party*, 173.

55. Bundy, *McDonald*, 209-213; Kansas City *Call*, Feb. 2, 1940; Fort Worth *Press*, July 5, 1950; Houston *Informer*, Oct. 18, 1930; July 15, 1950; Dallas *Express*, July 15, 1950; Dallas *Morning News*, Sept. 18, 1949; Texas Writers' Project, *Fort Worth*, 19285-19286; Arnett G. Lindsay, "The Negro in Banking," *Journal of Negro History*, XIV (Apr., 1929), 183; Muraskin, *Middle-Class Blacks*, 141-143.

56. Kansas City *Call*, Feb. 2, 1940; Texas Writers' Project, *Fort Worth*, 20690, 22455; Houston *Informer*, Jan. 29, 1927.

57. Houston *Informer*, Oct. 18, 1930; Texas Writers' Project, *Fort Worth*, 19285-19286; Dallas *Express*, June 26, 1926, July 2, 1927.

58. Houston *Informer*, June 29, 1929, Oct. 18, 1930, July 8, 1950; Kansas City *Call*, Feb. 2, 1940; according to "Ten Richest Negroes in America," 13, he also owned land in Dallas and Houston; Texas Writers' Project, *Fort Worth*, 20689, 20691, 22455, 22457; Dallas *Express*, July 15, 1950; *Negro Yearbook, 1952*, p. 382; "Death Comes to the World's Richest Negro," 66-68, 70.

59. Johnson to L. B. M., June 17, 1958, interview; *Christian Science Monitor*, Dec. 3, 1949; Dallas *Morning News*, Sept. 18, 1949, July 6, 1950; Kansas City *Call*, Feb. 2, 1940; Texas Writers' Project, *Fort Worth*, 20691-20692; Bundy, *McDonald*, 98-100; Murphy, "Negro Segregation Practices in Texas," 90; Munchus-Forde, "History of the Negro in Fort Worth," 140; Houston *Informer*, Apr. 18, 1936, July 8, 1950; Fort Worth *Star-Telegram*, July 6, 12, 1950. According to "Death Comes to the World's Richest Negro," 67, McDonald's financial decline came about thusly: "but generous to himself, to charity as well as to his numerous wives (he had five), he doled out his money liberally rather than have his heirs pay tremendous inheritance taxes." On the same page, the article argued, "legend has distorted much of 'Gooseneck's' amazing career, but it is an admitted fact that in later years he acquired a penchant for young brides '20 or under.' On each he lavished $3,000 fur coats, automobiles, jewelry and divorce settlements of $10,000. His marriage bargains were struck with only one pre-agreed requisite: each had to return his first wife's jewels when she decided to leave him." There is no other evidence to support these statements that I have located.

60. "From Poverty to Banker," V, 3.

61. William M. McDonald, speech at Shreveport, Louisiana, Jan. 1, 1919, cited

in Bundy, *McDonald*, 292-293. On McDonald's racial views, see also William Madison McDonald, "Letter in Answer to Questionnaire: Group Tactics and Ideals," *Messenger,* IX (Jan., 1927), 11, 13-14.

62. August Meier, *Negro Thought in America, 1880-1915: Racial Ideologies in the Age of Booker T. Washington* (Ann Arbor, 1966), 248, 255.

63. McDonald to W. L. Dixon, Mar. 14, 1911, in Bundy, *McDonald,* 201; Melvin James Banks, "The Pursuit of Equality: The Movement for First Class Citizenship in Texas, 1920-1950" (SSc.D. diss., Syracuse University, 1962), 138. The Reverend Mr. S. R. Prince declared at McDonald's funeral that "he was a racial patriot and did all he could for his race that he knew was an infant race." William ("Gooseneck Bill") McDonald Folder, Lewis Notes.

64. McDonald, speech at Dallas, Texas, in 1921, in Bundy, *McDonald,* 240.

Mary Branch. Courtesy Huston-Tillotson Library.

V

MARY BRANCH: Private College Educator

Olive D. Brown and Michael R. Heintze

Black education in a formal rather than an individual setting began before the Civil War with first private and later public schools conducted by both black and white teachers, usually on a segregated basis, for free blacks. After the war the Freedmen's Bureau and northern missionary societies extended instruction to the South with the aid of local black leaders. During the 1870s and 1880s segregated public schools with black teachers assumed most primary education, while the integrated religious organizations concentrated on secondary schools and colleges. From both levels of black education came leaders, such as L.C. Anderson, principal of Prairie View College, who founded state organizations like the Colored Teachers State Association of Texas, in 1884, and who worked to improve both the availability and the quality of instruction for black students. For the general history of black education and its leaders, see Henry Bullock, *A History of Negro Education in the South* (Cambridge, Mass., 1967).

Women assumed important roles in black education, as in other aspects of black life including family, civil rights, labor, government, and social concerns. They served as teachers beginning in the 1790s and became school founders and directors early in the nineteenth century. The black women of Texas have provided group leadership through women's clubs and religious societies and have included prominent figures such as Maud Cuney Hare in literature, Etta Motten in radio and movies, and

Barbara Jordan in politics. Thus, Mary Branch, the first black woman to serve as a college president in Texas, participated in a long tradition of black women as leaders in state and national education and community affairs. For the range of those activities, see Gerda Lerner (ed.), *Black Women in White America: A Documentary History* (New York, 1972).

The Editors

The Great Crash of 1929, followed by the Depression, struck individuals and institutions alike with dread. Businesses withered and died, bankrupting stockholders and erasing thousands of jobs. Banks closed on a moment's notice, impoverishing countless citizens who had thought themselves financially secure. In 1929 Tillotson College was experiencing its own version of the proverbial lean years as it struggled for its institutional life. At this juncture a bespectacled woman, fiftyish, buxom, self-assured, and possessed of indefatigable strength and courage, came to the capital of Texas. Her mission was to rescue a small Negro college on the brink of collapse. This woman's life, as well as her performance as president of Tillotson College, represents one of the truly noteworthy chapters in black, as well as women's, history.[1]

One of six children, Mary Elizabeth Branch was born in Farmville, Virginia, on May 20, 1881.[2] Although opportunities for Negro public education remained quite limited in the small college town, she and her brothers and sisters were among the more fortunate black children who attended the local elementary school. As members of the developing black middle class, her parents actively sought to instill in their children the fixed ideas they possessed about culture and advancement which manifested themselves in the acquisition of scholarly books. Among reading materials available for the children were works on religion, biography, history, and philosophy. These were found in the Branch home during a time and in a town where such educational opportunities were not open to blacks. Instructed to make the most of their lives, the children spent many of their evenings reading and interpreting passages selected by their parents. Mary became an avid reader and developed a lifelong interest in books.[3]

Mary Branch acquired from her parents not only a desire for education but also an inclination toward initiative and leadership.

Her father, Tazewell Branch, was born a slave near Farmville. Reared as a house servant, he learned to read and write in his master's home. As a young man Tazewell learned the trade of shoemaking and, ultimately, became a skilled craftsman and respected member of the slave community. After emancipation his reputation among whites and blacks in the area was such that he was urged to seek public office. Branch subsequently won election to the Virginia legislature in 1874 and 1876. He retired from party politics, however, when he observed that many of the politicians were corrupt. Branch then returned to Farmville, where he became an internal revenue collector.[4] According to Mary Branch, these honors were "forced upon him by his friends, black and white, who respected him highly for his intelligence, integrity, unusual common sense, and good judgment."[5] In many ways Tazewell Branch epitomized the type of Negro leader Booker T. Washington described in *Up from Slavery:*

> If one goes into any Southern town and asks for the leading and most reliable colored man in the community, I believe that in five cases out of ten he would be directed to a Negro who learned a trade in the days of slavery.[6]

After serving four years as a tax collector, the aged Branch returned to his craft, but soon found it difficult to support the family. Mary's mother, Harriett Branch, then took up the double burden of raising and supporting the family. She managed to accomplish this by performing a wide variety of domestic jobs in the community.[7]

Mary Branch was thirteen when she first "attended" college at the State College in Farmville.[8] She was there, however, not as a student but as an employee. As Mary Branch later noted, "I did attend the State College in Farmville, for my mother washed clothes for a number of girls and teachers, and I attended regularly to get clothes or to take them."[9] Eventually, she acquired a job as a maid in the college library. Working there amid the shelves of books, she was fascinated by the wealth of knowledge at her fingertips and became determined that she would somehow secure an education. In the following years she fulfilled her dream by finishing her high school studies at the normal school of Virginia State College in Petersburg.[10]

Being a perfectionist and having been exposed to a wide variety of literature at home and at school, Miss Branch became interested in the field of English. She appreciated the need for her people to be able to read and speak with precision. Thus, she began her career as an English teacher at the elementary school of Blackstone, Virginia, at a meager salary of $27.50 per month. From this humble beginning she was asked to join the faculty of her alma mater, Virginia State College. For twenty years she taught at Virginia State. Her popularity with the students was unrivaled, and her courses, known as "Branch's English," were always crowded, not because they were easy, but because they were the most challenging and interesting.[11]

In addition to her teaching duties, Branch served as housing director for the men's and women's dormitories. Her personality and charm drew countless students to her office, seeking advice and counsel on personal as well as academic matters. In the summers she kept busy by pursuing undergraduate work at the University of Pennsylvania, Columbia University, and the University of Chicago. From the latter she received a Bachelor of Philosophy degree in 1922 and a Master of Arts degree in English in 1925. She also began studies toward a doctorate in the School of Education.[12]

In the late 1920s, Mary Branch's career took another course when she accepted a social studies position at Sumner Junior College in Kansas City, Kansas. Then the following year, she was named dean of girls at Vashon High School, in St. Louis, which was then the largest school for Negro women in the country. Professionally speaking, Branch had now risen to the very pinnacle of teaching in the world of black education. Not only was the salary substantial, but there also existed the opportunity for professional, as well as personal, fulfillment. Since Vashon was located in the poorest of neighborhoods, her work was as much missionary as educational. For many students, meeting Branch was their first encounter with a teacher of any kind.[13] Her job offered a challenging opportunity to study young people as she advised, counseled, and even disciplined them.

Then in 1930 Mary Branch received a call from the American Missionary Association to become president of Tillotson College in Austin, Texas. The decision was difficult, since it would mean giving up the best income she had ever received as well as another offer from a local community college.[14] On two occasions she turned down AMA appeals, but in the end she relented, noting:

I thought of the numbers of white teachers who had gone South for years since the Civil War and worked among an alien race for no other reason than a Christian interest in the underprivileged. They had made far greater sacrifices than I would be called upon to make. I thought and prayed over the matter and finally got a definite feeling that I should go to Tillotson.[15]

Mary Branch knew that Tillotson was a declining institution, but beyond that she knew little else about her new responsibility. Tillotson College had been founded to provide educational training for blacks in the Austin area. It was one of several benevolent projects undertaken by the American Missionary Association, whose aim was to establish schools for freedmen throughout the South.[16] In 1871 the Reverend George Jeffrey Tillotson, a retired Congregational minister from Connecticut who was serving with the AMA, decided to tour Texas and select a site for another school[17] When he and a traveling companion, the Reverend Gustave D. Pike, arrived in Austin, the Reverend Mr. Tillotson was impressed by the view from atop a steep hill overlooking the Colorado River. Feeling that this location was ideal, Tillotson then raised some sixteen thousand dollars and purchased several acres of land, upon which Tillotson Collegiate and Normal Institute was established.[18]

Tillotson was officially chartered in February, 1877, but because of construction delays, did not open until January 17, 1881. Staffed by white administrators and teachers supplied by the American Missionary Association, the institution initially sought to provide Negro students of the Austin area with elementary and secondary instruction in traditional and industrial studies. By 1909 the school achieved collegiate status and became known as Tillotson College.[19]

Then after 1914 the college suddenly began to decline. A number of factors played a part in this downward spiral. To begin with, the pool of potential students for most southern black colleges was shrinking. Between 1914 and 1920 Texas and other southern states witnessed a significant black migration northward. This exodus resulted from a combination of evils which included low wages and poor job opportunities in the South; the tenant farming system; the rising tide of Jim Crowism and racial violence; widespread crop failures caused by droughts, heavy rains, and boll weevil infestations;

military recruitment for World War I; and war-related jobs in northern industrial centers. Consequently, college enrollments, especially of male students, fell, and some schools had to make adjustments. For Tillotson a change came in 1925, when it was reduced to a junior college.[20]

Another key to Tillotson's troubles was the American Missionary Association's appointment in 1925 of J.T. Hodges as president.[21] As the college's first black leader, Hodges could have written an important chapter in Tillotson's history had it not been for his lackluster and nepotistic leadership. Hodges lost much of his credibility and community support by appointing members of his family to important administrative posts and by remaining aloof from the townspeople. Charges of dormitory irregularities, high tuition, and nepotism finally forced Hodges's resignation in 1929, after the college had suffered additional enrollment damage. In 1926 as a result of declining enrollment and administrative problems, Tillotson converted to a women's college.[22]

Into this distressing and seemingly hopeless situation came Mary Branch. On July 1, 1930, she received her first glimpse of the challenge that awaited her. Entering the campus through the pitiful remnants of a fence, she made her way up a "gullied and scraggly path through underbrush so thick that a fox could—and did—hide in it."[23] The campus was composed of little more than half a dozen timeworn buildings, surrounded by old, weather-beaten mesquite trees. After touring these structures, Branch entered the administration building where she found a cramped, eight-by-ten-foot room which she discovered to be the president's office.[24]

A weaker person might have turned around and walked away, but Mary Branch remained. For her the school became a challenge which she accepted with hope and self-assurance. Given a free hand by the American Missionary Association, she laid out a five-year plan to upgrade the physical plant and attract more college students. The library became one of her first projects. There were barely two thousand volumes suitable for college research. By soliciting donations from friends, local businessmen, and civic groups, she expanded the library's holdings over the next fourteen years to more than twenty-one thousand volumes.[25] With her efforts old buildings such as the women's dormitory and the industrial shop were renovated, while other new ones arose. The laundry, college co-op, Home Management House, men's dormitory, several staff homes, and gymnasium[26] were all products of her leadership. The campus also sprouted new trees and shrubs as well as athletic fields.[27]

In order to attract more college students, President Branch initiated a number of institutional changes. First, she deleted the high school program and increased the college budget. Then she doubled the size on the faculty and required that all members have, at least, a master's degree. Teachers were sent throughout the Southwest to recruit qualified students, and scholarships were offered to assist the most needy. Students were also attracted to the campus through such events as "play day activities," which brought high school girls from around the state to participate in athletic events.[28] Finally, in 1935 the Branch administration reorganized Tillotson as a coeducational college once more. Because of such innovations, enrollment steadily grew from 140 students in 1930, to 362 in 1938, and to 502 in 1944.[29]

Branch was also successful in the field of student affairs. After 1930 Tillotson began to take on a more contemporary appearance as she abolished mandatory chapel,[30] permitted social fraternities and sororities,[31] and promoted the formation of academic and athletic clubs.[32] Yet her religious background, which had begun in the African Methodist Episcopal church and later included worship in the Episcopal and Congregational churches, endowed her with many conventional Christian and moral principles which she applied in dealing with students.

One such belief was that all students should be willing to work for, at least, a portion of their educational expenses.[33] Thus, almost every student at Tillotson held some job. Fortunately, President Branch displayed an uncanny ability for matching the right person with the right job. For example, an Austin student sought a job on campus, indicating that she desperately wanted a college education, but could do so only with financial assistance. The young woman possessed a keen sense of humor and never seemed to be serious about anything. Branch was concerned as to whether the student was actually serious about attending college; so she gave her the job of picking up trash around campus each day. The girl took the job, performed her task well, and continued to exhibit her sense of humor, despite being ridiculed by other students. She graduated from Tillot-

son, earned an advanced degree, and was hired by the Austin Independent School District.

Not all of Branch's efforts to aid young people were in this vein,
for her generosity and stewardship often led her to deal with others in
a much different manner. So, for another young woman who was
outwardly more serious than the "campus paper-picker," Miss
Branch provided funds for graduate study. For still another worthy
student, she assumed all financial responsibility for personal as well as
educational needs.

As another goal, Mary Branch sought to generate a positive,
working relationship with the surrounding community. To this end
she involved herself and her students in community affairs. Her interests were many and varied. She supported the work of charity
clubs, participated in forums, served on committees, and concerned
herself with city politics and public school operation. She established
a rapport with faculty members at the University of Texas, at the
nearby Negro college, Samuel Huston, and with public school administrators and teachers. She also brought noteworthy speakers and
artists of local, state, and national stature to the campus.[34] Although
her frankness, which often approached brusqueness, irritated some,
few ever thought of overlooking her in civic matters. Her contemporaries frequently sought her for advice, and many group decisions
often hung upon her opinion.

One such civic organization which claimed Branch's interest was
the Austin chapter of the National Association for the Advancement
of Colored People (NAACP). She served as chapter president in 1943,
encouraged the participation of her students, and sponsored a student chapter on campus. Likewise, the State Interracial Commission
of Texas claimed her as a member. Her involvement in civil rights activities was linked to the social conditions of that era. Spurred on by
the humiliations of Jim Crowism, Branch supported almost any plan
which might improve living conditions for black people. There is
evidence that she used her powers as the chief business officer of the
college to close accounts or boycott businesses where segregation was
enforced. Many times coworkers would venture to suggest a curtail-
ment of these activities, but such advice made her even more determined to proceed.[35]

During the Depression, Mary Branch devoted a great deal of her time to working with the New Deal's National Youth Administration (NYA), which provided part-time jobs and vocational training for needy high school and college students. In 1935 the NYA director for Texas, Lyndon B. Johnson, appointed her to the state's NYA Negro Advisory Board. Serving with such leading Negro figures as Joseph J. Rhoads, president of Bishop College, and L. V. Williams, principal of Booker T. Washington High School in Dallas, Mary Branch worked diligently to insure that the federal jobs program would equally benefit the state's black and white students. The Negro Advisory Board's efforts proved reasonably successful. By mid-1936 approximately 773 students in the state's Negro colleges were being assisted by the NYA.[36]

Mary Branch was equally resolute in her belief that individuals, as well as institutions, needed the cooperation and support of others. After Dr. Frederick Patterson of Tuskegee Institute approached her in 1944, seeking support for his idea of establishing the United Negro College Fund (UNCF), Tillotson was one of the first to join. The decision proved to be wise, since the UNCF became a potent force in the financial operation of its forty affiliate institutions.

Mary Branch's burden of presidential duties ran the gamut from overseeing garbage disposal to meeting with heads of state. The list of her responsibilites included:

> Selection and orientation of freshmen;
> Determining the basis for student selection;
> Interviewing candidates for admission;
> Student advising;
> Interviewing students sent by other faculty members concerning financial problems;
> Giving permission to students to leave campus;
> Providing worthwhile books and magazines for leisure reading;
> Entertaining college visitors;
> Supervising the college food service.[37]

This list represents only the responsibilites she shared with other staff members. The list of duties for which she was solely responsible was no less formidable:

Locating part-time employment for students;
Interviewing students desiring work;
Managing student work schedules;
Approving purchase of equipment for dormitories;
Selecting and approving heads of residential halls;
Making changes in the physical, social, and academic environment;
Raising funds;
Administering student loans and scholarship funds.[38]

It is evident that Mary Branch's duties were, to say the least, comprehensive. Perhaps the best explanation for this was that the economic climate of the 1930s placed undue pressures and responsibilities upon the heads of small institutions, and Tillotson was no exception. Tillotson was fortunate that it had an administrative leader of untiring strength, who possessed an innate curiosity concerning all circumstances affecting the institution under her direction.

The 1930s and early 1940s were hard, strange, and often frightening times. Yet through these years Mary Branch exhibited a strength and vision which brought recognition to her college. In 1931 the college was given unconditional senior college standing by the State Board of Education, and in 1933 the college was approved as a class "B" institution by the Southern Association of Colleges and Secondary Schools. Two years later Tillotson returned to a coeducational status and in 1936 was admitted to membership in the American Association of Colleges. Finally, in 1943 Tillotson received an "A" rating by the Southern Association of Colleges and Secondary Schools. This was an impressive succession of achievements for Branch's administration, and they did not go unrewarded. Along with these advances for the college, Branch acquired two honorary degrees—the first Doctor of Pedagogy bestowed by Virginia State College and a Doctor of Laws degree from Howard University.[39]

Her wish to make Tillotson a successful and respected college for the state's youth led Branch to encourage a coalition with Samuel Huston College, a Methodist Episcopal college for Negroes, which was also in Austin. The two were less than a mile apart, offered essentially the same curriculum, and faced the same need for supplementary funding and increased enrollment. Branch and Karl E. Downs, president of Samuel Huston, entered upon several cooperative programs such as sharing faculty members and presentations of speakers and artists. Although Branch and Downs both died before the colleges merged in 1952, they were a decisive force in the movement toward the creation of Huston-Tillotson College.

A review of the activities which claimed Branch's attention would seem to indicate that she had little time for social mingling. However, this was not the case. She somehow found the time to assist in the organization of a local book club, participated in the activities of her college sorority, Alpha Kappa Alpha, and joined a women's club. She played bridge and took regular strolls up and down the hills of the twenty-three acre campus, always stopping to chat with whomever she met. In short, she was a social being with an outgoing personality which could both attract and inspire.

At the height of her career, Mary Branch was suddenly struck by illness. In the summer of 1944, she sought medical consultation at Johns Hopkins University Hospital in Baltimore concerning a goiter ailment. While in the East, she decided to visit her two sisters in New Jersey. During her visit she again became seriously ill and was rushed to a local hospital where she died on July 6.[40]

Mary Branch's career as a college president placed her in an elite group of black women who successfully directed institutions of higher education. During the 1930s and 1940s, Branch had only two comparable contemporaries. One was Mary McLeod Bethune, who founded Bethune-Cookman College in Florida and who gained national prominence by serving as the director of the Division of Negro Affairs of the NYA under President Franklin D. Roosevelt and as a member of the Committee for National Defense under President Harry S. Truman.[41] The other was Artemisia Bowden, who, between 1902 and 1954, served Saint Philip's College in San Antonio as instructor, principal, dean, and president.[42] Mary Branch's contributions to Tillotson College, however, were equally impressive. The impact of her handiwork is clearly visible if one examines the enrollment statisitics between 1930 and 1944 for the various black colleges in Texas (see table 6.1).

As table 6.1 indicates, between 1930 and 1944, ten of the state's thirteen black colleges experienced varying declines in their enrollments, and one school, Guadalupe College in Seguin, was forc-

TABLE 6.1 Enrollment Statistics for Black Colleges in Texas, 1930-1944

INSTITUTION	ACADEMIC YEAR 1930-31	1932-33	1935-36	1936-37	1938-39	1940-41	1942-43	1944-45	PERCENT INCREASE OR DECREASE
Bishop College	350	490	448	608	539	452	331	231	-34%
Butler College	—	—	205	230	—	—	275	189	-7.8%
Guadalupe Baptist	—	100	175	—————Closed—————					-100%
Houston College	—	—	—	—	402	400	273	456	+13.4%
Jarvis Christian	226	—	242	190	147	181	163	136	-39.8%
Mary Allen Junior	185	254	146	163	135	150	112	143	-22.7%
Paul Quinn College	125	—	—	—	169	169	230	70	-44%
Prairie View State	1300	750	1056	986	1236	1329	1420	1243	-4%
Saint Philip's Junior	—	—	—	—	200	175	101	113	-43.5%
Samuel Huston College	300	—	259	259	310	310	310	270	-10%
Texas College	400	—	381	381	453	449	430	519	+29.7%
Tillotson College	140	168	209	275	362	584	465	502	+258.5%
Wiley College	715	362	500	480	557	420	367	500	-30%

Source: *Texas Almanac and State Industrial Guide,* (Dallas, 1930-1944).

ed to close.[43] Meanwhile, during Mary Branch's administration, Tillotson's enrollment soared from 140 in 1930 to 502 in 1944. This 258.5 percent increase in enrollment coupled with President Branch's improvements in the institution's faculty, staff, and facilities were the prime factors which convinced the Southern Association of Colleges and Secondary Schools to award Tillotson an "A" rating in 1943.[44]

Mary Branch's life at Tillotson College was punctuated with repeated efforts to bring education within the grasp of those who sought its benefits. Any person more timid or less curious, more retreating or less outspoken, more concerned about personal welfare or less concerned about the welfare of others, undoubtedly, would have failed. Coming to Texas when she did, facing the situations she met, and attacking the jobs at hand with all the vitality, strength, and experience she had, resulted in expanded vistas for a segment of America's population for whom little concern had been shown.

Students fortunate enough to have attended Tillotson during Mary Branch's administration gained a new perspective and vision of what they could hope and prepare for. She was, without question, the woman for the times.

NOTES

1. Unless otherwise indicated, the information in this essay is based upon the personal recollections of Olive Durden Brown. Mrs. Brown served as librarian at Tillotson College during the last three years of Mary Branch's administration but had known Branch since the week of her arrival in Austin in 1930.

2. Houston *Informer,* July 15, 1944, indicates that Mary Branch was born on May 20, 1882, but Thomas Yenser (ed.), *Who's Who in Colored America, A Biographical Dictionary of Notable Living Persons of African Descent in America, 1930-1932* (7 vols.; 3rd ed.; New York, 1933), 55, and J. M. Cattell (ed.), *Leaders in American Education* (New York, 1941), 111, give her year of birth as 1881.

3. Mary Jenness, *Twelve Negro Americans* (New York, 1936), 85-88.

4. Luther Porter Jackson, *Negro Officeholders in Virginia, 1865-1895* (Norfolk, Va., 1945), 5; Jenness, *Twelve Negro Americans,* 86-88.

5. Quoted in Jenness, *Twelve Negro Americans,* 88.

6. Booker T. Washington, *Up from Slavery: An Autobiography* (reprint ed., Garden City, N.Y., 1949), 121.

7. Jenness, *Twelve Negro Americans,* 88-89.

8. Ibid., 89.

9. Quoted in ibid.

10. *The Tillotson College Bulletin, A Memorial Issue* (Austin, Jan., 1945), 3.

11. Jenness, *Twelve Negro Americans,* 90-91.

12. Austin *American,* July 7, 1944; Mabel Crayton Williams, "The History of Tillotson College, 1881-1952" (M.A. thesis, Texas Southern University, 1967), 96.

13. William H. Jones, "Tillotson College, from 1930-1940: A Study of the Total Institution" (mimeographed; Austin, 1940), 9; *Tillotson College Bulletin,* 3; Jenness, *Twelve Negro Americans,* 92-93.

14. Jenness, *Twelve Negro Americans,* 93.

15. Quoted in ibid., 93-94.

16. Fred L. Brownlee, *New Day Ascending* (Boston, 1946), 176-197; Williams, "History of Tillotson College," 10.

17. According to Chrystine I. Shackles in Jones, "Tillotson College, from 1930-1940," p. 2, George Jeffrey Tillotson was born in Farmington, Connecticut, on February 5, 1805, and through his paternal grandmother, was descended through an unbroken line from Alfred the Great of England and Hugh Capet of France. Tillotson was a graduate of Yale College and Yale Divinity School.

18. In Plats, CCCMNIX, 817 (Travis County Courthouse, Austin, Texas), the property is described as being all of outlot 7, division B, bound by 657 feet of [East] Seventh Street on the south, 1,811 feet of Chicon Street on the east, 657 feet of [East]

Eleventh Street on the north, and 1,316 feet of Chalmers Street on the west; Reverend Gustave D. Pike to Reverend E. B. Wright, Feb. 8, 17, 24, 1876 (Archives, Huston-Tillotson College, Austin, Texas); Williams, "History of Tillotson College," 13-14; Jones, "Tillotson College, from 1930-1940," pp. 2-4.

19. Charter of Tillotson Collegiate and Normal Institute, Charter No. 803, Feb. 10, 1877, Secretary of State's Papers (Archives Division, Texas State Library, Austin); U.S., Department of the Interior, *Negro Education: A Study of the Private and Higher Schools for Colored People in the United States,* Bureau of Education Bulletin, 1916, No. 39 (1917; reprint ed., New York, 1969), 596; Frederick Eby, *The Development of Education in Texas* (New York, 1925), 276-277; C[ecil] E[ugene] Evans, *The Story of Texas Schools* (Austin, 1955), 216; Williams, "History of Tillotson College," 15.

20. Florette Henri, *Black Migration: Movement North, 1900-1920* (Garden City, N.Y., 1975), 49-80, 289-295; Evans, *Texas Schools,* 216; John Hope Franklin, *From Slavery to Freedom: A History of Negro Americans* (3rd ed.; New York, 1967), 455-456, 471-475, 546-547.

21. A native of Gonzales, J. T. Hodges graduated from Atlanta University and held positions at Prairie View State Normal And Industrial College and Houston College, Houston, before coming to Tillotson. See Williams, "History of Tillotson College," 80.

22. Ibid., 88-89.

23. Jenness, *Twelve Negro Americans,* 94.

24. Ibid., 94-95.

25. See Report: Lincoln Memorial Fund 1931-1932, 1932-1933 (Archives, Huston-Tillotson College, Austin); George F. Work to Branch, Feb. 19, 1934, Branch to Work, Feb. 21, 1934, Branch to Hortense Webster, Feb. 16, 1934, Branch to Texas Book Store, Feb. 26, 1934, Branch to Southwest Baking Company, Feb. 26, 1934, Branch to A. C. Baldwin and Sons, Feb. 26, 1934, Branch to W. H. Richardson and Company, Feb. 26, 1934, Branch to Gugenheim-Goldsmith, Feb. 26, 1934, Branch to John Bremond, Feb. 26, 1934, and Branch to F. W. Wilford, Mar. 20, 1934, Mary Branch Papers, (Archives, Huston-Tillotson College, Austin).

26. The gymnasium now bears her name.

27. Jenness, *Twelve Negro Americans,* 96-98.

28. Williams, "History of Tillotson College," 99.

29. *Texas Almanac and State Industrial Guide* (Dallas, 1931, 1939, 1945).

30. Jenness, *Twelve Negro Americans,* 98.

31. The national Greek letter organizations founded at Tillotson College were Omega Psi Fraternity (1936), Delta Sigma Theta Sorority (1936), Alpha Kappa Alpha Sorority (1939), Alpha Psi Alpha Fraternity (1939), Zeta Phi Beta Sorority (1940), Sigma Gamma Rho Sorority (1945), and Phi Beta Sigma Fraternity (1946). Williams, "History of Tillotson College," 105-106.

32. Clubs founded at Tillotson included the Delver Dramatics Club, Carver Science Club, Descartes Mathematics Club, Glee Club, Octette, Sextette, College Choir, YMCA, YWCA, E. E. Just Biology Club, Franco-Hispanic Society, Home Economics Club, Carter G. Woodson Historical Society, and Tillotson College Tennis

Club. Ibid., 107; *Catalogue of Tillotson College, 1937-1938* (Austin, 1937), 14.

33. Jenness, *Twelve Negro Americans,* 99.

34. For example, Mary Branch invited a local white Baptist minister, Reverend Blake Smith, and the noted black educator, Dr. Benjamin Mays of Atlanta, Georgia, to serve as commencement speakers. Austin *American-Statesman,* May 21, 1944; Williams, "History of Tillotson College," 111.

35. William Pickens to B. F. Caruthers, Nov. 30, 1936, Box G-200, NAACP Papers (Library of Congress, Washington, D.C.); *Crisis,* L (Feb., 1943), 58; Cattell, *Leaders in Education,* 111.

36. Branch to Lyndon B. Johnson, Mar. 11, 1936; Dallas *Gazette,* Mar. 7, 1936; San Antonio *Register,* Feb. 14, 1936; Marshall *Messenger,* Mar. 1, 1936; *Negro Labor News* (Houston), Dec. 31, 1935; Houston *Press,* Dec. 6, 1935; Houston *Defender,* Dec. 14, 1935; Houston *Informer,* Jan. 18, 1936; and NYA *Report,* 1936, pp. 1-4; all in Box 10, Papers (Lyndon B. Johnson Library, Austin, Texas).

37. Jones, "Tillotson College, from 1930-1940," pp. 68-83.

38. Ibid.

39. Chrystine I. Shackles, *Reminiscences of Huston-Tillotson College* (Austin, 1973), 33, 49; Jenness, *Twelve Negro Americans,* 95-99.

40. Austin *American-Statesman,* July 7, 1944.

41. Gerda Lerner (ed.), *Black Women in White America: A Documentary History* (New York, 1973), 134-135.

42. Clarence W. Norris, Jr., "St. Philip's College: A Case Study of a Historically Black Two-Year College" (Ph.D. diss., University of Southern California, 1975), 68-70, 82, 166, 193, 210.

43. Seguin *Enterprise,* Feb. 14, 21, 1936, Jan. 29, 1937.

44. *Texas Almanac and State Industrial Guide* (Dallas, 1930-1944).

W. R. Banks. Courtesy George R. Woolfolk.

VI

W.R. BANKS: Public College Educator

George R. Woolfolk

The Black Codes forbade the teaching of slaves to read and write. Appomattox changed that and with emancipation came the question of education of freedmen. The Freedmen's Bureau established Howard University, aided in creating Atlanta University, Fisk University, Talladega College, Tougaloo College, and Hampton Institute, as well as encouraging public school education throughout the South. All told, it was estimated that by the Freedmen's Bureau's demise in 1872 around a million blacks were enrolled in public schools. The bureau's activities and the eager quest of black folks for education clearly repudiated white assertions that blacks neither wanted nor could attain academic skills. The question now was who would direct the education of the blacks and what sort of education would be granted to them.

The overseeing of black education passed to whites. This decision guaranteed that black schools in the South would be separate and unequal. It meant, too, that black educators could not alienate their white overlords. Thus grew the black man's dilemma: how do you control your fate when the power structure controls the purse strings? Educators, such as W. R. Banks, addressed this question daily.

When Banks accepted the presidency of Prairie View, he must have been aware of its problems. The act that established Texas Agricultural and Mechanical College also provided for a black land-grant school. Prairie View never functioned as such, however. Supervised by the directors of A&M College, it served at various times in its early history as a teachers' training normal school, as a trade school, as a combination high school and college, and as a technical institute. Its mission, as far as whites were concerned, seemed clear: prepare the blacks for their proper (inferior) place in society.

How W. R. Banks succeeded in this difficult environment is the theme of Professor Woolfolk's essay. In undertaking such a task, he asks the reader to evaluate carefully what is the role of black leadership and can it be cast in terms of accommodation versus protest. He asks, furthermore, could Banks or any other black leader, either in the past or future, have actual control over decision making without financial independence from white power structures.

In addition to works cited in Woolfolk's notes, readers will find information upon the issue of leadership and education in Alwyn Barr's *Black Texans: A History of Negroes in Texas, 1528-1971* (Austin, 1973); "Educating Black Americans," in *The Black American Reference Book,* Mabel M. Smythe, ed., (New York, 1976), 410-452; and National Association of State Universities and Land Grant Colleges, *State Universities and Black Americans* (Atlanta, 1968).

The Editors

There are few concepts in our society that are under more serious scrutiny than the concept of leadership.[1] This is particularly true for blacks after the dominant illusion of monolithic leadership came to a shattering end with the tragic death of the Reverend Martin Luther King, Jr. This myth had substance only because it could both capture the minority fancy and provide a useful channel for minority manipulation. Few people comprehended the diverse varieties and potential options for leadership implicit in black society.

Authentic black leadership was not encouraged by the white majority. The mythical black spokesman has been the product of a selective process that kept him alienated from his own people. The discussion of his authenticity and viability is pertinent now because at last the black leader has the option of operating from a power base that is built upon black group consciousness, a willingness to accept group discipline, and desire for self-selected leadership.

Analysis of black leadership began with a false assumption of dichotomy—"accommodationists" and "protesters."[2] The merits of activism versus accommodation have become the central theme of an expanding literature and are accompanied by an attack upon the black middle class for shirking the natural responsibility of leadership inherent in its social status. Related to that view is a critique of black self-respect and masculinity which underscores exclusion from the normal world of leadership. New devotees of street or cult leadership have made a fetish of activism and hold in scorn all leadership prototypes which provided substantive access to the open society.

To understand the supposedly "accommodationist" black leaders in earlier periods of white domination requires an appreciation of their travail and sacrifices. Booker T. Washington understood that power of leadership comes from the masses. Without their capacity to support a leader, middle-class efforts to build a power base for black dignity and credibility were doomed to failure. A black leader in those circumstances became a client of a sponsor, subjected to whims and power needs alien to his own people's best interests. The only escape from that dilemma was to play power brokers against each other with a skill in maneuver between superior and inferior, while at the same time never seeming to pit one against the other. Leaders of the Washington genre, like W. R. Banks, surreptitiously pressured a guilt-ridden North to act as a counterweight to the raw irresponsibility of southern politicos.

Ashamed of the weakness that allowed blacks to maneuver them into rational patterns of social behavior, white southerners often reacted irrationally by forcing blacks into public submission and subverting, where possible, plans and programs for their social betterment. To their credit, men like Banks were willing to take the risk of this struggle in the interest of a people fickle and undependable in a showdown because of a dream for their progress and eventual liberation. Many black leaders lost the gamble and were rewarded by both personal danger and the destruction of their plans and programs.

In Northeast Georgia on August 8, 1881, the second born of thirteen children of J. M. and Laura Banks discovered America in the hill town of Hartwell.[3] They named him Willette Rutherford Banks.

He was born in the heroic age of Negro education. His father, a Georgia Populist and the founder of the Colored Zion Elementary School, which W. R. attended as a boy, was an exemplary symbol of the strivings of Negroes in the post-Reconstruction South. For twenty years W. R. Banks worked within a twenty-mile radius of Hartwell, preparing to follow his father's path to Atlanta University.

Banks entered a southern outpost of the classical tradition in Negro education where Horace Bumstead and E. T. Ware were making their mark and W. E. B. DuBois was to pioneer the inquiry method to solve black problems. Banks entered the eighth grade at Atlanta University in 1901 by examination, and in the succeeding eight years he became a varsity debater, all southeast center of the football squad,[4] member of the YMCA, and managed and edited the school paper. Here he met Clovinia Virginia Perry, who brought both love and culture into the life of this hill-town boy. He also gave his heart to DuBois, whose educational conference, involvement in the Niagara movement and the NAACP, and book, *The Souls of Black Folk,* left an indelible mark upon the mind and spirit of this impressionable youth.[5]

Following Banks's graduation from Atlanta in June, 1909, E. T. Ware, president of Atlanta University, recommended him for a teaching job at Fort Valley Normal and Industrial Institute. His duties at the Georgia school included teaching five subjects, being business manager, coaching athletics, supervising the farm, teaching Sunday School, being dean of men, and leading prayer meetings. There he received his first lessons in practical life. He left the position in 1912 with the unshakable conviction that the value of an able man could be measured by the number of related and unrelated positions he could hold in the institutional framework.

In 1912 a vacancy occurred in the principalship of Kowaliga Community School in Elmore County, Alabama. President Ware recommended Banks to Oswald Garrison Villard as a man who knew how to work with rural people. Banks's acceptance brought him into contact with northern philanthropic financing and with community divisions which he healed.[6]

Membership in the Colored Methodist Episcopal church gave Banks his next administrative experience. The church's secretary of the Education Board, an intimate friend of the Banks family, suggested Banks to Bishop R. A. Carter for the presidency of Texas College at Tyler. Banks was elected in May, 1915, and arrived there in August. He found the board of a hundred-plus trustees composed of preachers and a few laymen and larger than the seventy-five-member student body. Banks was further dismayed to find a small faculty underpaid or unpaid in a ramshackle plant. The plight of the school during Banks's tenure forced him to become a master of fly-by-night financing, a builder, and a recruiter par excellence. The student body became the second largest among the state's black college community. Therefore, by the time he left in 1926, Banks had made a reputation for himself in black educational circles across the state.

W. R. Banks was prepared neither by temperament nor training for the peculiarities of state-supported education when in 1926 he was offered the principalship at Prairie View, the only state-supported college for blacks. His prior experience had been with denominational private schools which emphasized liberal arts and teacher training. The fiscal freedom and educational initiative he had previously exercised poorly prepared him for the restraints imposed by the rules and regulations of Texas A&M College, Prairie View's parent institution. He had been trained in the Old South tradition where the president was a demigod, lord of a patrimony including everything in his sight and under the sound of his voice. He was not prepared for the faculty anarchy, the educational expression of political Fergusonism,[7] which had wrecked the administration of his predecessor, J. G. Osborne.

The James Ferguson political machine lent an air of Jacksonian egalitarianism to the folksy ruralism of a program which seemed liberal because if found itself sometimes on the side of the commoner. Calling Sears and Roebuck and the Fergusons the best friends the Negro ever had, "Farmer Jim" Ferguson held Texas politics in his hand for two decades after 1914 and frequently interfered in the affairs of Prairie View.

As has been true in so many southern states, blacks of doubtful political morality and social-personal ethics played the dirty game of educational politics. Though material gains were small and risks were high, the doubtful prestige of standing in the shadow of the seats of the mighty and using their power and glory for personal ends became the logical goals of some of those suffering from the ills of disfran-

chisement. Educational politics always loomed large in Negro thinking because it was accepted as the main channel and, in the case of
the Negro in the post-Reconstruction South, almost the only channel
through which the fruits of the American dream could be realized.
The silt of racism often choked this channel, and the leadership it
produced was often motivated by ideas of racial progress antithetical
to those held by the mass of Negroes. Such was the case shortly before
Banks went to Prairie View; at that time a nationwide movement
among Negroes for self-determination began to develop.

The monopoly of the politics of religion and education among
Negroes was shattered because mobility and urbanization intensified
interest in the American dream.[8] The result was a new consciousness
which showed itself in a demand to fight in World War I, the Marcus
Garvey movement, the "New Negro" movement in literature, Carter
Woodson's Negro history and culture movement, and the leftward
swing of the Randolph-Owen coalition that swept blacks beyond the
simple accommodation of the religion-education leadership. Political
stirrings in Texas, typified by court suits against the white primary
brought by Dr. L. A. Nixon of El Paso, made younger black leaders
skeptical of older models.

Banks was among those young blacks who sensed a new day.[9]
Men in Methodism sensed it and felt free to talk to Banks about the
short-comings of the old order. At that time Banks was seeking a new
avenue for his talents. Thus, he welcomed the Prairie View opportunity as "a divine call to a field of larger service" despite Bishop
Carter's admonition, "You know that you are going to a political
hotbed at Prairie View, where a single misstep politically will mean
that you will hunt you another job."[10]

Although the principalship at Prairie View had a bad reputation, several capable young men were recommended for it, including
faculty member E. B. Evans and J. J. Rhoads, a high school principal
and future president of Bishop College. Indeed, the Colored Teachers
State Association set up a search committee for the post. Many blacks
mistakenly thought they had a role in Banks's getting the job.[11] From
the time that A&M President T. O. Walton began his correspondence
with Banks about the job, however, Jackson Davis and Leo M. Favrot,
field agents of the General Education Board, had the inside track in
urging Banks's nomination. Only the strength of that Rockefeller in-

terest in the improvement of southern education convinced Walton to turn his back on Harold Tarver, the nominee of the A&M board member from San Antonio who had been a friend of Walton's for twenty-five years and was responsible for his presidency.

Succeeding a helter-skelter philanthropic evolution of solutions to southern cultural poverty, the General Education Board's statesmanlike grasp of the problem was clearly revealed in its support of secondary education, rural education, college education, and the farm demonstration work developed by Seaman Knapp of Terrell. The efforts for blacks were part of the total program.[12] The General Education Board encouraged southern states to publically support elementary and vocational education for blacks to cure the hit-or-miss effort of private philanthropy and chose centers like Hampton and Tuskegee to train personnel for future needs. The cooperation of the General Education Board with the Slater, Jeanes, and Rosenwald funds further stimulated the revolution in black public education.

Feeling that its work in elementary and secondary education was firmly grounded and sure that its aid made strategically located private colleges seed-beds for its policies, the General Education Board sought to promote teacher training with grants enabling public colleges to attract additional funds for buildings, maintenance, and facilities. Davis and Favot were convinced of the key position of the enlightened teacher in the black uplift movement and were determined that the state land-grant and normal schools should take on the task. There was no doubt in their minds that W. R. Banks was the man for Prairie View.[13] President Walton brought Banks's name before the A&M board at the November meeting of 1925. Banks was elected "provided the Prairie View Committee and President Walton satisfied themselves about Banks' attitude toward the race question as some reports were made to the Board questioning his position on the matter."[14] By the time of Banks's final election on June 1, 1926, he had written enough letters to Walton claiming closeness to Booker T. Washington to scotch some black attempts to smear him with ties to DuBois. Thus, Walton could assure the A&M board of directors that Banks was "safe" on the race question.

Banks's election as the seventh principal of Prairie View brought some plain speaking from his superior. Walton thought the job had gotten too large for a Negro since the school gave him more trouble than all his other obligations. Walton said that blacks needed a real leader, and Banks promised to try to be one. The promise was easier than fulfillment.[15] Osborne left him some able men and women, E. B. Evans, Charles Lewis, Dr. J. M. Franklin, C. L. Wilson, and many others. But Banks was a liberal arts man thrust into a land-grant situation. More serious still was the necessity to confront the faculty anarchy and gross academic and personal amorality which had embedded itself in the very core of the institution.[16]

One of the last of the great Negro pioneers in minority techniques, Banks posed, as an answer to faculty anarchy, a type of intolerance, self-opinion, and the keeping of his own counsel, which, while lasting long after the problem had gone, found terse expression in his phrase, "keep them on a cold trail." Banks also had a friend at court, Henry C. Schuhmacher of the Houston grocery firm, who for years was the A&M board member invidiously called "Prairie View lover."[17] While assiduously cultivating the idea of being "safe" as a matter of strategy, Banks adroitly emphasized the serious development of southern education through the network of foundation activity centered around the General Education Board and federally sponsored programs for the land-grant college movement. Banks would have been odd indeed if, since he came to educational maturity at the turn of the century, his administration in philosophy, organization, and action did not reflect much of the Tuskegee idea. Banks may have given DuBois his heart, but he gave Booker Taliaferro Washington his head.

Banks took office at a time when participation of black colleges in the land-grant movement offered opportunities for perceptive administrators to work together[18] and pressure their own boards away from the narrow provincialism affecting state ratings and regional progress.[19] By the time Banks entered the picture, the Association of Negro Land-Grant Colleges had become the Conference of Presidents of Land-Grant Colleges. Led by John M. Gandy and John W. Davis, the organization became a floating seminar for the consideration by these black leaders of the frustrations and inadequacies of state-supported education.[20]

Investigation became the new weapon. College heads like Banks could explore the entire range of school activities as he did in Arthur J. Klein's Bureau of Education Survey of Black Colleges in 1927. Getting a favorable judgment on his secondary and college programs helped Prairie View look good in the Klein report.[21] He was not home free, but his deficiencies did not take the bloom off the rose. The Association of Land-Grant Colleges and Universities' determination to study its members thoroughly (with federal money) gave the seventeen black institutions the chance to reappraise their objectives and functions. When the black presidents established an advisory committee, Banks was off again as an investigative field agent. As good as was the opportunity to show recalcitrant "boards" the real need of land-grant college orientation, the revelation came too late. The "teaching" function, cheaper and well established, would remain dominant because the depression would make impossible the addition of scientific dimensions to the black land-grant colleges. The A&M board did instruct Walton and Schuhmacher to examine, improve, and add to the curriculum at Prairie View.[22]

The situation was made for the Banks touch. He could turn to his foundations and suggest that his teachers be remembered when training money was available, and he could ask A&M's board for plant improvement. He was alarmed at how low the salaries were at Prairie View, especially since review by the Southern Association must come as a logical part of his drive to upgrade the college. Classes were overloaded, and plant facilities and faculty housing left much to be desired. Just as he pivoted between the Rockefeller coalition and the state for staff improvement, so he hoped to execute the same maneuver to improve the physical plant.

Banks asked the General Education Board to provide $125,000 for a projected $364,000 building program which was to include a girls' dormitory, hosptial and nursing quarters, boys' dormitory, boys' trade building, renovating two boys' halls, mess hall annex and equipment, addition to steam-light-power plant, community center, furniture for boys' and girls' dormitories, and equipment for the hosptial. Continuing the work begun by Osborne, Banks got $100,000 from the General Education Board and the remainder from the state through the A&M board. His idea of "cleanup" included the planting of trees and shrubs as well as the fortuitous assistance of an accidental fire to clear away an old building. Needless to say, Banks brought to bear on students the same critical eye that would have put the Geneva Consistory to shame. Because Methodist morality, serious scholarship, and athletics had influenced him, he encouraged, "Y's," "baseball-football," and "honor societies," from scientific to debating, to compete with each other in the general atmosphere of spiritual earnestness that pervaded any Banks school.

True to his promise to President Walton to provide leadership for the Negro citizens of Texas, Banks did not limit his talents to the campus. To be sure, the idea of a program of service to the citizens of the state was not original with Banks. Indeed, given the time and circumstances, the leadership of his predecessors L. C. Anderson and E. L. Blackshear in the field of positive social action was superior to Banks's conception. Banks saw clearer than any of his predecessors that the ultimate answer was not a state answer but one that lay in the broader field of national action. Despite Walton's growing protest that he spent too much time off campus and out of Texas, Banks persisted in maintaining his contacts with the broader currents of national action and thought.

Banks was encouraged by the dedicated staff he found on his arrival. The cooperative Extension Service for Negroes at Prairie View,[23] with the legendary Mary E. V. Hunter and C. H. Waller; the Texas Interscholastic League of Colored Schools;[24] the summer normals, institutes, and schools—all of these fired Banks's imagination, though giving little room for innovation. Banks worked around the edges, even mistakenly designating April 1929 as the fiftieth anniversary of the college and celebrating it with a barebones frugality which became the hallmark of his administration.

Searching for some initiative in the state arena, Banks thought to reproduce, perhaps in format and content, the great DuBois conferences at Atlanta University. Having been elected president of the Colored Teachers State Association, Banks sensed the opportunity of combining the Atlanta idea with the efforts of the National Association of Teachers in Colored Schools, fostered by the General Education Board. The national association's president, John W. Davis, wanted state facts gathered for monthly reports and annual meetings. After a series of discussions, Banks's mind flowed beyond the immediate needs, and he penned letters to several foundations for approval.[25] The conference was approved by outside contacts and the State Board of Education. Banks was ready. His matter-of-fact letter to Walton suggested the spring of 1930 as the date of the first "conference," with the "object . . . . to make an analysis and a thorough study of the present educational system and opportunities for the colored youth of Texas."[26] Walton rose to the bait and accepted the idea, seeing in it an opportunity for Texas blacks to accept the natural leadership of Prairie View in the crucial areas of educational progress. Only 165 people attended the first conference, but Banks had laid the foundation for one of his most significant contributions to the life of the college and the development of black education in the state.

Time is seldom kind to a man who dreams, and Banks was no exception. The Great Depression, worldwide in its scope, placed Banks in a terrible dilemma. The voice of the New York squire, Franklin Roosevelt, tried to put fear in perspective and offered a bewildered nation hope with his proposed New Deal. The massive shift of blacks to the Democratic party was reflected in "black cabinets," themselves reflecting a deeper soberness which intuitively sensed the winds of change. Needless to say, black intellectuals began to take a long look at their colleges.[27]

The presidents not only agreed with DuBois that "the Negro college has today neither intelligence nor comprehension" of "the tremendous organization of industry, commerce, capital, and credit which today forms a super-organization dominating and ruling the universe," but agonized over the irrationality of their programs and the primitiveness of their plants.[28] The black land-grant college presidents, in a series of meetings as the depression deepened, found the personal courage to admit the irrelevance of their operations. When Banks was president at the thirteenth annual meeting in Washington, D.C., he faced the same hard truths as he did at home.[29] Governors Ross Sterling, Miriam Ferguson, and James Allred had to stand for economy, but the General Education Board and the Rosenwald Fund could help relieve the general gloom.

Banks was to find that hard times tended to intensify problems that had public repercussions. The case of a student named Tyree Slaughter brought Banks under fire from a member of the board, Judge Byrd E. White, which forced Walton to intervene to protect Banks. Banks discovered that Walton was considering the replacement of Dr. J. M. Franklin with a white hospital director because the high quality of services had attracted some white women as patients. Schuhmacher fended off the attack. Depreciation cut into the state warrants the state paid his staff, and one day Banks could not meet his payroll. Teachers and programs fell before this dilemma. And what of the grandiose schemes he had for the building of a modern college? Despite adroit handling of his surplus funds, neither the state nor A&M could come to his rescue. Master by instinct of depression economics, Banks used both his students[30] and the lumber from older buildings to push his building program along.[31]

Behind the facade of constant and feverish activity on all fronts, in Banks's mind the supreme imperative was: could he, amid these distractions and frustrations, build a college in the real sense of the word? The final test of his skill lay in securing accreditation for Prairie View. Since he understood that the Texas imprimature would not do, Banks knew it would have to come from the Southern Association of Colleges. His constant pleas to College Station for improvement received a dramatic boost from a survey of state agencies made by Griffenhagen and Associates of Chicago and authorized by the legislature. The report was a critical exposé of Banks's resources for accreditation.[32]

Griffenhagen was satisfied with the outreach program of the college and thought that the state had not been as generous with the only black college it supported as with the white colleges. If the money was properly managed, however, it would efficiently do the job. The college was inadequate in the vital areas of instruction, management, and plant facilities. The qualifications of the staff were questionable at both undergraduate and graduate levels; the library collection was too small; and the plant was as badly scattered as its structures were poorly planned. The power plant was insufficient. Worst still, the supervision from College Station seemed unsympathetic and inconsistent when viewed from the standpoint of the needs of black education. The Griffenhagen report recommended that Prairie View be removed from the oversight of the A&M board of directors, the president, the supervising engineer and the supervising accountant because waste and maladministration had characterized the actions of these officers toward Prairie View.

The depression was no time for salient display of virtuosity in maneuver among the philanthropic foundations, and Banks had sense enough to know it. In his campaign for accreditation he also saw the need for a more adroit use of key members of the board and top faculty and officials surrounding the A&M president. Banks listed as potential supporters Henry C. Schuhmacher; F. M. Law; S. C. Bailey, A&M executive secretary; and Dean Charles E. Friley, for he knew intuitively the word of a black leader was never taken upon its own merits.

With the help of Friley, Banks presented his unauthorized plans for a "school of Arts and Sciences" (knowing that his more ambitious plans had no chance of acceptance) to Dr. Arthur D. Wright, a Dartmouth savant who was acting for the Southern Association, in January, 1931. Wright's vagueness and noncommittal attitude suggested the possibility of trouble. Carefully making his plans, Banks, flanked by A&M's Dean Friley and representatives of the State Board of Education, faced Dr. Fred McCuistion of the Southern Association at a May conference. Immediately it became apparent that the library, salaries, and qualifications of the faculty were, as Banks already knew, suspect. Backed by promises of aid from the parent school, Banks began laying plans and making assurances of efforts to upgrade Prairie View's position before a December, 1932, meeting of the Southern Association; thus McCuistion left in good spirits.

Banks opened a campaign of letter writing to his College Station supporters[33] concerning the library, the budget,[34] the salary scale, the pride of the system, and the pride of the Prairie View family. Banks wondered if the promise of one white man to another would prevail. Before long he knew the answer. The faithful Schuhmacher wrote that the A&M board refused to raise salaries: "I am sorry that I was unable to get the Board to meet your views, but the stand was so decided that I immediately saw that it was futile for me to make any further attempt."[35] But all of Banks's efforts had not been in vain. As if in anticipation of the Christmas holiday, the singing wires brought news from Nashville on December 6, 1934, "Congratulations: Southern Association voted Prairie View State College Class "A" Rating." The nine-year struggle was over, although it had not resulted in complete victory.

To a man of Banks's mettle, public honesty was as important as private honesty; and this rating without honor, regardless of what the public thought, was almost as bad as no rating at all. Unfortunately, the second-class "A" rating he wrung from the association not only was indicative of the pattern of accreditation that was to prevail for

most of the Negro colleges of the South, but also highlighted the
spiritual relations of Banks's administration with College Station.
Somehow, despite his best efforts, the officials of the Agricultural
and Mechanical College managed to water down his victories either
with indifference of attitude or execution so that the results always
fell short of the dream. Angry about the implications of the "pit-
tance" he could pay his staff for his dream of a modern college, Banks
let the mask drop and lashed out with the remark, "We have men at
Prairie View who find it difficult to meet their grocery bill."

By the mid-1930s Banks's reputation as a builder was still intact,
and his great skill in prodding the state to support Prairie View
through using the philanthropic agencies in New York, Washington,
and Chicago was still useful. Despite low salaries, he had upgraded
the faculty and provided a jerry-built collection of structures to house
them. He had labored with his contemporaries to build a greater consciousness of mission. Through fire and blood and chicanery and the
studied insult of nonsupport or half-hearted support for his program,
this gaunt, determined man had built a better institution for the
education of blacks within the limited pattern of a segregated system.
For many years he had perfected his skills to suit such a pattern of
education. Could he find the skills to meet the situation should the
rules of the game suddenly change?

The New Deal released an inner dynamism in American society
which bade fair to radically change the world Banks understood. Suddenly blacks found themselves wept over by liberals who called for
programs of social action, the political trademark of pragmatic
liberalism. The politics of recovery blurred the color line from "black
cabinets" to radical unions. Impassioned court fights also erupted
over jury exclusion, residential segregation, library exclusion, swimming pools, railroads, police forces, and the use of black doctors of
hospital facilities. Could the segregated schools with their cadre of ill-
prepared teachers and culturally deprived students escape the attention of aroused blacks?

In the late 1920s and early 1930s, there had been a few court
cases in the border and northeastern states on discrimination in
primary and secondary education. But by the late 1930s the National
Association for the Advancement of Colored People (NAACP) was
perfecting a departure in litigation calculated to override state

recalcitrancy through "an action for a declaratory judgment and injunction, based upon the equal protection clause of the 14th Amendment, and section 43 of Title 8 of the United States Code."[36]

It was inevitable that the application of the same principle to litigation in higher professional education would come in a few spectacular cases. Anticipating the problem, Missouri (1921 and 1929) and West Virginia (1927) opted for out-of-state aid for blacks. North Carolina's Guy B. Johnson saw the dilemma as one of increasing black demands on the one hand and inadequacy of the black colleges on the other. The Supreme Court ruled in December, 1938 (*Lloyd Gaines* v. *University of Missouri*), that the southern states, even though most stood for either aid in out-of-state (South) or "regional" schools, must educate blacks in their own states.[37]

The handwriting was on the wall. North Carolina, Maryland, and Virginia by 1939 had instituted graduate programs at black colleges. Black land-grant presidents, fully aware of the poverty-stricken South's capacity for intellectual amorality, warned at the Howard conclave in 1937: "It would seem a wise precaution to assure the adequacy and effectiveness of the undergraduate program before advancing into the graduate field."[38]

In time the presidents ceased to warn against the move to add graduate professional programs to their institutions, and many like Banks sought to exploit the trend for all it was worth. The growing sense of the need for justice for blacks that both the Texas Centennial and the coming war engendered found evidence in a soul-searching of the "separate but equal" doctrine. Texas liberals were prepared to follow the other southern states. Governor Allred admitted that Texas had not been fair with blacks and suggested either out-of-state aid or improvement of Texas institutions.[39] The legislature chose out-of-state aid.

The crisis had come. Banks, like all of his contemporaries, had, in the best Booker T. Washington tradition, spent the greater part of their lives executing that most dangerous and difficult of all maneuvers—running with both the hounds and the hares. Moreover, Banks was not a man of great intellectual stature. Instead, from the days of his Atlanta University studies, his talents rested in the quicksilver arena of judging and handling men in a fairly stable, if not rigid, social system. It was Banks's misfortune that the milieu he understood best was shattering under the impact of the depression and emerging world conflagration. Discovering that both federal agencies and foundations were together in sanctioning the new departure, Banks tried to salvage what he could from a situation that, on its face, seemed to be the expansion of opportunity, but which in essence could result in the denial of opportunity to the masses of Negroes in the state.

Say what one will in the defense of Banks's position, the real dilemma of the black college is clearly revealed here. The black publically supported college can never be an institution of higher learning, in the real sense of the word, so long as it is not the master of its own destiny, so long as it cannot call its soul its own. Before damning black leadership in higher education for lack of creative statesmanship and a positive educational initiative, one must remember that the only alternative would have been, pending the development of true social enlightenment in the South, personal destruction and institutional emasculation. The choice for Banks was not an easy one. He chose to go along. He thought it was better for Prairie View to get half a loaf than none at all.

Banks's turnaround was three pronged. In the face of black skeptics, he opted for a graduate program on the grounds, first, that Negro Texans were too poor to go North and could be better trained in Texas to face southern conditions.[40] Second, northern schools already were alarmed at the possible black tide and were getting ready to block it. Third, Prairie View should set its schedules to serve as a shock absorber for the state after the *Gaines* ruling.[41]

Banks's position is better understood in the light of the General Education Board's and Southern Association of Colleges' determination to establish regional centers of graduate study for blacks. Meeting at Durham with the directors of education for Negroes in the states of Arkansas, Louisiana, Mississippi, Oklahoma, and Texas, the association chose Prairie View as the regional center for professional studies in administration, supervision, guidance, and curriculum building.

With Banks's orthodoxy no longer in doubt, Walton was happy. Calling Prairie View the leading college for blacks in the South and the nation, he said, with tongue in cheek, that it stood third in Texas only to Rice and the University of Texas. The Forty-fifth Legislature voted nine thousand dollars for graduate work for each year of the biennium. Black leaders in denominational schools and white liberals opened the fight for out-of-state aid. Banks knew he was losing valuable support. But his knowledge of what the General Education Board and the Rosenwald Fund were prepared to do sustained his most respectable reason for the graduate effort: it would strengthen the undergraduate program at Prairie View. In June, 1938, Banks opened the graduate school with thirty-five students.

Only time could tell whether Banks had been a statesman or a politician. Time already had taught that ambiguity in the matter of convictions, created by the peculiar demand for "safety" in leadership by Banks's superiors, could reflect itself in an intellectual schizophrenia which for years to come would stand as a roadblock to real maturity and educational responsibility in black institutions of higher learning. Since truth must always be qualified by what is likely to give offense, and pecuniary considerations must always have priority over moral and spiritual judgments in the name of survival, Negro institutions were forced to substitute the prudence of mediocrity for intellectual honesty. Banks's frustration at having to settle for less than first class was like that experienced by the Old Man of the Sea. It was his cross. He bore it well.

Banks's last years as president of Prairie View coincided with the worldwide offensive against totalitarian rule. Since 1926 he had stood at the helm of the institution that had taken most of the shocks of college and graduate school education for Negroes, and with some degree of success. His answer to the intellectual provincialism of the college and the inadequacy of its plant had been, at first, a delicate balancing and pressuring of state officials through eastern philanthropic foundations and the federal government. When he saw the growing weakness of this approach, Banks feigned an ideological rapprochement with his superiors because he had little faith in their sense of justice. Nor did he have any more in the promises of white southern liberalism, or in the support of his own people should he take a bold stand in their defense.

Banks never really adjusted to the tempo or extent of change wrought by the war. Time was to demonstrate that he never understood or appreciated the full meaning of integration for his people. Banks had lived in a segregated world too long. The contagion of "protest," which had long manifested itself in the statesmanship of Texas Negroes, stripped Banks of all illusions that anything but a bold strike for social justice for his people was futile. yet, paradoxically, he clung tenaciously to the cautious wisdom of the heroic couplet which runs "Be not the first by whom the new is tried." To that extent Banks became the symbol of the black educational activist, standing on the threshold of the fulfillment of democracy, yet afraid of the future. Realizing that he had been one of the chief beneficiaries of the segregated world and that his experience had been one of limited contact with the white world, he feared subtle, less overt techniques of the denial of opportunity and the demands of unrestricted competition.

When the United States entered the war in December, 1941, the worst fears of blacks were soon realized. Detroit; Mobile; Beaumont; Harlem; Columbia, Tennessee; and Athens, Alabama, became the scene of riots, with the new and odd dimensions of blacks fighting back.[42] It was clear that blacks were going to have to fight for freedom. The issue of Executive Order 8802, a response to A. Philip Randolph's threatened march on Washington against job discrimination, was only symptomatic of new black resistance. The new black stance caused a reconsideration of manpower needs by the armed services. In addition, many antidiscrimination suits were filed across the nation, ranging from peonage, through travel, to breach of the white primary by *Smith* v. *Allwright*.

Fortuitously, Gunnar Myrdal finished the Carnegie Corporation commissioned *The American Dilemma: The Negro Problem and Modern Democracy*, championing a new racial rationale based on basic American ideals, sociology, and anthropology. Following quickly, Rayford Logan and his associates took the opportunity, through sponsorship of University of North Carolina Press, to say *What the Negro Wants*. Summing up the ideas of his associates, Logan said, "Negroes in the United States want first class citizenship."[43]

Could Negro land-grant presidents be insensitive to such a heady atmosphere? Would they not be thrilled by DuBois's call for a cooperative research program in the black colleges to substitute for "perpetually indignant and passionate agitation against wrong, a persistent planned scientific procedure to emanciptate American Negroes by using the same thought and methods which are making for the emancipation of the laboring classes throughout the world?''

Emboldened by their newfound freedom to speak out, land-grant presidents asked, on the one hand, for racial harmony and the winning of the war and, on the other, for what appeared to be black nationalism, but what in reality was the full moral obligation implied by Myrdal and Logan and his associates.[44] Because many white southern political leaders were in revolt against the New Deal and alarmed about the implications of World War II, Banks and the other presidents sensed the value of caution, but saw the first line of defense in the schoolroom and the ballot box.

The ideological mix and the sparse distribution of blacks in Texas encouraged Banks to take his last gamble to bring Prairie View to the forefront of black education. Time was running out, and the passing years, so unkind to the aged, were pregnant with the opportunity for revolution. The 1939 study on higher education for blacks, underscoring its inadequacy at all levels, was a simple reminder that the task was unfinished. Banks also understood that he was surrounded by men for whom his superiors showed greater appreciation. All of these factors resulted in a new urgency and plain speaking in his relations with Texas A&M. An inadequate budget in 1941 and E. M. Norris's graduate school report brought the magic words out of Banks's bag, ''I feel that the situation is of such gravity that it precipitates an emergency.''

Life teaches a peculiar wisdom from which man learns to have faith in the success of his own peculiar formulas. Could not Banks again combine northern philanthropy with Texas liberalism to break at last the logjam that stood in the way of national credibility for Prairie View?[45] Remembering the power of ''surveys'' in southern education, Banks wrote Jackson Davis of the General Education Board for one thousand dollars to survey Negro education in Texas. Stating that President Homer Rainey of the University of Texas, President Walton of A&M, the State Board of Education, and the Commission on Interracial Cooperation were interested, he suggested Leo Favrot to direct the study. The calculated gamble worked like magic. Banks again was in business.

Banks graciously accepted the advice from Austin and College Station that a conference precede the request for foundation funds because of his previous conference on graduate study. All of the relevant committees in the state met and came to the conclusion that Banks wanted, all improvements in black higher education should be concentrated at Prairie View. A black faction led by J. J. Rhoads wanted another black college altogether.[46] But, with all the colleges and the public school authorities as cosponsors of the study, the chance for success appeared imminent.

The committee investigating the needs of Negro education brought in the suggestion that Prairie View be made a university. The Forty-ninth Legislature obliged with the necessary action, ". . . providing for the establishment of courses in law, medicine, engineering, pharmacy, journalism or any other generally recognized college course taught at the University of Texas."[47] A&M's board was to put this mandate into operation and see to it that these courses were "substantially equivalent" to those at the University of Texas in Austin.

Banks could have been satisfied with this solution if the legislature had implemented its action with appropriate financing. The "new college" faction, though dissatisfied, seemed stalemated, though the rumor of a test case of the University of Texas in Austin was in the wind. A&M had submitted to the Forty-ninth Legislature a budget figure of $853,260 for the biennium to fund Prairie View. By summer, 1945, it was clear that the board's figure would be reduced by the legislature to $558,080. The State Board of Education had suggested $560,000 for salaries alone at Prairie View. Spurred at last into a flurry of action, Banks, who had never been offered the opportunity of meeting the board of directors, prepared a flood of papers directly to the legislature and the Free Conference Committee over the heads of his superiors, although he had been warned by an A&M dean that it might cost him the chance to continue beyond the official retirement age. Banks won his point with the legislature, securing in the $900,000 it granted even more money than A&M had requested for Prairie View.

In the spring of 1946 A&M announced Banks's retirement at the end of the state's allotted tenure. Yet he never ceased to pursue the goal of improved education for blacks. In 1947 he became vice-chairman of the board of regents for Texas State University for Negroes, later Texas Southern University. Although he continued to live at Prairie View, he served on the boards of Atlanta University,

Morehouse College, and Paine College, all in Georgia. He died on October 16, 1969, in Corsicana and was buried at Memorial Park in Prairie View.

But by the time of Banks's retirement, the NAACP was making the move through the *Sweatt* case that would outlaw the world for which Banks had fought. Banks never had conceived of the day when schools like Prairie View might no longer be of use in the changing South. What he really wanted was separate but equal education for blacks. He had no fundamental objections to the black elite being trained at the best schools, but he intuitively, if not fully intellectually, understood the barriers to substantive cultural change among the masses. Such a position would always keep the realist in Negro education at the halfway house. Trying to keep a foot in both camps places some pressures upon educational statesmanship, which result inevitably in twilight zones of academic excellence and professional integrity.

And what of the Prairie View W. R. Banks had created? He had done what he could to make it a multipurpose teacher-training college despite its ill-kept, outdated plant and a constantly changing faculty that was easily raided by other colleges and the public schools which could offer better incomes. Banks knew that his legacy was only a "passable" Negro school. How much of this situation was due to the times is difficult to say. Poorer states in the Old South had done much better in general facilities for Negro populations less progressive or enlightened. It is also difficult to assess the interplay of personalities at the policy level. Perhaps if Banks had been better understood or liked by his superiors, more might have been accomplished. Yet Banks left a long shadow upon the future of Prairie View.

It would be misleading and incorrect to label men like Banks pure and unadulterated accommodationists. The Booker Washington syndrome, correctly delineated, was a dangerous maneuver of running with the hares and the hounds. Such leaders as Banks could do what the current black activist could never do intellectually or actively. They could bring the overpowering influence of the board rooms of northern capital as leverage for social action plans while living in the midst of pressures so unremitting as to stagger the imagination. They fed on this danger, and in its school they became adroit and wise. Men like Banks often led in the dark because the very nature of their strategy, if fully known, would have destroyed both the value of their tactics and the power of their influence.

Their stance of "public safety" was the quid pro quo for what even their southern superiors, though overawed by the national connections of these black men, demanded: a ceremonial bending of the knee which the unwary and superficial student of our time has foolishly called accommodation. The new black secular leadership cannot hope to gain the moral stature and the sheer gut courage of the leaders of the Banks era.

NOTES

1. "In Quest of Leadership," *Time* (July 15, 1974), 22-23. The serious attempts to analyze black leadership began with Gunnar Myrdal, who divided it between accommodation and protest in his *An American Dilemma: The Negro Problem and Modern Democracy* (New York, 1944), 507-508, 720-726, 772-774. With deeper perception Oliver C. Cox observed, "No contemporary leader of major significance then can be totally void of at least a modicum of the spirit of 'Uncle Tom.' " Oliver Cromwell Cox, *Caste, Class, and Race: A Study in Social Dynamics* (Garden City, N.Y., 1948), 573.

In *The Negro Leadership Class* (Englewood Cliffs, N.J., 1963), pp. 58, 74, 165, Daniel C. Thompson introduced the concept of the leadership cadre and the stratifications within it, while Robert Penn Warren observed that, even in protest, leaders must find vulnerable points and avoid showdown situations. Robert Penn Warren, *Who Speaks for the Negro?* (New York, 1965), 408-409. Martin Luther King, Jr., called Myrdal's dichotomy unnatural and suggested a synthesis of public virtues into one individual in *Where Do We Go from Here: Chaos or Community?* (New York, 1967), 149. Seemingly oblivious to the risk involved, Lerone Bennett, Jr., offered "revolt"—"a refusal to accept"—as a new means of liberation in his *Confrontation: Black and White* (Chicago, 1965).

2. Psychological analysis of black emasculation is ambivalent. Some studies propose solutions to this dilemma. Others argue that emasculation began in slavery and is beyond recovery. Abram Kardiner and Lionel Ovesey cataloged the influences of slavery and emphasized the concepts of self-hate and guilt feelings about success in their *The Mark of Oppression: A Psychosocial Study of the American Negro* (New York, 1951), 46-47, 365. The need to suppress aggression to avoid retaliation was detailed by Bertram P. Koron, who stated that therefore close contacts among males, a *sine qua non* of leadership, are avoided lest they erupt in pysical aggression. Bertram P. Karon, *The Negro Personality: A Rigorous Investigation of the Effects of Culture* (New York, 1968), 172.

The most dramatic statement of this trend appears in William H. Grier and Price M. Cobbs, *Black Rage* (New York, 1965), 59: "Whereas the white man regards his manhood as an ordained right, the black man is engaged in a never ending battle for its possession." The recent debate over the existence of a "Sambo" complex under slavery reflects the influence of this psychological concern on the writing of history.

3. W. R. Banks, *News Letters,* 1931-1939 (W. R. Banks Library, Prairie View A & M University, Prairie View, Texas), May, 1931 (hereafter cited as *News Letters,* [date]). These *News Letters* are bound in two volumes to 1944 and constitute a valuable month by month account of the public happenings of the Banks administration.

4. George A. Towns to Van Edward Sims, Mar. 22, 1950, W. R. Banks Papers (Archives, Texas College Library, Tyler, Texas).

5. Myrdal, *American Dilemma,* 742-744.

6. Banks to G. R. W., Feb. 18, 1950, interview.

7. V. O. Key, Jr. and Alexander Heard, *Southern Politics in State and Nation* (New York, 1949), 262-268.

8. Myrdal, *American Dilemma,* 745-750; Monroe N. Work (ed.), *Negro Year Book, . . . 1931-1932* (Tuskegee, 1931), 58, 70, 99-102.

9. J. A. Lester, registrar, Meharry Medical College to Banks, July 13, 1926, Ray S. Tomlin, president, Paine College, to Banks, July 2, 12, 1926, Banks to Bishop John W. McKinney, June 30, July 14, 1926, Bishop R. A. Carter, Fourth Episcopal District, C.M.E. Church, to Banks, July 15, 1926, Banks Papers. Said Bishop Carter, "I am sorry that your betting on the wrong horse in St. Louis in 1922 has so disgusted you, and also the way the horse has treated you for the last four years, that you have decided to get out of the educational work of the C.M.E. church. However, I cannot blame you much. Things have gotten so rotten until some more of us would like to make a change if we could get an acceptable one."

10. Carter to Banks, July 15, 1926, F. R. Barnwell to Banks, July 15, 1926, Banks Papers; Houston *Informer,* June 26, 1926.

11. Mabel Kilpatrick, a Blackshear student remained certain that had not the members of the staff at Prairie View and her father collected the data proving Harold Tarver's unfitness for the post of principal, he, and not Banks, would have followed Osborne to the principalship.

12. Robert D. Calkins, "Historical Review, 1902-1947," in General Education Board, *Annual Report, 1947-1948* (New York, n.d.), 41-42, 48-63, *Annual Report,* 1946, (New York, n.d.), x-xiv, xv-xix; George A. Works et al., *Texas Educational Survey Report,* vol. I, *Organization and Administration* (Austin, 1925), 291-296; Leo M. Favrot, "Securing an Adequate Supply of Prepared Teachers for Negro Rural Schools," in National Education Association of the United States, *Addresses and Proceedings* of the Fifty-eighth Annual Meeting, held at Salt Lake City, Utah, July 4-10, 1920, vol. LVIII (Washington, D.C., 1920), 292-295; "Dr. Jackson Davis, Noted Educator, Dies of Heart Attack," *The Quarterly Review of Higher Education among Negroes,* XV, (July, 1947), 240; Journal of Negro History, XXXII (July, 1947), 401-403.

13. "There are two reasons why I believe that you are going to make success of this work. One reason is that as an administrator you keep fully informed about the details of the situation with which you are dealing. The other reason is that you are

inclined to accord to teacher-training its rightful place in a college." Favrot to Banks, July 20, 1926, Banks Papers. There is some indication that T. D. Walton looked upon Banks's administrative reputation as a solution to an impossible supervisory problem, as he explained to James W. Bass, collector, Internal Revenue Department at Austin, who was having trouble getting the free alcohol report. Walton to Bass, July 14, 1926, Banks Papers. Walton also wrote to J. R. Reid, chairman, Board of Examiners, State Department of Education, concerning his hopes for Banks in raising the standards of the college. Walton to Reid, Dec. 16, 1926.

14. Minutes of Board of Directors, Texas A & M Univeristy, Nov. 10, 1926 (Archives, Texas A & M University, College Station, Texas); Banks to Walton, Nov. 11, 1926, Banks Papers.

15. Ella P. Baker to Banks, July 2, 1926, Banks Papers.

16. Peyton Irving, Jr., state college examiner, to Walton, Jan. 8, 1927, ibid.

17. The interest of the Schuhmacher family in Prairie View was enlightened and symbolic of the better public consciousness of many other white people of Texas. The family spent many pleasant days on the campus, and the warm friendship is clearly revealed in the Banks-Schuhmacher letters. Banks to Henry C. Schuhmacher, May 21, 1929, Jan. 7, 1931, Schuhmacher to Banks, Jan. 10, 1931, ibid.

18. Irving to Banks, June 4, Oct. 2, 1926, L. W. Rogers, first assistant state superintendent to Banks, July 13, 1926, Banks to Walton, Feb. 8, 1927, ibid; Walter J. Greenleaf, *Land-Grant Colleges, Year Ended June 30, 1926,* Department of the Interior, Bureau of Education, Bulletin, 1927, No. 37 (Washington, D.C., 1927), 60-63 (hereafter cited as *Land-Grant Colleges*). *Land-Grant Colleges,* Bulletin 1925, No. 44, pp. 58-62; *Land-Grant Colleges and Universities, 1928,* Bulletin, 1929, No. 13, 64-67; Luther H. Foster, C. E. Mitchell, and W. J. Hale, "Report of Committee on Survey of Administrative, Business, and Financial Operations in Negro Land-Grant Colleges" (manuscript copy of report submitted at the Washington meeting in 1926); Presidents of Negro Land-Grant Colleges, *Proceedings of the Fourteenth Annual Conference,* Petersburg, Va., Nov. 10-11, 1936, pp. 93-107 (hereafter cited as Presidents, *Annual Conference,* date).

19. At the Greensboro meeting, in collaboration with the Federal Fifth Conference on Negro Land-Grant College Training, Osborne read a paper on "How Can We Strengthen Our Faculties."

20. The Washington report demanded competence in surpervising boards; presidential responsibility in general administration, fiscal matters, and employment; national solidarity of presidents and their fiscal agents; and academic responsibility for the instructional program and staff.

21. Arthur J. Klein, chief of the Division of Higher Education of the Bureau of Education, with a distinguished group of educators, among whom was William B. Bizzell, president of the University of Oklahoma and former president of Texas A & M, did this study with the cooperation of nineteen state departments of education, seventy-nine Negro colleges and universities, the Association of Colleges for Negro Youth, the Phelps-Stokes Fund, and the educational boards and foundations of seven church bodies.

22. Shcuhmacher to Banks, Jan. 7, 1931, Banks to Schuhmacher, Jan. 13, 1931, Banks Papers.

23. H. S. Estelle to G. R. W., Apr. 5, 1950, interview; M. V. Brown to G. R. W., Apr. 17, 1950, interview; typescript released by the Cooperative Extension Service for Negroes in Texas, Prairie View A & M College, Prairie View, Texas; Mrs. M. E. V. Hunter to G. R. W., Sept. 21, 1950, interview.

24. Prairie View State Normal and Industrial College, *Rules and Regulations of the Texas Interscholastic League of Colored Schools of Texas* (Prairie View, 1941), 5-8.

25. E. R. Embree to Banks, Dec. 31, 1929, W. W. Alexander to Banks, Dec. 18, 1929, Arthur J. Klein to Banks, Dec. 20, 1929, J. H. Dillard to Banks, Dec. 20, 1929, N. C. Newbold to Banks, Dec. 28, 1929; H. C. Sargent, federal agent for agricultural education, to Banks, Jan. 8, 1930, Thomas E. Jones, president of Fisk University, to Banks, Jan. 16, 1930; L. W. Rogers to Banks, Jan. 22, 1930, T. M. Campbell field agent, Extension Services of the U.S. Department of Agriculture, Feb. 6, 1930, Banks Papers.

26. Banks to Walton, Jan. 3, 1930, Walton to Banks, Jan. 8, 1930, ibid. Walton's statesmanlike endorsement marks the high tide of Banks's honeymoon at Prairie View.

27. W. E. Burghardt DuBois, "Education and Work," *Journal of Negro Education,* I (Apr. 1, 1932), 62. The NAACP's Durham Fact Finding of April, 1930, voiced a similar pronouncement in its report when it said, "There must be a revision of educational ideals so as to emphasize more persistently the education of the Negro masses for economic efficiency. The economic competition of the present machine age makes it most imperative that special measures be taken to fit for the exactions of a technical industrial order." Work (ed.), *Negro Yearbook, . . . 1931-1932,* p. 32.

28. Kelly Miller, "The Past, Present and Future of the Negro College," *Journal of Negro Education,* II (July, 1933), 414; Frank Horne, "The Industrial School in the South," *Opportunity: Journal of Negro Life,* (May, 1935), 136-139.

29. Presidents, *Eleventh Annual Conference,* Nov., 1933; Presidents, Thirteenth Annual Conference, Nov., 1935.

30. F. E. Griesecke to Banks, Oct. 18, 1933, Banks Papers.

31. Banks to Walton, Feb. 1, 1934, ibid. Besides those mentioned above, Banks built Anderson Hall in 1933 and Alta Vista, an apartment building for male instructors, in 1935.

32. Griffenhagen and Associates, *The Government of the State of Texas* (Austin, 1932) (hereafter cited as Griffenhagen Report). This is the most notable survey made by this Chicago group. Though in thirteen volumes, only three dealt with higher education. Part XI of the study is concerned with the Agricultural and Mechanical College of Texas and its affiliates. Chapter XII, covering pp. 257-318, is the report on Prairie View Normal and Industrial College.

33. Banks to Walton, Apr. 1, 1932, Banks Papers. Fred McCuistion was scheduled to come to the college in May, 1932, and Banks called Friley to his defense. Both felt that cutting back and strength would enable the college to meet the Southern Association's requirements.

34. Banks to S. C. Bailey, July 4, 1932, Banks to Walton, June 3, 1932 (budgetary statement), Banks to Dean Charles E. Friley, July 4, 1932; Friley to Walton, July 5, 1932, supporting Banks's statement on the necessities for meeting the Southern Association's demands, Banks Papers.

35. Shcuhmacher to Banks, July 14, 1932, ibid. This is a rather pathetic letter and shows the attempt of this friend to let Banks down gently. The missive reads in part: "I suppose you have been informed by this time that the Board would not approve the salary budget as proposed by you. They took a very decided stand on the fact that now was not the time to increase the salary of anyone."

36. The six cases, a majority of which were settled by consent decrees, were as follows: *Gibbs* v. *Board of Education, Montgomery County, Maryland; Brown* v. *Board of Education, Calvert County, Maryland; Griffin* v. *Ocala County School Board, Florida; Black* v. *School Board, Norfolk, Virginia; Cook* v. *Prince County School Board, Maryland.* The full effect of the "declaratory judgment" procedure was seen in the *Mills* v. *Anne Arundel County, Maryland.* The crowning success of *Alston* v. *Norfolk School Board* cannot be overlooked. Jessie Parkhurst Guzman (ed.), *Negro Year Book, . . . 1941-1946,* pp. 62-67.

37. Guzman (ed.), *Negro Year Book, 1941-1946,* p. 97.

38. Presidents, *Fifteenth Annual Conference,* Nov. 15-17, 1937, pp. 96-97.

39. James V. Allred, *Legislative Messages of Hon. James V. Allred, Governor of Texas 1935-1939* (Austin, n.d.), 241-242.

40. Banks to Walton, May 26, 1936, Banks Papers.

41. Banks to Walton, Jan. 28, Feb. 3, Apr. 20, July 18, 1939, ibid.

42. Guzman (ed.), *Negro Year Book, 1941-1946,* p. 232-257.

43. Rayford W. Logan, "The Negro Wants First-Class Citizenship," in *What the Negro Wants,* ed. Logan (Chapel Hill, N.C., 1944), 14, passim.

44. Presidents, *Twenty-second Annual Conference,* Oct. 1944, pp. 117-125; Presidents, *Twenty-third Annual Conference,* Oct., 1945, pp. 88-92.

45. Walton to Homer P. Rainey, president, University of Texas, May 6, 1942, Jackson Davis to Banks, May 8, 1942, Banks to Davis, May 19, 1942, Walton to Banks, May 21, Nov. 9, 1942, Banks to Walton, May 25, Nov. 6, 1942, Banks Papers.

46. The Steering Committee was composed of the following persons: Dean B. F. Pittenger, University of Texas; Dean Thomas Dudley Brooks, Texas A & M; Mrs. Wessendoff, Columbus; Dr. Gordon Worley, executive secretary, State Board of Education; J. J. Rhoads, Bishop College; and W. R. Banks, Prairie View.

47. Texas, Legislature, *General and Special Laws of the State of Texas Passed by the Regular Session of the Forty-ninth Legislature* (Austin, 1945), chap. 308, Senate Bill No. 228 (became law June 1, 1945).

Heman Marion Sweatt. Courtesy Barker
Texas History Center.

VII

HEMAN MARION SWEATT: Civil Rights Plaintiff

Michael L. Gillette

The efforts of black people to gain full civil rights in the United States began with petitions and court cases during the American Revolution. The struggle continued by means of the abolitionist movement, black conventions, and local protests throughout the nineteenth century. Permanent civil rights organizations, such as the National Association for the Advancement of Colored People, began to arise early in the twentieth century. Black Texans attained a significant role in the movement after the Civil War. Especially during the period from the 1920s through the 1940s, they challenged the structure of disfranchisement and discrimination in court cases against the white primary and segregation in public colleges. A brief history of civil rights movements is Lerone Bennett, Jr., *Confrontation: Black and White* (Chicago, 1965).

Black people achieved leadership in civil rights through a variety of roles including crusading newspaper editors, stump speakers, protest leaders, and group organizers. Frederick Douglass exemplified a combination of these abilities in the nineteenth century, as did W. E. B. DuBois in the twentieth century. The attorneys who successfully devoted themselves to civil rights cases, like Thurgood Marshall, also became important figures in the movement. Lerone Bennett, Jr., describes several civil rights leaders in his *Pioneers in Protest* (Chicago, 1968).

Plaintiffs in civil rights cases have often remained shadowy figures, despite the fact that they bore a major burden of public attention and psychological pressure as well as the commitment of time to see a court case through the several trial and appeal stages. The black Texan who first confronted disfranchisement in the 1920s and 1930s is the subject of Conrey Bryson's *Lawrence Nixon and the White Primary* (El Paso, 1974). Heman Sweatt, who challenged the segregation of public education in the 1940s, probably faced even greater pressures because improvements in mass communication focused more attention on his case. Thus, a biographical rather than legal approach clarifies the background influences and character which motivated and sustained him amid those pressures.

The Editors

Finding plaintiffs for civil rights lawsuits was no easy task for the NAACP in the 1940s. Few blacks were willing to have their lives disrupted by an endless succession of meetings and court appearances. The racial hostility that a Negro routinely encountered intensified once he became a plaintiff. As such he placed his job in jeopardy and subjected his family to harassment by whites who regarded him as a troublemaker and a symbol of racial agitation. He became a target for pranksters and extremists.[1]

It was especially difficult to find a plaintiff for an education lawsuit. That the volunteer had to be qualified academically for admission to the segregated institution usually meant that he was eligible to attend a more prestigious university elsewhere. While a plaintiff in a voting rights case could return to anonymity after his court victory, the legal proceedings were only half of the education plaintiff's trial. Once admitted to a white school, he had to attend the institution, compete academically, and endure whatever threats and insults came his way. Finally, there was the greater risk in being a plaintiff in an education suit. Although many white southerners conceded that the Negro should have the right to vote, the thought of school integration incited their deepest feelings of prejudice.[2]

It is clear that not only did a lack of plaintiffs prevent NAACP attorneys from filing more lawsuits than they did but that the suitability of the plaintiff often affected the suit's outcome. Donald Murray served admirably in his suit against the University of

Maryland law school. In 1938 Lloyd L. Gaines won the right to attend the University of Missouri law school, but he vanished after the Supreme Court's decision and thus prevented a proper resolution of the case. Although the circumstances of his disappearance are uncertain, several NAACP lawyers believed that he had deserted them at a crucial moment. If Ada Sipuel Fisher earned her attorneys' esteem for her role as a plaintiff, George W. McLaurin's conduct during his lawsuit was a keen disappointment to the NAACP. His deficient academic performance, repeated demands for money, and unimpressive courtroom testimony made him less than the ideal plaintiff.[3]

In Texas a challenge was long overdue. The University of Texas's ranking law school was preeminent in legal education within the state and its alumni included an impressive array of leading lawyers, jurists, and politicians. Desegregating the institution had been a chief objective of NAACP leaders since their establishment of a statewide organization in 1937. But only after the successful *Smith* v. *Allwright* litigation against the Democratic white primary did the association focus its attention on the fight for equal education. Even then NAACP officials searched for a qualified plaintiff for almost a year before a volunteer actually applied.[4]

The Texas State Conference of NAACP Branches launched the endeavor early in 1945, when its executive committee assigned William J. Durham, its resident counsel, to prepare an opinion on the possibility of a suit against the university. On April 9, A. Maceo Smith, the state's NAACP leader and executive secretary, sent Thurgood Marshall a copy of Durham's brief to review and declared that the State Conference was now ready for legal action. Requesting Marshall to come to Texas, Smith added that "we want to go about it in the same manner that we handled the Texas Primary Case."[5]

Simultaneously, Carter W. Wesley, publisher of the Houston *Informer,* took the initiative through other organizations. In March the Southern and Western regions of the Negro Newspaper Publishers Association met in Jackson, Mississippi. Resolving to work toward equalization of opportunities at all educational levels, the conferees denounced the principle of dual school systems. They also outlined plans for a second meeting to be held in Memphis under the auspices of the Southern Negro Conference for Equalization of Education, an organization headed by Wesley. With the intention of forming a South-wide legal committee, Wesley invited attorneys A. P. Tureaud, A. T. Walden, Arthur Shores, W. J. Durham, and Thurgood Marshall to the Memphis meeting on May 13. Although Marshall and Durham were not present, John J. Jones, president of the Texas State Conference, did attend.[6]

Within two weeks the State conference regained the limelight when its executive committee met in Dallas on June 2, 1945. The principals were Smith, Wesley, Durham, Jones, and Marshall from the NAACP's national office. Amid carefully orchestrated publicity, they formulated the major plans for a lawsuit against the University of Texas. Smith announced that a suit following the *Gaines* precedent would be filed to secure the equalization of educational opportunities at the graduate and professional level. To finance the litigation, they established an educational equalization fund with a preliminary goal of ten thousand dollars. As they adjourned they appraised the meeting as "one of the most successful and profitable in the history of the organization."[7]

In the next few weeks the executive committee drew up a contract retaining Durham as counsel for the proposed action. They set his fee at one thousand dollars plus expenses for litigation at the district court level, and five hundred dollars for the appellate work. Although the State Conference would assume the financial responsibilities, the agreement specified that the suit would be prosecuted in cooperation with the national NAACP and "in conformity with its policies and procedures."[8]

Throughout the summer of 1945, the State Conference worked to secure money and a plaintiff. With substantial publicity from Wesley's newspapers, which printed weekly tallies of the fund-raising drive, the conference collected almost four thousand dollars by October. The task of finding a suitable plaintiff proved to be more difficult. The object of the search had to have a bachelor's degree from an accredited college. Not only did he have to consent to the legal action, but he also had to be willing to attend the university after the suit was won. Smith, Wesley, and Kenneth Lampkin, an Austin attorney, comprised a committee responsible for selecting a plaintiff. By mid-August they had interviewed five individuals, but not one met the qualifications. Another candidate, Grover Washington, "measured up in every respect, but the disapproval of his family caused him to withdraw.'' Smith next suggested that Durham's young legal associate, Crawford B. Bunkley, Jr., apply to the university for a master's degree in law. A graduate of the University of Michigan law school, Bunkley, while unenthusiastic, was willing to apply so that the case would not be held up for want of a plaintiff. When Marshall learned of the idea, he cautioned that the university regulations regarding a master's program be examined, since universities sometimes reserve the right to select the students for such programs. Ultimately the lawyers abandoned this proposal.[9]

By summer's end they still had found no plaintiff, and the search continued into the fall of 1945. ''The plaintiff is our biggest worry,'' wrote Durham, as he disclosed plans to confer with the Carter Wesley in the hope that they could find a suitable candidate. By September 26 Marshall concluded that since they had found no one for the law school, they should consider filing a lawsuit at one of the lower educational levels. He asked Wesley for suggestions regarding what type of discrimination in elementary or high school they should attack first in Texas and the best location to do this. When the NAACP Regional Training Conference convened in Fort Worth on October 5-7, a prospective plaintiff still eluded the association's leaders. Finally, on October 12, 1945, Marshall received welcome news from Lulu White, the NAACP's state director of branches, who wrote: ''I think I have a plaintiff for the Educational Case. I have sent the name to Durham.''[10] The name was that of Heman Marion Sweatt, a thirty-three-year-old Houston mail carrier.

In size and appearance, Sweatt was an unlikely challenger to face the state of Texas. Bespectacled and prematurely balding, he was slightly built and less than five and a half feet in height. He was serious-minded, bookish, and taciturn, but was nevertheless articulate, dignified, and well liked by his associates. At the heart of his decision to become the plaintiff lay his sensitivity to the injustice he had known since his youth and the example his father had set by fighting it. Heman's father, James Leonard Sweatt, was born in Waxahachie in 1870. After graduating from Prairie View, he took a job as a teacher and principal at a small school in Beaumont. The prospect of a larger salary lured him to Houston, where he became a railway mail clerk and married Ella Rose Perry, a native Houstonian. Heman, the fourth of their six children, was born on December 11, 1912. He was named after his mother's brother, Heman Perry, a prominent Atlanta businessman and founder of Standard Life Insurance Company.[11] Yet Heman Sweatt's friends and family would always call him by the nickname, Bill.

Shortly before Heman's birth, his father helped organize black railway mail clerks. The group began as a local fellowship of Negro clerks who were based in Houston. Without "rules, by-laws, regulations, or taxations," members simply met once a month to discuss their common problems. A white insurance company, the Mutual Benefit Association, served as the catalyst for expanding the organization by adopting a "Caucasian clause" in 1910. This provision, which another insurance company subsequently adopted, barred the issuance of insurance policies to black clerks. In response the group of thirty-five clerks met in the summer of 1912 and decided to provide the nucleus for a national organization. Sweatt and others contacted Negro clerks throughout the South with the goals of establishing insurance provisions and a means of presenting grievances to the Post Office Department. They scheduled an organizational meeting for October, 1913, in Chattanooga, Tennessee, where they formally established the National Alliance of Postal Employees and elected Houstonian Henry L. Mims its first president.[12]

A forceful man of great dignity, James L. Sweatt set an example of social activism for his children to follow. Even in retirement he continued to raise his voice against both racist white postmasters and his own fellow blacks who failed to resist such prejudice. Addressing the broader issue of racism that all Negroes faced, he urged that the alliance serve as an instrument of protest "to combat the disciminations nurtured by society generally." Active in civic affairs, he was a charter member of the Houston NAACP branch and a member of the African Methodist Episcopal church.[13]

He built a large home on Chenevert Street for his family. In this sparcely populated area, the Sweatts were isolated from the bulk of Houston's Negro community. As white families settled around them, the elder Sweatt constructed a high, white picket fence to protect his children from the fights that inevitably occurred. While white neighbors used the playground facilities at nearby Baldwin Park, segregation compelled Heman to walk several miles to Emancipation Park, the only such facility for Negroes.[14]

Schooling presented similar inconveniences. On his two-mile walks to Douglass Elementary School, Heman passed two all-white schools which he could not attend. One of them, Longfellow School, was only blocks from his home. In 1930 he graduated from Jack Yates High School.

The elder Sweatt's belief in higher education was such that he encouraged all his children to go to college. John, his oldest son, attended Iowa State College in Ames, where he studied under George Washington Carver. Erma went to Columbia University; Jack, to the University of Michigan; and Wendell, to the University of Nevada. "All of my children had to go out of this state to get their training," Sweatt's father once observed, "when their white playmates got the same training at less cost and trouble right here in Texas."[15]

Heman selected Wiley College, a private institution in Marshall and the first black college in the state to receive accreditation. Marshall, which was also then the location of Bishop College, was a center of black intellectual life in Texas in the 1930s. The faculty at Wiley College included such men as James Leonard Farmer, James H. Morton, and Melvin B. Tolson. A biology major, Sweatt studied science under Morton, a civil rights activist who later became president of the Austin NAACP branch. Sweatt's most inspiring teacher, however, was Melvin B. Tolson, the brilliant English professor, poet laureate of Liberia, and author of *Harlem Gallery*. When directed against racial discrimination, Tolson's eloquence was devastating. Whether speaking to black students in his classes or to white students at the University of Texas, the gentle genius captivated his audiences with his satirical wit, his imagery, and his piercing analysis. Sweatt, in retrospect, believed that no one, with the exception of his father, had influenced him as much as Tolson had. The mentor, in turn, acknowledged his responsibility for having contributed to Sweatt's "contamination."[16]

After graudating from Wiley in 1934, Heman pursued a variety of occupations. He first took a job as a porter at Sakowitz, a Houston clothing store, where he had worked during previous summer vacations. In 1936 his brother Jack left a teaching position in Cleburne to attend the University of Michigan. Heman filled the vacancy at the school, which included all grades from kindergarten through high school. For a year he taught and served as acting principal at what he regarded as "the most unsupervised school system for blacks that heaven ever conceived." With his pedagogic enthusiasm dampened, he decided to attend graduate school at the University of Michigan. He had originally intended to go to medical school with financial help from Heman Perry, but when his uncle's Standard Life Insurance Company failed, this prospect dimmed. Viewing Michigan's public health curriculum as a suitable alternative, Sweatt matriculated there in the fall of 1937. While living at 210 Glenn Street in Ann Arbor, he became acquainted with Lloyd Gaines, a fellow student whose lawsuit against the University of Missouri was before the Supreme Court. While Gaines's knowledge of and interest in civil rights issues impressed Sweatt, his egotistical manner did not. Later, when pursuing his own lawsuit, he resolved to discipline himself to avoid appearing arrogant.[17]

Sweatt's stay in Michigan was short-lived. The harsh winter kept him in poor health, and after completing the second semester, he returned to Houston for the summer. He found temporary employment in the post office as a substitute carrier, then decided not to return to Ann Arbor. In April, 1940, he married Constantine Mitchell, his high school sweetheart. They bought a house at 3402 Delano Street in Houston.[18]

Sweatt had experienced racial discrimination in its many forms. He had encountered it on buses and streetcars, in his job, and in other daily activity. Yet, if he was familiar with racial injustice, he also knew its adversaries. Lulu B. White, the mainstay of the Houston NAACP chapter, was a family friend, as was her husband, Julius, a tough businessman and plaintiff in several white primary lawsuits. Two other plaintiffs in similar litigation were also acquaintances of Sweatt. Richard R. Grovey was his barber, and Lonnie E. Smith his dentist. Carter W. Wesley, the outspoken publisher, was a friend of James Leonard Sweatt, and Heman wrote several columns for Wesley's *Informer*.[19]

Sweatt's involvement with the NAACP spanned several decades. As a boy he had attended Houston branch meetings with his father. During the early 1940s he became increasingly active in the association. He helped raise funds for white primary lawsuits and participated in voter registration drives. When the NAACP youth council sponsored a mass meeting to commemorate National Negro Youth

Week in May, 1944, Sweatt delivered the principal address. He asserted that no longer would the Negro have to bear an inferiority complex imposed by educators "who spend sleepless nights developing tests aimed at providing mental inferiority of Negro to white," instead of ". . . opening equal doors of opportunity."[20]

Sweatt's primary concern, however, was the problem of discrimination against blacks in the post office. In order to be promoted to supervisory positions, an employee first had to be a clerk. Yet postmasters systematically exluded Negroes from becoming clerks, thus relegating them to the lower position of postal carriers. As local secretary of the National Alliance of Postal Employees, Sweatt and his colleagues continued his father's work. They enumerated their grievances in conferences with the postmaster. In March, 1944, Sweatt, with the assistance of attorney Francis Scott Key Whittaker, prepared a documentation of their case, citing national postal regulations and policies.[21] This involvement sharpened his interest in the law as a means of challenging discrimination. By mid-1945 he had decided that instead of remaining a postman he would like to go to law school. He contemplated attending the University of Michigan law school but decided against doing so when his father suffered a serious heart attack.

In a conversation with William J. Durham, Sweatt explored the possibility of acquiring a legal education in Texas. The attorney advised seeking admission to the University of Texas law school. He knew that the university was vulnerable, since there was no law school for blacks in the state. Under the *Gaines* precedent, Texas would either have to provide a separate school for Sweatt or admit him to the university.

Later that fall Sweatt decided not only to apply to the university but also to serve as the NAACP's plaintiff if rejected on the basis of race. He made his decision during a meeting at Wesley Chapel in what he later described as a "brash moment." On that occasion Lulu White spoke to a group of Houston blacks, appealing for a volunteer to file a lawsuit against the university. When no one else showed a willingness to do so, Sweatt stood up and announced that he would.[22]

After NAACP officials notified Durham of this development, he and White apparently met with Sweatt at the latter's home, where they discussed plans in further detail. Durham had several reasons to be optimistic about the situation. He had known Sweatt and his family for a number of years and was confident that the postman would make an excellent plaintiff. Also as Durham reviewed for Sweatt the status of similar legal actions in other states and the association's plans to file additional lawsuits, it became evident that the odds of winning were favorable.

If Sweatt was eager to volunteer as a guinea pig, his wife was not. Knowing that such action would result in financial insecurity, she feared that her husband might lose his job and even their house. She also worried that they would become victims of racial violence. Nevertheless, when confronted with her husband's determination, she reluctantly acquiesced.[23]

Sweatt's family received the news with characteristic shows of support. When his father learned of the decision, he heartily approved and expressed pride that his family would be associated with the action. Sensing that Heman would need the family's full support, James Leonard Sweatt suggested a family gathering to inform the others and weigh their reactions. The discussion took place during a large Sunday dinner. After the elder Sweatt announced his son's decision, various members of the family offered their views. Sweatt's mother voiced her unqualified agreement, so did Erma, his sister. Jack, on the other hand, believed that Heman, at age thirty-three, was too old and had been away from school too long to take on law school. The role should be left to a younger student. John also opposed the decision, but for different reasons. In his opinion the modest resources of the Sweatt family were no match for the state of Texas or American racism. "The only way this white man is going to be whipped," John declared, "is for Uncle Joe Stalin to come over here and just blow the hell out of him!"[24] Nevertheless, the conversation concluded with all the Sweatts pledging their support.

Toward the end of 1945 NAACP leaders continued their fundraising and legal preparations, increasingly drawing Sweatt into their considerations. As they evaluated his college records, they reviewed the university's admission requirements. Sweatt and his wife traveled to Dallas for a meeting with A. Maceo Smith and Durham. They agreed that the association would assume responsibility for the litigation and legal fees and signed a contract to this effect. The organization was to underwrite his travel expenses and other costs incidental to the case. Although the association could not contract to pay Sweatt's educational expenses, Smith as an individual assured him that arrangements would be made. Nevertheless, before Sweatt would give final approval to proceeding with the lawsuit, he wanted first an opportunity to talk with his employer.[25]

Early in November Durham announced that he was ready to file the lawsuit as soon as the NAACP executive committee gave him the "green light." By mid-February the fund totaled $7,200, and Carter Wesley hinted in the *Informer* that the suit would be filed within the next thirty days.[26] It was now only a matter of waiting until time to register for the spring semester.

The climax came on February 26, 1946, when Heman Sweatt attempted to register at the University of Texas. Upon his arrival in Austin, he went first to Samuel Huston College, where he joined an NAACP delegation. The group, which included R. A. Hester, Lulu White, and Dr. B. E. Howell, among others, accompanied Sweatt to the university campus. At the registrar's office they met with President T. S. Painter and other university officials. Hester, as spokesman for the blacks, asked what the state had done to provide graduate and professional education for Negroes. With inferior educations, black youths and GIs returning from the war were having to compete with others in the state for jobs. They needed improved educational opportunities. When Painter explained that nothing was available except the out-of-state scholarships, Hester replied that this provision was inadequate and unsatisfactory. It not only cost blacks more money to live in other sections of the country but travel home was more difficult because of the additional distance. Hester added that most of those who went away to study in more liberal states decided to stay there; thus Texas Negroes never received any advantage from that training. The delegation presented recommendations that Prairie View be divorced from Texas A&M College and developed into a vocational and technical college. They also advocated the establishment of a graduate and professional school for blacks in some large urban center.[27]

After Hester completed his statement, a dialogue ensued. Painter suggested that a small beginning ought to be made and then courses added as demand indicated, believing that a limited graduate program could be set up by September. The committee refused to accede to a compromise predicated on a lack of funds. Then, upon a signal from Hester, Sweatt asked permission to speak. He declared that "the state has the money, and the law and the constitution provide for me to have the training." He needed the education, he said; it was a serious problem. "I cannot go out of state to school, and I cannot wait indefinitely until some provision is made."[28] He concluded by presenting his transcript and requesting admission to the university's law school.

In an attempt to dissuade Sweatt from applying, registrar E. J. Matthews assured him that funds would be made available for education elsewhere. Boasting that he had no more "than the normal amount of prejudice against Negroes," he warned blacks against losing everything if a lawsuit were filed. Likewise, Vice-President J. C. Dolley advised Sweatt to think twice and to choose the course that offered him the most promise of success. After Sweatt declined their alternative, the conference ended with Painter's holding the application until he could obtain a ruling from the attorney general.[29]

The NAACP delegates tried to represent the registration attempt as a coincidence. They thought that Sweatt was merely going along as an interested observer, they claimed. His application, Hester declared, "was just as much of a surprise to us." Mrs. White added that while the NAACP was not contemplating a lawsuit, Sweatt's plans were another matter. Joining the charade, Sweatt declared that his action was taken as an individual and that he was not affiliated with any "crusading Negro group." He did not want to be a guinea pig in the segregation question. "I just went to Austin to try to become a student at the university because that's the only place I can get the training I want." His sole desire was to occupy one seat in a classroom of a law school and eventually to practice law in Texas. Although the blacks never mentioned their intention to file a lawsuit, the well-orchestrated timing of Sweatt's application caused university officials to realize that one was in the making. "It is apparent," Painter wrote Attorney General Grover Sellers, "that this is to be a test case on the question of admission of Negro students in the higher educational institutions of the State."[30]

In requesting an attorney general's opinion, Painter stated that Sweatt was "duly qualified...except for the fact that he is a Negro." Sellers announced his ruling on March 16: he decided to uphold

"Texas' wise and long-continued policy of segregation."[31] Sweatt could, however, apply for legal training at Prairie View, and if none were provided then he could legally attend the University of Texas. But, in Sellers's view, a suitable law course could be set up at the Negro college in forty-eight hours.

The attorney general's ruling set events in motion. Painter mailed it, along with an official letter of rejection to Sweatt, who sent a copy to Durham. The lawyer then informed Maceo Smith that it was time to prepare the petition to file suit. He also recommended that the association have blacks apply for admission to the university's schools of medicine, engineering, journalism, and every other professional school. On May 16, 1946, Sweatt filed suit against Theophilus Shickel Painter and other officials in the 126th District Court, of Travis County, where Judge Roy C. Archer presided. The petition sought a writ of mandamus compelling university officials to admit Sweatt to the institution's law school.[32]

The pace of court proceedings was ponderously slow. After the first hearing on June 17, 1946, Judge Archer declined to grant the writ. Although he declared that the state's refusal to admit Sweatt to the university constituted a denial of his Fourteenth Amendment rights, Archer gave the state six months to provide a "substantially equal" course of legal instruction. When a second hearing was held at the trial level after six months had expired, there was still no law school for blacks. Yet Archer dismissed Sweatt's petition, ruling that a resolution passed by the Texas A&M board of directors to provide legal education for Negroes on demand had satisfied the state's obligation.[33] The plaintiff appealed the judgment, and on March 26, 1947, the Court of Civil Appeals set aside the trial court's ruling without prejudice and remanded the case to the lower court for a new trial. The remand was a critical juncture of the litigation, for it gave both sides an opportunity to alter their strategies and introduce new facts at the trial level. Attorney General Price Daniel had requested the remand because the status of higher educational facilities had changed, but this development can best be explained by tracing briefly the state's responses to black pressure on education.

Since the *Gaines* decision, Texas's white newspapers had discussed a possible legal action by Negroes to open the University of Texas. In 1945 such speculation increased, as editorials commented on the lack of graduate and professional courses for Negroes. Some black leaders, reports stated, were planning a lawsuit. Sensing trouble, the state legislature responded by introducing Senate Bill 228 on March 7, 1945. This measure authorized the Negro institution at Prairie View to teach any course in law, medicine, engineering, pharmacy, journalism, or any other subjects then taught at the University of Texas. Furthermore, to give added semblance of equality, legislators changed the name of Prairie View State Normal and Industrial College to Prairie View University. After Senator L. J. Sulak of La Grange sounded the alarm that there were already a few applications from Negroes pending at the University of Texas, the senate voted unanimously for the bill's passage. The House, with only five dissenting votes, followed suit on May 30, and Governor Coke Stevenson attached his signature.[34]

To the NAACP, S.B. 228 left much to be desired. Although the legislation increased the biennial appropriation for Prairie View, it did not specifically allocate any funds for implementing a new graduate and professional school curriculum. In fact, the bill merely authorized the school to provide such courses as Negro applicants demanded.

In response to Judge Archer's initial ruling, the board of directors of Texas A&M passed a resolution providing for Negro legal training in Houston. They arranged for two Negro attorneys, William C. Dickson and H. S. Davis, Jr., to teach such a curriculum in their law offices at 409½ Milam Street. Although the "law school" opened in February, 1947, no students applied. Then the legislature, deciding that S.B. 228 had to be materially supplemented, passed another bill in March, 1947. This measure, S.B. 140, provided for the establishment of a new three-million-dollar Negro university, including a law school, to be located in Houston. Thus was born Texas State University for Negroes, which made use of the existing land and buildings of Houston College for Negroes.[35] It would later become Texas Southern University.

Yet in order to have a facility ready by the time of the impending trial, the state hastily set up a temporary law school in Austin. Officials leased the basement of a building on East Thirteenth Street from a petroleum company, ordered a law library of ten thousand volumes, and made interim provisions for students to use the library of the Texas Supreme Court. They assigned three University of Texas law professors to teach courses on a part-time basis in addition to their teaching responsibilities at the university. University of Texas law school dean Charles McCormick and librarian Helen Hargrave received appointments as dean and librarian of the basement school. They worked to obtain accreditation for the institution. When the basement school opened its doors for registration on March 10, 1947, its most noticeable deficiency was students. There were none. After no one matriculated in the first week, officials announced that there would be no deadline for enrollment. Heman Sweatt received a registered letter announcing the school's opening and inviting him to apply.[36] Instead of replying he took the letter to Durham in Dallas. A number of Negroes did inquire about the law school, but none could be persuaded to register for the spring semester. The NAACP, and its Austin branch in particular, worked assiduously to discourage applications.

Even though the basement law school had not students, by the time of the remand, the state at least had a physical facility to compare with the University of Texas. While the state had raised the stakes in an effort to retain segregation, the NAACP altered its original strategy to make segregation per se the major issue. What began as a lawsuit demanding equal educational opportunities under the *Plessy* and *Gaines* decisions evolved into an attack on the "separate but equal" doctrine. The new approach held that segregation was inherently discriminatory and, therefore, a violation of the "equal protection" clause of the Fourteenth Amendment.

Thurgood Marshall and the other NAACP lawyers at an Atlanta conference in April, 1946, decided to abandon the earlier tangential approach in favor of the frontal assault on segregation. They concluded that their suits demanding equal facilities had not resulted in overturning segregation, as they had hoped. They had succeeded only in creating a rash of Jim Crow schools.[37] Although the *Sweatt* suit became the first to follow the frontal assault strategy, the lawyers did not actually modify the case until it was remanded to the district court in March, 1947.

Even then it was not so much the lawyers' decision in Atlanta but a series of complex factors in Texas that led to implementation of the frontal assault. First of all, circumstances had changed. At the outset of the suit, the absence of any Negro law school facility had virtually guaranteed victory under the *Gaines* precedent. Yet the establishment of the basement school enabled the state to contend at least that it met the provisions of the *Gaines* ruling. Second, the state's Court of Civil Appeals placed the burden of attacking segregation per se on the NAACP lawyers. During the initial appeal, the chief justice construed the NAACP's position as "arguing that segregation and discrimination were tied up together and could not be separated." Then the case was remanded to the district court to be retried on the merits. At that point the lower-court judge concluded that it was now "wide open." Marshall, reacting to these pronouncements, declared, "Whether we like it or not, we are now faced with the proposition of going to the question of segregation as such."[38]

Although he realized that overturning segregation would require several years and a number of cases, he favored this approach and was especially interested in experimenting with evidence showing the inevitable financial, social, and cultural discrimination that accompanied segregation. Using the analogy of a personal injury suit, Marshall believed that the NAACP would have to prove damages or demonstrate that segregation was harmful.[39]

Another influential factor was Marshall's belief that black Texans overwhelmingly opposed segregation, more so than Negroes in any other NAACP state. Their support was crucial since they would have to finance the lawsuit which ultimately cost $34,000. It also enabled Sweatt's lawyers to counter the attorney general's claim that the Negroes of Texas favored segregation. Yet, despite Marshall's impression, black public opinion was by no means unanimous. A statewide Belden poll, taken in January, 1947, reported that Negroes, eight to five, favored the creation of a separate university over blacks' admission to the University of Texas.[40]

Nevertheless, many black Texans who did oppose segregation contributed to the NAACP's cause. The association conducted statewide fund-raising campaigns to cover legal fees, travel expenses, printing bills, and court costs. While the State Conference and its affiliate branches paid some of these expenses from their treasuries, they also raised larger sums specifically for the *Sweatt* case.

Sweatt himself participated as a frequent speaker at NAACP

fund-raising rallies. He spoke in San Antonio and Beaumont and at the immensely successful mass meeting in Austin in December, 1946. On the latter occasion, he shared the platform with Jim Smith, University of Texas student body president, and J. Frank Dobie, the distinguished folklorist and critic of the university's administration. Sweatt used the opportunity to emphasize that intermarriage was not one of his motives in the lawsuit. Introducing his wife, he declared, "I want to get a legal education at the university, not a wife."[41]

In addition to NAACP rallies, he participated in the legal proceedings. After the remand to the district court, he went to Austin for the trial on the merits which was held May 12-16, 1947. He stayed at the home of Dr. Louis Mitchell, where the NAACP attorneys planned their strategy, interviewed their witnesses, and prepared their plaintiff for his testimony. Imitating the attorney general and his assistants, Sweatt's lawyers cross-examined him and coached him on appropriate responses. Before he had given a deposition in June, 1946, they had counseled him to assert that he would attend a segregated law school at Prairie View if it were equal to that of the University of Texas. But in May, 1947, when the attack shifted to segregation per se, they advised Sweatt to testify that he did not believe that there could be equality under segregation and would not attend a Jim Crow law school.[42]

Observing his battery of NAACP lawyers during the trial heightened the plaintiff's interest in law. There was W. Robert Ming, from the University of Chicago, who furnished several expert witnesses. W. J. Durham and his two young associates, C. B. Bunkley, Jr., and Harry Bellinger, bore the responsibility of conforming the case to Texas procedure, which out-of-state NAACP lawyers found quite knotty and different from any other state in their experience. Marshall, his assistant, Robert L. Carter, and other members of the NAACP legal staff, wrote most of the brief. And with the aid of Durham, Marshall provided direction for the entire case.[43] Finally, there was James M. Nabrit, Jr., from the Howard University law school, who could draw from his own intimate knowledge of legal education.

In directing the examination of witnesses, Nabrit was able to demonstrate the inequality of the basement law school. Through relentless cross-examination, he forced Charles T. McCormick, dean of the two law schools, to acknowledge the basement school's part-time nature, absence of extracurricular activities, inadequate library, and lack of accreditation and prestige. By the time McCormick left the stand, the state's case lay virtually demolished. So devastating was Nabrit's style of interrogation that Marshall himself questioned Helen Hargrave. He feared that another Nabrit performance, one which concentrated on a white woman, would create unfavorable press reaction in Texas.[44]

Lawyers for the plaintiff presented their witnesses. Some of them, such as Earl G. Harrison, confined their testimony to aspects of legal education and comparisons of the two schools. Others contributed a broader range of sociological evidence. Donald Murray, once a plaintiff himself, testified that he had not been ostracized after his admission to the University of Maryland law school. Robert Redfield, testifying on the general inappropriateness of segregation in education, asserted that there were no differences in the scholastic ability of the races and that segregation was injurious to the student as well as to the community which practiced it. Charles Thompson, dean of the Howard University graduate school, presented the findings of his research on higher education for Negroes in Texas, which demonstrated the discriminatory effects of segregation.[45]

In his interrogation of witnesses, Price Daniel attempted to prove that Maceo Smith and his cohorts in the NAACP had actually instigated the lawsuit (which of course they had) and that they had discouraged Sweatt and others from attending the basement law school. Yet the attorney general could no more verify these assertions than he could prove that Sweatt did not genuinely desire to attend law school. And as Marshall argued, as long as the plaintiff expected to attend the university, his motives for doing so were immaterial.[46]

Daniel, in attempting to establish the basement school's equality, stressed its opportunities for individual instruction with a teacher-student ratio of three to one. Harrison, however, replied by emphasizing the importance of class discussion and interchange of ideas under the case method of study. It was mistaken, he said, "even absurd to speak of any institution that has one student as a law school."[47]

As the litigation wore on, the strain of being the plaintiff took its toll on Sweatt. While on his job, he encountered pressures and even threats on his life. At home he and his wife were harassed by malicious notes and telephone calls. Vandals defaced the Sweatt house with paint and smashed windows. Sweatt's health, which had been bad for several years, worsened as the tension mounted. His ulcers required him to be hospitalized, and finally, in late 1947 he resigned from the postal service. Although poor health brought on financial difficulties for Sweatt, Carter Wesley sensed his situation and gave him a job in the *Informer*'s circulation department. He worked on the newspaper staff for almost a year, then returned to the post office. If Sweatt and the irascible publisher occasionally clashed over Wesley's attacks on the NAACP's strategy and his impulsive editorial assaults on virtually everyone, they remained on friendly terms. He continued to rely on Wesley for legal advice when Durham was unavailable. But Sweatt was deeply committed to the NAACP's policy of opposing all forms of segregation, while Wesley advocated simultaneous efforts to make Jim Crow facilities as equal as possible.[48]

Publicity from the lawsuit brought Sweatt both celebrity status and notoriety. In addition to the Texas press, several out-of-state newspapers, including the New York *Herald-Tribune,* sent reporters to interview him. After a writer for *Life* magazine drafted an article that made Sweatt appear ungrateful for refusing to attend the basement law school, Marshall and other NAACP officials "worked day and night to change it," and they succeeded. When *Life* published the more generous version in the September 29, 1947 issue, Sweatt delivered the usual subscription copies on his mail route, unaware of the magazine's contents. The most publicity came from the black weeklies, particularly Wesley's Houston *Informer* and Dallas *Express.* The latter selected Sweatt as its Texan of the Year in 1946, noting that he represented the fact that "the days of Old Black Joe are really gone."[49]

Sweatt himself wrote an article which appeared in the University of Texas magazine, *Texas Ranger.* Entitled "Why I Want to Attend The University of Texas," the essay concluded that his reason was the same as that of other Texans studying there. it was the best law school in the state and the only one that could offer him training equal to that available to other students. He played down his opposition to segregation, asserting that "my personal concern with segregation does not exceed my immediate interest in a first class legal education."[50]

"Playing the game," was Sweatt's subsequent characterization of these public statements. To increase public support he avoided voicing his views on segregation. He emphasized his genuine intention to study law to maximize the chances of winning the lawsuit. And he de-emphasized the NAACP's role in the litigation to avoid having the association charged with violating barratry laws. Aware of the "cost of a careless word to the present educational struggle of Negroes of Texas," Sweatt wrote privately that he had been "very cautious in his every action."[51] Perhaps the inability to express his attitudes openly contributed to the tension and frustration he felt.

Only in conversation and correspondence with friends did he reveal the range of his feelings. When he did so, there emerged not merely a postman who desired to be a lawyer but a sensitive, determined, and often radical civil rights activist. He emphatically reassured NAACP officials that he could be depended upon to attend the University of Texas if the suit were won. Even willing to risk physical harm, he declared that he could think of no greater cause for which to give himself without count of cost. In a letter to Walter White, Sweatt reviewed his earlier experiences with discrimination, then characterized his role in the litigation as "more than an abstract Guinea Pig." He was grasping at the rare opportunity in a lifetime of struggle behind the wall of segregation. He was determined to make a contribution to the progress of the American Negro. Blacks, he contended, are not really individuals in the eyes of others. "We live as a group," and what affects one, affects the whole group. He had been excluded not because he himself was objectionable, but because "the group I belonged to was not wanted." Accordingly, Sweatt had in mind one objective: to abolish segregation. Rejecting suggestions of compromising and accepting a separate law school, he argued that "half-loaf philosophy leads only to half-loaf preparation." He believed that blacks had come as far as they had only because they had chosen the radical method and that they must continue to aim their gun at the door of the state's main university. This course was the only way to gain entrance to that university. At the same time it would force the greatest possible equality under the system of segregation.[52]

The reports Sweatt received from students attending Texas State

University for Negroes bolstered his determination, for they told him of the school's inadequacy. Yet the acceptance of the Jim Crow institution by other blacks and their pressures on him to be satisfied with it disheartened him. Some Negroes commented on what good the *Sweatt* case had done, as though the suit were finished. Others advised him that he was out on a limb by himself. "If my alliance with the NAACP in the current educational problem wasn't rooted in very firm soil," he confided, "the present sight of Negro Ph.D.s flocking here madly for the self-fattening dollars being invested in Jim Crow education would make me toss in the towel of disgust." Nevertheless, as he wrote Marshall, "my interest in seeing this movement through cannot be diverted by anything."[53]

In his racial aspirations and in his political beliefs, Sweatt had much in common with the liberal and radical elements in Texas. He undoubtedly felt the influence of Lulu White, whose leadership he regarded as "a reservoir for keeping my own strength alive." Never cast as a moderate, White publicly denounced "the facist ideas held deep in the hearts of lawmakers and inherent in the political machinery of our state." Along with Lulu White, J. Frank Dobie, and others, Sweatt supported the movement to have Henry Wallace's Progressive party placed on the ballot in Texas in the 1948 presidential election. So many of the people he agreed with were accused of being communistic that Sweatt was loath to deny that he himself was one. Yet he concluded that for him to give a lecture on Marxism would be as "nonsensical as a Bilboic thesis on Democracy."[54]

Sweatt and his attorneys were not discouraged when Archer denied the petition on June 17, 1947, nor when the Court of Civil Appeals and the Texas Supreme Court reaffirmed the lower court's ruling. They realized that their only chance of winning would be at the level of the U.S. Supreme Court, which in November, 1949, granted the petitioner's writ of certiorari. After a delay the Court ultimately rescheduled the case for oral argument on April 4, 1950. Sweatt initially did not plan to attend the hearing, believing that neither his health nor his financial resources were equal to the trip. Although the NAACP launched a fund-raising drive to pay his travel expenses to Washington, he refused to endorse the scheme. His presence in court merely as an observer, he believed, was not important enough to justify soliciting contributions. Marshall, however, urged Sweatt and his wife to make the trip. In the *Sipuel* hearing the petitioner's presence had been helpful because of "certain fast-moving developments," and Marshall was certain that Sweatt's attendance would be valuable to his case. So, with travel money, provided by NAACP, the Sweatts took the train to Washington. On the Saturday night before the scheduled argument, they went to Howard University for a traditional mock hearing. There, sympathetic faculty members, attorneys, and judges tried to anticipate the questions of the nine justices, while Durham and Marshall rehearsed their presentations.[55]

The next hearing was not for practice. When the Supreme Court convened at noon on April 4, 1950, Durham began with his remarks, but Marshall soon took over and carried the weight of the argument.[56] As they had done in their brief, the NAACP attorneys contended that Sweatt was not offered equal education and could not receive it in a separate law school. Nor did it matter whether the state built a law school the exact equal of the University of Texas in books, in seats, and in faculty. If it were a segregated law school, it would be unequal.

E. Jake Jacobson, an assistant attorney general, initiated the respondents' presentation. He attempted to justify the state's separation by race and to prove that the basement school and its permanent counterpart in Houston were equal to the University of Texas. Another assistant, Joe Greenhill, presented a historical argument justifying segregation in education under the Fourteenth Amendment. The hearing lasted an hour and a half. At its conclusion both sides, including the plaintiff, his wife, and interested observers, posed together for a photograph. It was now a matter of waiting for the Court's decision.

Two months later Heman Sweatt was delivering mail in Houston when the Supreme Court, on June 5, 1950, announced its ruling. He heard the news first from his wife, then began listening to reports on the radio. Next Thurgood Marshall telephoned him with words of congratulations. "We won the big one," the counsel said. The state would now have to "age law schools like good whiskey."[57]

Chief Justice Fred Vinson, speaking for a unanimous Court, concluded that Negro law students were not offered substantial equality in educational opportunities. In six tangible features—the number of faculty, the opportunity for specialization, the scope of the library, the variety of courses, the size of the student body, and the availability of law review and similar activities—the University of Texas law school was superior. Moreover, the Court went beyond a physical comparison to consider "those qualities which are incapable of objective measurement but which make for greatness in a law school."[58] Here the Court cited the reputation of the faculty, the experience of the administration, the position and influence of the alumni, the standing in the community, and the traditions and prestige of the University of Texas which made it "one of the nation's ranking law schools." Finally, the chief justice discussed the practical nature of the legal profession and the importance of a law student's interaction and exchange of views with other individuals who would become the lawyers, witnesses, jurors, judges, and state officials with whom he would inevitably be dealing in the practice of law. To exclude the petitioner from the racial group that made up 85 percent of the Texas population—the race with which the petitioner would have to work as a lawyer—would be a denial of his rights under the Fourteenth Amendment.

The *Sweatt* decision along with rulings in two companion cases, *McLaurin* v. *Oklahoma State Regents* and *Henderson* v. *United States Interstate Commerce Commission and Southern Railway*, significantly eroded the doctrine of "separate but equal." Taken together, the three decisions, in Marshall's words, "did one of the finest jobs of gutting the *Plessy* decision that I know of." All three decisions, the lawyer added, "are replete with road markings telling us where to go next." Three weeks later he announced an all-out attack on segregation at all educational levels "from law school to kindergarten."[59]

Despite Marshall's confidence, the legal implications of the *Sweatt* decision were by no means clear when announced by the Court. Since it had refused to overturn *Plessy* v. *Ferguson*, segregation per se remained legal as long as it offered equality. At the same time the Court applied the "separate but equal" doctrine so rigidly that it required absolute rather than nominal equality of treatment. The justices could have decided to admit Sweatt to the white law school merely on the basis of its physical superiority. Instead they weighed such intangibles as Sweatt's interaction with white law students who represented the future judges, officials, and attorneys with whom he would have to work. This consideration meant, in effect, that with regard to the nation's law schools separate was not equal. Yet the application of this rule to other areas also had relevance. Were not others who were deprived of interaction with future doctors, teachers, engineers, and social workers handicapped by this lack of association? If this interaction constituted a basic part of the individual's education, was it not even more essential that it also take place during the earlier, more formative years of primary and secondary education? Subsequent Chief Justice Earl Warren made precisely this point in the *Brown* v. *Board of Education of Topeka* opinion. Alluding to *Sweatt* and *McLaurin,* he asserted that "such considerations apply with added force to children in grade and high schools." Not only did *Sweatt* serve as a precedent for the *Brown* decision, which overturned *Plessy* v. *Ferguson,* but also the Court's focus on intangible factors in the *Brown* ruling was a logical extension of the rationale in *Sweatt.*[60]

The fact that in the physical comparison of the two law schools the justices found inequality is also significant. They demonstrated their willingness to exact a standard of absolute equality and to reexamine the facts carefully and overturn findings of lower courts.[61] Consider the Court's careful scrutiny of the holdings of the libraries, number and qualifications of the faculties, number and variety of courses, as well as extracurricular activities. This precise standard of examination raised the cost of segregation, while at the same time increasing its vulnerability.

Both the state of Texas and the NAACP had gained experience and insight since Heman Sweatt had applied for admission to the University of Texas law school in 1946. The state, from its contract arrangement in Houston and basement law school in Austin to the multimillion-dollar Texas State University for Negroes, had learned the cost of "separate but equal." The *Sweatt* ruling saved the state from further financial extravagance entailed in a strict compliance with the *Plessy* doctrine. The expense angle had already come into focus when Herman Barnett applied to medical school in 1949. Confronted with the alternative of creating a costly Jim Crow medical facility for one student, state officials responded by violating the Texas segregation statute. Although Barnett's registration listed affiliation with the Jim Crow school, he was in fact attending classes with white students in the Galveston institution.[62]

For its part the NAACP had become increasingly resourceful in attacking segregated education. Not only had the organization arranged Barnett's application to medical school, but it was also searching for a qualified Negro to apply to the university's engineering school at the time of the *Sweatt* decision. Having learned of the university's "atom smasher," they reasoned that the state would have to duplicate the nuclear facility or admit the black student. In neighboring Oklahoma the NAACP had even found a solution to the physical isolation within the classroom. Association officials arranged for a black student to enroll in the University of Oklahoma's marching band.[63]

In practical terms the *Sweatt* decision compelled the University of Texas and similar state institutions to admit Negroes to graduate and professional schools. Accordingly, Horace Heath enrolled in the government department for work on his Ph.D., and John Chase in a graduate program in architecture during the summer session of 1950. They were the University of Texas's first Negro students since October, 1938, when George Allen registered by mail and attended classes for two weeks before confused university officials decided to remove him. University officials also changed Barnett's registration to the University of Texas medical school.[64]

Sweatt heralded the Court's decision as a "milestone in the progress of democracy." He reiterated his intention to enroll in the university in September "without malice toward anybody." Speculating that he would ultimately practice law in Houston after graduation, he expressed his desire to participate in other cases to break down segregation. But first he would have to complete law school. At age thirty-seven he was not only four and a half years older than when he had first applied, but the ordeal of being the plaintiff had weakened him physically and emotionally. When he had first filed the lawsuit, he had felt that he "could lick the world." Now he regarded himself as a "complete emotional wreck."[54]

Amid the flashing lights of photographers' cameras, Sweatt registered on September 19, 1950. From his first day on the Austin campus, he experienced a mixed reception. While some professors, such as Jerre Williams and Charles McCormick, befriended and encouraged him, others insulted him. The new dean, Page Keeton, first demonstrated his hostility by rebuking Sweatt for the publicity attending his registration and warning him against any "NAACP showmanship." Although Keeton had been helpful to Marshall during the *Sweatt* and *Sipuel* cases, he perhaps feared that Sweatt's presence would reduce alumni endowments. The attitudes of fellow students were also varied. If a few were abusive, most were agreeable toward him. He and other black students encountered little or no difficulty at drinking fountains, lounges, campus eating places, and football games. Sweatt even received an appointment to serve on the class social committee.[66]

There were, of course, incidents, the ugliest of which occurred on the first Friday night of the semester. After studying late in the library, he started walking toward his car. Waiting for him across the street was a large crowd with a burning cross. Accompanied by a white friend, Sweatt reached his car unharmed but then discovered that his tires had been slashed.[67]

If such distractions made it difficult for Sweatt to concentrate on his studies, he nevertheless worked hard. If he found the curriculum time-consuming, it was also interesting. He particularly liked his courses in torts and property. Yet the technical and abstract nature of the material bothered him, as did the immense pressure he felt to excel. Like many of his classmates, he did not excel. After receiving failing grades during his first year, he returned in the fall of 1951 to audit the courses in which he had been deficient. He enrolled again as a regular student in the spring, but it was his last semester. Bitterly disappointed by his failure, Sweatt blamed himself, although there were many factors that affected his performance. Throughout his stay at the university he was plagued by ill health. Besides his ulcers, an appendectomy forced him to miss class for seven weeks. Financial problems added to his burden. Texas groups and individuals had helped the NAACP raise eleven thousand dollars for a Sweatt Victory Fund to underwrite his education, but the disbursement process was cumbersome. His monthly checks frequently arrived late, leaving him penniless in the meantime. These multiple pressures increased the tension between Sweatt and his wife. Their strife finally reached the stage that Constantine returned to Houston, and a divorce followed. In the summer of 1952 Sweatt also went back to Houston with his professional hopes crushed and his personal life shattered.[68]

Remarkably, he did not abandon his interest in education. That fall he received a scholarship to study at Atlanta University's Graduate School of Social Work. He decided that he could be equally as happy "learning what makes people tick in their relationships and how to help them achieve goals against a society that resists change."[69] After earning a master's degree in 1954, he moved to Cleveland, where he worked for the NAACP and the National Urban League. He later returned to Atlanta and became assistant director of the Urban League's Southern Regional Office, a position he still holds at the time of this writing. In his community organizational work, he utilizes many of the skills that he developed in the voter registration drives, the Postal Alliance, and the NAACP in the 1940s. He also teaches classes at Atlanta University. Remarried, he lives comfortably with his family in suburban Atlanta.

Heman Marion Sweatt's stature stems from the significance of his lawsuit. Neither a skillful legal strategist like Thurgood Marshall nor a dynamic organizer like Lulu White, he was primarily an instrument of the NAACP's legal offensive. A plaintiff's main attributes were a willingness to volunteer to file suit and a resolve to remain steadfast and stay quiet throughout the litigation. Yet he was an essential part of the struggle for black civil rights. As Marshall wrote to Sweatt shortly after the Court's ruling: "If it had not been for your courage and your refusal to be swayed by the others, this victory would not have been possible."[70]

The plaintiff personalized the issue of segregation. He as an individual stood as the victim of discrimination as well as the alternative to segregated education. The public perceived Heman Sweatt in particular, not merely Negroes in general, as seeking admission to the University of Texas law school. He was constantly under the scrutiny of the courts and the public. In his formal testimony, his public posture, his statements to the press, and his cooperation with NAACP officials and attorneys, Sweatt served his cause well. His failure in law school, although a devastating blow to him, was of secondary importance. The fact that he did attend after the decision and persisted for two years at least demonstrated his earnestness in seeking the right to attend the institution.

What explains Sweatt's willingness to become a plaintiff? The influence of his father stands out as the greatest factor. James Leonard

Sweatt's example of activism in the Postal Alliance and his admiring son's desire to do likewise must count heavily. Sweatt's own experiences in the Postal Alliance, in the NAACP voter registration drives, and in his contact with Carter Wesley and Lulu White were steps that led him to the courtroom. Moveover, he possessed a keen desire for achievement and public recognition. In the month that he filed the lawsuit, he promised a total commitment so "that generations of young people coming behind me will not be able to say that I failed them." On reflecting in later years, he observed that he had "given a great deal to my race and the cause of democracy."[71]

Sweatt was at once a casualty and a beneficiary of the lawsuit that bore his name. He gained the right to attend the University of Texas law school and in the process earned public esteem and the identification as a hero among blacks. His prominence aided his subsequent work in the field of civil rights. At the same time the experience exacted a devastating toll. The constant strain jeopardized his health, disrupted his marriage, and temporarily scarred him with a sense of frustration and failure. "I don't think anyone can possibly realize the wear and tear on personal emotions one suffers in going through six years of this kind of struggle," observed Sweatt, who maintains that the burden is too great for one individual to bear.[72] Yet the episode that nearly destroyed him also conferred distinction and a justifiable sense of pride and achievement.

NOTES

1. In this essay the terms "black" and "Negro" are used interchangeably at the suggestion of Justice Thurgood Marshall.

2. NAACP strategists attempted to minimize whites' hostility by initiating lawsuits at the graduate and professional level where they believed they would encounter less friction and opposition. They also felt that higher education suits, especially against law schools, offered the best chances of victory. Thurgood Marshall to Erwin N. Griswold, June 14, 1948, NAACP Files (Library of Congress, Washington, D.C.).

3. Thurgood Marshall, "An Evaluation of Recent Efforts to Achieve Racial Integration in Education through Resort to the Courts," *Journal of Negro Education,* XXI (Summer, 1952), 318; Marshall to G. James Fleming, Nov. 5, 1947, Marshall to Heman M. Sweatt, Sept. 30, 1947, Roscoe Dunjee to Marshall, June 13, 1949, June 6, 1950, Marshall to Dungee, June 8, 1950, NAACP Files; *Sipuel* v. *Board of Regents,* 332 U.S. 631; *Fisher* v. *Hurst,* 333 U.S. 147; *McLaurin* v. *Oklahoma State Regents,* 339 U.S. 637.

4. Juanita Jackson to Walter White, Apr. 22, 1937, Minutes of Texas State Conference of Branches, NAACP, June 18, 19, 1937, Charles Houston to C. F. Richardson, Oct. 8, 1937, NAACP Files; *Smith* v. *Allwright,* 321 U.S. 649 (1944).

5. A. Maceo Smith to Marshall, Apr. 9, 1945 (quotation), NAACP Files.

6. Dallas *Express,* Mar. 31, May 19, 1945, Dec. 28, 1946; Carter W. Wesley to A. P. Tureaud and others, May 1, 1945, NAACP Files.

7. Wesley to Marshall, Dec. 23, 1946, NAACP Files; Marshall to M. L. G., Oct. 31, 1974, interview; Dallas *Express,* June 9 (quotation), 30, 1945.

8. Smith to Marshall, June 28, 1945, Suggested Agreement signed by John J. Jones and W. J. Durham, undated copy (quotation), NAACP Files.

9. Dallas *Express,* June 9, 30, Oct. 13, 1945; *Informer* (Houston), Jan. 22, Feb. 12, 1946; Smith to J. J. Jones, July 31, 1945, Smith to Marshall, Aug. 17, 1945 (quotation), C. B. Bunkley, Jr., to Marshall, Aug. 27, 1945, Marshall to Durham, Aug. 21, 1945, NAACP Files.

10. Durham to Marshall, Aug. 6, 1945 (first quotation), Marshall to Wesley, Sept. 26, 1945, Minutes of Texas NAACP Board Meeting, Fort Worth, Texas, Oct. 7, 1945, Lulu B. White to Marshall, Oct. 10, 1945 (second quotation), NAACP Files.

11. Heman M. Sweatt to M. L. G., Feb. 10, 1973, interview; Text of Address by Heman M. Sweatt to the Student Bar Association of Texas Southern University, Apr. 29, 1972.

12. *Postal Alliance,* Oct., 1946 (quotation), Oct., 1947, Oct. 1949, and July, 1950; *Informer* (Houston), July 24, 1951; Sweatt to M. L. G., Feb. 10, 1973, interview. A somewhat different version of the founding of the Postal Alliance appears in Cornellius Hendricks, ''The National Alliance of Postal and Federal Employees,'' *Crisis,* LXXXIV (Apr., 1977), 148; Walter Powell to M. L. G., June 9, July 15, 1973, interview.

13. *Postal Alliance,* Mar., 1946, Oct., 1947; Sweatt to White, Sept. 3, 1948, NAACP Files; Sweatt to M. L. G., Feb. 10, 1973, interview.

14. Sweatt to M. L. G., Feb. 10, 1973, interview.

15. Douglass Hall, ''The Sweatts—A Family of Texas Fighters,'' *Afro Magazine,* Mar. 20, 1948, M-11.

16. Sweatt to M. L. G., Feb. 10, 1973, interview; Ben N. Ramey to M. L. G., July 28, 29, 1973, interview.

17. Sweatt to M. L. G., Feb. 10, 1973, interview; Sweatt to White, Sept. 3, 1948, NAACP Files; *Missouri ex rel. Gaines* v. *Canada,* 305 U.S. 337 (1938).

18. Constantine Mitchell to M. L. G., Oct. 20, 1973, interview; Sweatt to M. L. G., Feb. 10, 1973, interview.

19. Sweatt to M. L. G., Feb. 10, 1973, interview; Dallas *Express,* Sept. 15, 29, 1945.

20. *Informer* (Houston), May 6, 1944.

21. Walter Powell, William Day, Byron and Rannie Cook, T. B. Allen to M. L. G., July 15, 1973, interview; Sweatt to M. L. G., Feb. 10, 1973, interview; Brief of the Houston Local Branch of the National Alliance of Postal Employees Submitted to the Honorable John Dunlop, postmaster of the Houston Post Office, Mar., 1944, copy in author's possession.

22. Sweatt to M. L. G., Feb. 20, 1973, interview.

23. Mitchell to M. L. G., Oct. 20, 1973, interview; Sweatt to M. L. G., Feb. 10, 1973, interview.

24. Sweatt to M. L. G., Feb. 10, 1973, interview (quotation); Mitchell to M. L. G., Oct. 20, 1973, interview.

25. Durham to Marshall, Jan. 28, 1946, Smith to Lulu White, Nov. 19, 1945, NAACP Files; Mitchell to M. L. G., Oct. 20, 1973, interview; Sweatt to M. L. G., Feb. 10, 1973, interview.

26. Dallas *Express,* Nov. 3, 1945; *Informer* (Houston), Feb. 12, 1946.

27. Sweatt to M. L. G., Feb. 10, 1973, interview; James H. Morton to M. L. G., Nov. 17, 24, 1971, interview; *Defender* (Houston), Mar. 9, 1946; Dallas *Express,* Mar. 9, 1946.

28. *Defender* (Houston), Mar. 9, 1946.

29. Ibid.

30. Ibid. (first quotation); Dallas *Morning News,* Feb. 28, 1946; Dallas *Express,* Mar. 9, 1946; *Daily Texan* (Austin), Mar. 3, 1946 (second quotation); Houston *Post,* Feb. 28, 1946 (third and fourth quotations).

31. Austin *American,* Mar. 17, 1946; *Daily Texan* (Austin), Mar. 19, 1946.

32. Durham to Marshall, Apr. 2, 1946, NAACP Files; *Brief for the Petitioner, Sweatt* v. *Painter, 339 U.S. 629, In the Supreme Court of the United States, October Term 1949,* No. 44, p. 2.

33. Dallas *Express,* Dec. 21, 1946.

34. Dallas *Morning News,* Dec. 14, 1938, Apr. 24, 1939, Feb. 4, Mar. 20, Apr. 24, and May 1, 1945. For the text of Senate Bill No. 228, see Texas, Legislature, *General and Special Laws of the State of Texas passed by the Regular Session of the Forty-ninth Legislature* (Austin, 1945), chaps. 308, 506 (hereafter cited as Texas, *Laws,* date).

35. *Daily Texan* (Austin), Sept. 19, 1950; *Sweatt* v. *Painter, Transcript of Record,* 23-30 (hereafter cited as *Transcript of Record*); Texas *Laws,* 1947, chap. 29, 36.

36. E. J. Matthews to Sweatt, Mar. 3, 1947, in *Transcript of Record,* 372-374.

37. James M. Nabrit, Jr., "The Negro: The Present Situation and Recent Gains," in *Discrimination in Higher Education,* Southern Conference on Discrimination in Higher Education (New Orleans, 1950), 25; Marshall, "An Evaluation of Recent Efforts," 318-319; Annual Report of Legal Department—1946, Digest of Proceedings in Atlanta Conference, Marshall to Wesley, Jan. 7, 1947, Marshall to Wesley, Oct. 3, 1947, Marshall to Wesley, Oct. 16, 1947, NAACP Files; Marshall to M. L. G., Oct. 31, 1974, interview.

38. Marshall to William H. Hastie, Apr. 3, 1947 (quotations), Marshall, Memorandum in re: University of Texas Case, Apr. 24, 1947, NAACP Files; Marshall to M. L. G., Oct. 31, 1974, interview.

39. Marshall to Griswold, June 14, 1948, Marshall to Hastie, Apr. 3, 1947, NAACP Files; Marshall to M. L. G., Oct. 31, 1974, interview.

40. Marshall to Hastie, Apr. 3, 1947, Marshall to Wesley, Oct. 16, 1947, NAACP Files; U. Simpson Tate to Mrs. H. M. Justice, Aug. 14, 1951, Juanita Craft

Papers (Archives, University of Texas at Austin); Statewide Survey of Public Opinion, Jan. 26, 1947, in *Brief of the Respondents in Opposition to Petition for Writ of Certiorari in The Supreme Court, October Term, 1948*, No. 667, pp. 86-87.

41. *Texas Spectator* (Austin), Dec. 20, 1946 (quotation).

42. C. B. Bunkley, Jr., to M. L. G., Mar. 23, 1973, interview; Marshall to M. L. G., Oct. 31, 1974, interview.

43. Ibid.; Sweatt to M. L. G., Feb. 10, 1973, interview; Harry Bellinger to M. L. G., May 27, 1974, interview.

44. *Transcript of Record*, 86-111; Sweatt to M. L. G., Feb. 10, 1973, interview; Bunkley to M. L. G., Mar. 23, 1973, interview.

45. Judge Archer later excluded the testimony of Redfield and Thompson as being beyond the scope of the pleadings. *Transcript of Record*, 441.

46. Ibid., 182-183.

46. Ibid., 216-217.

48. Mitchell to M. L. G., Oct. 20, 1973, interview; Sweatt to M. L. G., Feb. 10, 1973, interview; Wesley to Marshall, Dec. 23, 1946, Oct. 8, 1947, NAACP Files.

49. Sweatt to White, June 9, 1947, Marshall to Sweatt, Sept. 30, 1947, (first quotation), NAACP Files; Sweatt to M. L. G., Feb. 10, 1973, interview; Dallas *Express*, Dec. 28, 1946 (second quotation).

50. *Texas Ranger*, LX (Sept., 1947), 20, 40, 42.

51. Sweatt to M. L. G., Feb. 10, 1973, interview (first quotation); Sweatt to Lulu B. White, Nov. 8, 1946 (second quotation), NAACP Files.

52. Sweatt to Lulu B. White, July 25, 1946; Sweatt to Walter White, June 9, 1947 (first and third quotations), NAACP Files; *Daily Texan* (Austin), Sept. 19, 1950 (second quotation).

53. Sweatt to Lulu B. White, July 25, 1946, Sweatt to Marshall, Sept. 19, 1947, Sweatt to Walter White, Sept. 3, 1948 (first quotation), Sweatt to Marshall, Feb. 19, 1949 (second quotation), NAACP Files.

54. Sweatt to Lulu B. White, July 25, 1946 (first quotation), Sweatt to Walter White, Nov. 8, 1946 (third quotation), NAACP Files; *Postal Alliance*, July, 1950, p. 6 (second quotation). "Bilboic democracy" is a reference to Theodore G. Bilbo, a Mississippi governor and U.S. senator known for his espousal of white supremacy.

55. Sweatt to Marshall, Mar. 1, 1950, Marshall to Sweatt, Mar. 7, 1950 (quotation), NAACP Files; Francis Williams to M. L. G., Oct. 20, 1973, interview.

56. A transcript of the oral argument is in the *Sweatt* v. *Painter* file of the Attorney General of Texas.

57. Sweatt to M. L. G., Feb. 10, 1973, interview.

58. *Supreme Court Reporter*, LXX, 850.

59. In *McLaurin* the Court ruled that a Negro attending the University of Oklahoma graduate school was entitled to the same treatment as other students and must not be set apart from them. 339 U.S. 737 (1950). In *Henderson* racial segregation in railroad dining cars was ruled unconstitutional. 330 U.S. 816, 843 (1950). Marshall to Charles Bunn, June 12, 1950 (first quotation), Marshall to Lem Graves, Jr., July 5, 1950 (second quotation), NAACP Files.

60. John P. Roche, "Education, Segregation and the Supreme Court—A

Political Analysis," *University of Pennsylvania Law Review,* IC (May, 1951), 958; *Brown* v. *Board of Education of Topeka,* 347 U.S. 483 (quotation).

61. Roche, "Education, Segregation and the Supreme Court," 952-956.

62. T. S. Painter to Herman Barnett, Aug. 19, 1949, NAACP Files.

63. Donald Jones to James M. Nabrit, Jan. 14, 1949, Dunjee to George Cross, Oct. 22, 1949, Dunjee to Marshall, Nov. 19, 1949, NAACP Files.

64. *Informer* (Houston), June 10, 1950; Dallas *Express,* Oct. 15, 22, 29, 1938; *Daily Texan* (Austin), June 7, 9, 1950.

65. Dallas *Morning News,* June 6, 1950 (first and second quotations); Houston *Post,* June 11, 1950; *Daily Texan* (Austin), Sept. 19, 20, 1950; Sweatt to M. L. G., Feb. 10, 1973, interview (third quotation).

66. Sweatt to M. L. G., Feb. 10, 1973, interview (quotation); Marshall to M. L. G., Oct. 31, 1974, interview; Marshall to Sweatt, June 3, 1950, Sweatt to Marshall, Oct. 28, 1950, NAACP Files.

67. Sweatt to M. L. G., Feb. 10, 1973, interview; Sweatt to Marshall, Oct. 30, 1950, NAACP Files.

68. Sweatt to M. L. G., Feb. 10, 1973, interview; *Negro Labor News* (Houston), Feb. 4, 1956; Sweatt to Marshall, Oct. 28, 1950, NAACP Files; *Daily Texan* (Austin), July 11, 1952; *Informer* (Houston), Oct. 10, 1950, Sept. 26, 1950, Jan. 23, 1951, June 17, 1952; Walter Powell to M. L. G., June 9, July 15, 1973, interview; Mitchell to M. L. G., Oct. 20, 1973, interview; Ben and May Ramey to M. L. G., July 28, 29, 1973, interview.

69. Sweatt to M. L. G., Feb. 10, 1973, interview.

70. Marshall to Sweatt, June 8, 1950 (quotation), NAACP Files.

71. Text of address by Heman M. Sweatt to the Student Bar Association of Texas Southern University, Apr. 29, 1972; Sweatt to Smith, Mar. 19, 1946 (first quotation), NAACP Files; "The Strange Case of Heman Sweatt," *Jet,* Feb. 2, 1956, p. 14 (second quotation); Sweatt to M. L. G., Feb. 10, 1973, interview.

72. *Negro Labor News* (Houston), Oct. 28, 1961 (quotation); Sweatt to M. L. G., Feb. 10, 1973, interview.

John Biggers. Courtesy John Biggers.

VIII

JOHN BIGGERS: Artist

Frank H. Wardlaw

John Biggers certainly ranks as a major Texas artist. The issue, however, may be one of what is black art and is it separate from art in America.

The institution of slavery prevented most black Americans from becoming painters. Scipio Moorhead, generally regarded as a practitioner of "history painting," Joshua Johnston, an early portrait painter, and Robert S. Duncanson, who painted landscapes, demonstrate the types of motifs chosen by early black artists. These men looked to the existing artistic mainstream for inspiration and direction. Thus, before 1920, black artists were a small number of individuals looking for survival and not innovation. Consequently, nineteenth-century black artists left no collective sense (i.e., Afro-American art) to their artistic descendants.

Along with the migration to northern cities and the formation of black ghettos, there grew a black awareness. It manifested itself in the Harlem Renaissance in literature, in Marcus Garvey's back to Africa movement, and in the formation of the Harmon Foundation, committed to the encouragement of minority arts. The foundation exhibited black artists and aided the newly developing art departments at Fisk and Howard universities.

Black art remained diverse, however. Some black artists joined the movement toward the left in art in the 1930s. Others looked to African art for inspiration, while still others explored more deeply native black American scenes. Biggers did both.

The new art departments continued to grow under adverse circumstances. And by the 1960s one could argue that a tradition of Afro-American art existed. Although it may have been inchoate, it did represent much of the black nationalism of the 1960s, and black artists did not fear the selection of subjects that represented their own past. By the 1970s more black Americans had entered the academic and museum fields. Their efforts produced more shows and activities that exhibited the work of black artists. One critic has maintained that they had an "impact. . . in presenting black America to the larger public, thereby achieving greater recognition of the quality, beauty, and power of black cultural life." (Edmund B. Gaither, "Afro-American Art" in *The Black American*, Mabel E. Smythe, ed., [New York, 1976], p. 343). In that sense a field of Afro-American art now is part of the larger artistic scene.

In 1976 a distinguished art critic summarized the problems faced in evaluating Afro-American art as separate from fine arts in the United States. He listed them as the absence of a detailed art history of the genre, a collection of a body of work that would allow detailed criticism, a shortage of people committed to the field, and the need for professional art institutions that would preserve and guarantee the survival of Afro-American art. Edmund Gaither meant museum activities, of course, and the publication of essays and biographies on Afro-American art that would lead to a full-length monograph. Wardlaw and Biggers would agree, probably, but they would argue, too, that Biggers's fine work at Texas Southern University formed just such a base as Gaither requested.

For more information on Biggers's work, see John Biggers and Carroll Simms with John Edward Weems, *Black Art in Houston: The Texas Southern Experience* (College Station, 1978). For general surveys see James A. Porter, *Modern Negro Art* (New York, 1969), and Alan L. Locke, *The Negro in Art* (Washington, D.C., 1940). More specialized works include Marion Perkins, *Problems of the Black Artists* (Chicago, 1971), and Edmund B. Gaither, *Afro-American Artists, New York and Boston* (Boston, 1970).   The Editors

John Thomas Biggers is an important artist. The fact that he is black is significantly but definitely secondary. He is unquestionably the most important artist of his race to have lived in Texas. His national reputation, though considerable, would probably have been towering indeed had he not chosen over the last three decades to sublimate his personal artistic achievement and pour himself into building a truly distinctive undergraduate art program at Texas Southern University in Houston.

It has been said that most artistic achievement stems from unhappy childhood. It would be easy to speculate—for those who do not know him—that John Biggers's art was the product of rebellion against the desperate poverty of a black family in the South during the depths of the depression and that it represented an isolated flowering of talent under intolerable circumstances. Nothing could be further from the truth. His boyhood was happy and productive. The foundations of his career were laid in his home by a mother and father who believed in hard work, in education, and in self-expression, whose faith in God and in themselves never wavered, and who transmitted these values to their children. The Biggerses' home was a place of warmth and love and self-respect and joy of life.

The achievements of John Biggers are also the achievements of his remarkable parents, Paul Andrew and Cora Finger Biggers. Paul Andrew Biggers was born on a tenant farm in York County, South Carolina, in 1881. His mother was a former slave, half-black, half-Cherokee; his father was a white farmer who had owned her until emancipation. However, Paul always looked upon his mother's husband, a man named Jim Britt, as his real father. All of Paul's brothers and sisters, with the exception of his twin brother Sandy, were Britts. John barely remembers his grandmother, but he recalls vividly her husband, Britt, a hard-working, warm, and happy man who was fun for kids to be around.

John also remembers very well his maternal grandmother, Elizabeth Finger Whitworth. "She lived alone on her farm until she was seventy-seven," John recalls. "She smoked a pipe and took wine and whiskey on occasion. All of us children loved to visit her because of her kindness and good cooking. We learned to pick cotton on her farm."[1]

The notion that hard work was harmful to children would have seemed absurd to the Britts and the Biggerses, all of whom worked from the time that they could swing a hoe or tote a cotton sack. When Paul Biggers was about six years old, he was working with his step-father in the woods getting wood for a sawmill when a tree fell the wrong way and crushed his leg against the trunk of another tree. His leg was crudely amputated above the knee. He never had an artificial limb, not even a peg leg, but spent the rest of his life on one leg and a crutch. "We never thought of Papa as being crippled or even handicapped," John remembers. "He was more active and productive than any two-legged man I ever knew. He even pitched horseshoes and played baseball with us boys."

When Paul Biggers was about eighteen years old he rode a mule across the North Carolina line to Lincoln Academy and entered school. A most unusual institution, Lincoln Academy was founded by the American Missionary Association (AMA) soon after the Civil War for the education of former slaves and their children. It was situated at the foot of Crowder's Mountain near King's Mountain, the Revolutionary War battleground, right on the South Carolina line. Paul, with his mule and his crutch, remained at Lincoln Academy, working and studying, until graduation. There he met his wife, John's mother, who walked two miles each way from her parents' farm near Bessemer City, North Carolina. Later Paul and Cora Biggers were to send four of their children, including John, to Lincoln Academy.

After graduation from Lincoln, Paul Biggers went to work as a carpenter, farmer, and shoemaker—all skills he had acquired at Lincoln along with a love of reading and an unquenchable thirst for knowledge. In the summers he attended Livingston College at Salisbury, North Carolina, where he studied Greek and Latin, among other things, and where he acquired certificates to teach and to preach. He grew up a Methodist but, after his marriage to Cora Finger in 1909, joined the Baptist church with her. Cora was a strong woman.

After their marriage Paul taught school in Wilkesboro, but for several months each year, he worked in the West Virginia coal mines for extra cash to augment his meager salary. In the meantime, his twin brother, Sandy, had moved to Gastonia, North Carolina, then a semirural cotton mill town with a large Negro population. He persuaded Paul and Cora to move to Gastonia.

Paul acquired a lot across the street from his brother, and with his own hands, built a house into which he, Cora, and their two oldest children moved. Paul added to the house room by room as the family grew. It ended up with five rooms, and he and Cora raised seven children in it. John, the youngest child, was born on April 13, 1924.

Paul Biggers was too busy to worry about being poor and disadvantaged. He and Cora always figured that you accepted the situation into which God had let you be born and did the best you could with it. Paul Biggers was a many-faceted man. From the time he moved to Gastonia until his final illness, he taught full time at several rural schools in Gaston County, always preaching at a church in the neighborhood of the school. He never accepted money for preaching; that was against his principles. He did, however, accept gifts of food from his flock. He always had a little farm somewhere in the county and worked it himself. And he always maintained a little shoe repair shop from which most of the family's meager supply of cash was derived.

At home in Gastonia the Biggers family kept an extensive garden in which they grew sweet potatoes, white potatoes, pumpkins, corn, okra, squash, collard greens, "creasy" greens, and other vegetables. They always had a cow, which was kept in bottomlands along a near-by creek with the neighbors' cows. They had hogs, too, which were kept in a communal hog pen about one mile away. The yard was filled with chickens, ducks, turkeys, and rabbits. As soon as the children could walk well, they were put to work in the garden. The kids always milked the cow and churned the butter. Each had his own little garden plot, his own chickens, rabbits, and pigeons, for whose care he had personal responsibility. Hog-killing time was a glorious occasion. It was a community affair with several families cooperating. The kids cleaned chitterlings, made liver pudding and sausage, and rendered lard, while Mama and Papa cured bacon and hams.

Although there never was much cash in the Biggerses' home, there was always plenty of good things to eat.

John Biggers remembers when, about 1936, Gastonia passed an ordinance banning cows, chickens, pigs, etc., from the city. "This was done in the name of sanitation," he said, "but it broke the back of our little community. Things were never the same again."

Cora Biggers spent her years taking care of the family, washing, ironing, sewing, and cooking. During the worst of the depression and during her husband's last illness, she worked as a domestic servant and took in washing and ironing. The kids helped with that too. John vividly remembers drawing and hauling water from the well on freezing mornings to fill the wash pots. (The only time he ever heard his mother swear was when he stumbled one cold morning and splashed half a bucket of ice water on her. "Damn you, boy!" she said.)

Coal and wood were all they had for fuel, and the coal smoke frequently begrimed the freshly washed sheets, making it necessary to wash them again.

But all was not work in the Biggerses' home. Both parents were avid readers and were determined that their children not grow up in ignorance. From early childhood the youngsters were forced to read two hours a day. At first John hated it—he was a slow reader in comparison with his siblings—but eventually he came to take great joy in reading, a pleasure which has lasted all his life, and read well before he entered school. How they acquired them John does not know, but the Biggers family had an unusually large collection of books, many of them religious, many of them the ordinary children's books of the day. As a little boy he delighted in *Aesop's Fables* and Joel Chandler Harris's folk tales. While John was still in elementary school, Charles Dickens fed his imagination, the essential element of the artist, with *David Copperfield* and *A Tale of Two Cities*.

The evenings were filled with reading. Paul read to the children, and they read aloud to each other. Each had the ambition of reading the Bible from cover to cover, and most of them accomplished this feat.

The Biggers youngsters played all the usual children's games. They particularly loved horseshoes and baseball. Papa participated in these games; to this day John does not know how he found the time to do it.

The evenings were wonderful and warm. Paul Biggers had a fine voice and organized a group of singers who moved around the neighborhood from house to house singing spirituals and rounds and "notes." (The singing of music from shaped notes was an absorbing pastime in the rural South in those days). Paul was a sort of unofficial neighborhood counselor to whom people brought their troubles.

John hung around his father constantly and listened to the grown folks talk. "It was an atmosphere of great warmth," he remembers. "My perception of the value of individuals came largely from my father and later was reflected in my art. This was one of the most important influences in my life."

Paul continued his study of Latin and Greek throughout his life, largely for the purpose of tracking down scriptural references. John remembers frequent sessions at which his father expounded the scriptures with the aid of Latin and Greek to groups of neighbors, some of whom were illiterate men who had been "called" to preach.

Cora had absorbed a large dose of puritanism from her white Yankee teachers at Lincoln Academy. She had a strongly developed sense of moral rectitude. She believed that the body was God's holy vessel and that it should not be violated by stimulants of any kind, tobacco, alcohol, even coffee and tea. She was a great drinker of hot water all her life. Despite her rigid puritanism, Cora was a warm, serene woman. "She saw beauty in practically everything and was quick to point it out to her children. The beauties and wonders of nature constantly enriched her life and ours as well. She was not an artist, but she had an artist's perception of the beautiful. The atmosphere she and Papa created in our home was an important force in my life as an artist."

Paul was much more flexible than his wife, except in matters of religion. He was a strict fundamentalist. The Bible was the word of God.

There were six children in the Biggers family in addition to John: Sylvester Paul, James Converse, Ferrie Elizabeth, Lillian Cora, Sarah Juanita, and Joseph Calvin. They were a close-knit family, supporting John's career and sharing in his accomplishments throughout their lives.

John Biggers's first artistic endeavor came when he was a small child. Every year he and his brothers and sisters would recreate the city of Gastonia out of the clay under their house, complete with streets and buildings, mules and horse-drawn wagons, and cars, and featuring Gastonia's two seven-story skyscrapers. It was an arduous and a happy enterprise.

When John Biggers was four years old he entered Highland Elementary School in Gastonia accompanied by his six-year-old brother. He remembers it as a good school which gave the pupils what they needed. Its main objective was to turn out people who could read, write, spell, and figure. They were drilled unmercifully in these fundamentals. Discipline was rigid. Biggers thinks Highland did much more for its pupils than modern schools which cater permissively to the desires of individual pupils and fail to give them the things which are basic to success in further education and in life.

One of the most important teachers in John Biggers's life was his second grade teacher, Mrs. Blue, who dedicated a part of every day to drawing. The method and the motivation she employed were simple. In those days every box of Arm and Hammer Baking Soda contained a picture of a bird. Mrs. Blue's class spent many hours copying these bird pictures. When they became pretty good at copying, they drew the birds from memory. By the time the year was over, John Biggers was drawing more than a hundred species of birds from memory. He was perhaps the best bird artist in the class, but there were two or three others about as good. One of the others, James Samuel Miller, has been John's lifelong friend. He is now principal of an integrated elementary school in Gastonia.

All the Biggers children could draw, although John was the only one to become an artist. For years in that grammar school all the posters were drawn and lettered by the Biggers kids. Sylvester, the oldest boy, copied scenes from the Bible and pictures of Christ in color, and nearly every home in the neighborhood had one of his pictures hanging in it. In Hawaii during World War II, Joe, the third boy, made a good thing out of painting scenes on coconuts and selling them to tourists and servicemen.

Where did John Biggers's talent come from? From God, of course, with some assistance from Mama and Papa. John recalls that his father was a natural draftsman, that his handwriting was beautiful and precise, and that he made excellent drawings of things he was going to build. "But it was the atmosphere in our home which was most important, the insistence that we respect ourselves and other people too, the insistence on high standards, the unwavering belief in right, in the truly Christian way of life. In these things I perceive the basic impulses for creativity."

Paul Biggers died in 1936 after a devastating period of illness. He had diabetes, and it went untreated. First he lost his one good leg to gangrene. Then he lost his sight. Then his life flickered out. But he never lost his spirit, his faith, his love. John remembers him as a great man.

John Biggers looks back at his boyhood in Gastonia and thinks of the good things in life that it brought him. He does not think of it in terms of poverty, injustice, and deprivation, although those elements were certainly present.

"We never really thought much about race," he said. "The black people lived in their own separate world. Ours was a warm world, a close world. For the most part we took care of our own. We accepted the differences in races as a matter of fact. That's the way the world was. Usually we just stayed on our side of town.

"Nearly every Negro family had a special relationship with a white family, usually a family for whom we had worked through the years. When we encountered a problem which we couldn't handle, we usually turned to our special white friends for help, and usually got it. Anything to do with the law came in that category, for the law was controlled completely by white men. People in power have always had to speak for people out of power. I suppose it was a paternalistic relationship, a carry-over from slavery, but we didn't feel demeaned by it. The world was so different then from the way it is now that there really is no basis for comparison."

While relationships with whites, particularly rural whites, were generally relaxed, Gastonia's Negroes usually steered clear of the cotton mill hands. They had come down out of the mountain coves and fastnesses a generation before—straight out of the Elizabethan age—and were cold-eyed, clannish, and violent people who had never really known black people and regarded them with deep suspicion.

During the labor unrest of the 1920s and 1930s, violence broke out repeatedly as unions began to organize the workers and the mill owners resisted. People were killed, including the chief of police. The Biggerses and their neighbors regarded these happenings with great puzzlement. The general reaction was "what can you expect? All those white people over there are crazy anyhow."

"The Negro community in Gastonia had a special quality about it that made young people who left want to come back to live. That is still true today. I know that, after all the years and all the changes, I still think of Gastonia as home.''

In 1937, the year after their father died, John and his older brother Joe entered Lincoln Academy for high school training. John worked half-time, Joe two-thirds time, to help pay expenses. To take care of the rest of the cost of her children's schooling, Mrs. Biggers worked as a matron for girls at a Negro orphanage in Oxford, two hundred miles east of Gastonia. She continued this assistance even during their college days.

Nestling at the foot of Crowder's Mountain, six miles east of Gastonia and four miles west of King's Mountain, Lincoln Academy consisted of about twelve buildings, three of them substantial brick structures. It had its own farm, shops, and barns. Everyone had to work, even students whose parents were able to pay their full bills. Students milked the cows, cared for and butchered the cattle, worked in the laundry, repaired the roads and the buildings. They kept the plant in tip-top shape.

Lincoln Academy had about 250 boarding students and an equal number of day students who commuted from nearby communities. The curriculum was the usual high school variety plus music, home economics, agriculture, and mechanical and industrial arts. Teachers included both blacks and whites. Discipline was extremely rigid, and the ultimate punishment was being sent home. For lesser offenses restriction to certain areas of the campus for a semester was common, and students caught in minor infractions of the rules were sentenced to extra work, frequently on rock piles from which road building materials were derived. During these work sentences students could not attend classes and had to catch up on their own.

John Biggers, a mischievous, high-spirited boy, was constantly in trouble with the authorities for offenses ranging from smoking to being "off limits" in areas of the women's campus where boys weren't allowed. John was sentenced to the rock pile for a month for smoking and was frequently out of class for minor infractions. The only reason he wasn't sent home was that he always stayed on the honor roll.

John's regular work was as a fireman in the boiler rooms; there was no central heating. He also kept up the tennis courts and worked as a janitor in the carpentry shop where he was introduced to cabinet-making, which was as close to art as he came; he found it challenging and rewarding.

"The atmosphere at Lincoln was wonderful," John remembers. "It made college later on somewhat anticlimatic. When I got to college I had already experienced the feeling of entering into a new adventure in learning. The students lived happily together and worked in common purpose. There were broadening cultural experiences, too. Symphony orchestras and great artists such as Roland Hayes and Marian Anderson would stop off at Lincoln for concerts between engagements in Charlotte and Atlanta or other cities. I am sure they weren't paid much, if anything. There were outstanding public speakers, too, national figures like Howard Thurmond and Walter White."

John Biggers took an active part in the athletic program, which included football, basketball, baseball, and, surprisingly, tennis and swimming. The clay tennis courts, the upkeep of which was John's special assignment, were among the best in the South. The swimming pool, dug by the students, was fed by strong springs in a natural valley. People came from as far away as Charlotte to swim in it. There weren't many places where Negroes could swim in those days.

"Henry Westerband became my ideal," John said. "An athlete and musician, he could draw and paint. He put on overalls every day and worked with the students on the roads. He could work with his mind and his hands. He taught me furniture making, and heightened my sense of aesthetics in the process. The furniture we made had to be both functional and beautiful.

"The only creative work I had at Lincoln was in cabinetmaking, working from my own designs. I kept on drawing, but it was mostly copying. I didn't know what art was. Art, I thought, was making pictures. It had nothing to do with creative expression."

Lincoln did contribute many things, however, that later flowered in John Biggers's art. Another strong man, Bill Drone, influenced him greatly. Drone taught agriculture officially, but he really taught ecology, although he did not call it that. "He taught us living biology," Biggers said, "the interrelationship of man, plants, and animals, the meaning of the natural world.

"All my life, as I have thought of the meaning of man and of beauty—the things with which my art has been concerned—I felt that the foundations were laid in those days. Lincoln took up where Papa and Mama left off."

John Biggers's understanding of his African heritage, which later was to revolutionize his art, had its beginning at Lincoln also. The president, Henry C. McDowell, had spent twenty years in Angola and brought to Lincoln an enlightened point of view about Africa. "Black Americans generally thought of their African background as somehow being shameful and regarded Africans as savages. Dr. McDowell came through with a positive approach to our African heritage which was brand new to me. He brought some students from Africa to the campus. We lived intimately with them and learned to our surprise that they were basically the same as we were."

Lincoln Academy equipped most of its graduates to go to college, but it was even more deeply concerned with giving them the knowledge and the skills with which to make a living. It was, John Biggers thinks, a wonderful school which performed a mighty service in its time. Its doors were closed permanently in 1951. It had always depended for its existence, in addition to contributions made through AMA, on appropriations from Gaston County and the state of North Carolina. But the state built a big new consolidated school about four miles away, and public support for Lincoln was withdrawn. It could not survive on private funds alone.

The plant which had been a happy home for two generations of the Biggers family has fallen into ruins. John thinks sorrowfully about the academy's death and privately doubts whether that big new public high school can do as much for his people as Lincoln did. But perhaps it had served its time, he thinks, and would be an anachronism in these confusing years with their constantly shifting values.

When John Biggers left Lincoln, he planned to become a plumber. "My ambition was to get a good stable job," he said. He learned something about plumbing during his four years' experience as a fireman in the campus boiler room (where he also passed many night and early morning hours copying engravings from the New York *Times*). He had also worked during the summers as an assistant to a plumber in Gastonia. There was good money in plumbing.

But somehow he decided to go on to college. His first choice was Tuskegee Institute in Alabama, but McDowell thought Biggers would have broader opportunities at Hampton Institute in Virginia. Hampton was a private college founded after the Civil War for the education of black freedmen and American Indians. Its founder was John Chapman Armstrong, a former Yankee general who had commanded black troops during the war. The Indians largely faded out of the picture in Hampton's early years and were remembered by black students chiefly through the names of the two oldest dormitories on campus, Wigwam and Wynona, and the Indian burial ground; apparently an unusual number of Indian students had died.

Hampton was chiefly important to John Biggers for two reasons: he met Hazel, his wife, there, and it was there that he met Victor Lowenfeld, who, with the exception of his father, had a greater influence on his life than any other man.

Victor Lowenfeld was an Austrian Jew, a psychologist, and an artist who had come to the United States to teach at Harvard for a year. During that year he decided that working with Negro students would be an unusual and interesting challenge. He joined the Hampton faculty as professor of psychology in 1940, the year before John Biggers entered as a freshman. There was no instruction in art then. Lowenfeld asked Dr. Arthur Howe, the president, for permission to organize an art class. "All right, if you want to waste your time," was Howe's response. "These people aren't interested in art." Lowenfeld put a notice on the bulletin board, offering a noncredit art class at night. Of the slightly more than 800 students at Hampton, about 750 showed up for the class, presenting Lowenfeld with a monumental task in cutting the class down to manageable size. The next year Lowenfeld's art class was offered for credit.

Lowenfeld was an accomplished painter and a superb teacher. Later his book *Creative and Mental Growth* was to become one of the foundations of modern art education; it has been translated into most of the major languages of the world. (Incidentally several of Biggers's drawings were used to illustrate the early editions of this work, not as examples of black art but as design.)

At first Lowenfeld had the art department to himself. There was, however, a talented graduate student in building and construction, Joe Gilliard, whose specialty was woodwork and whose skill on the wood lathe was remarkable. Lowenfeld asked Gilliard to make a pottery wheel, and Gilliard soon acquired great skill in making pots. He became Lowenfeld's first assistant.

John Biggers studied drawing and painting under Lowenfeld

and ceramics under Joe Gilliard. He became firmly committed to art during his Hampton years. He learned from Lowenfeld that art was not just making pictures, but was a means of self-realization, of fulfillment.

"I began to see art not primarily as an individual expression of talent but as a responsibility to reflect the spirit and style of the Negro people," he said. "It became an awesome responsibility to me, not a fun thing at all."

John Biggers's experience at Hampton was interrupted by two and a half years' service in the navy in World War II, but even there he continued his experience in art. In the navy he was a visual arts specialist and worked mostly under Joe Gilliard, his ceramics teacher at Hampton and a naval petty officer, making three-dimensional models of machinery for instructional purposes. Gilliard and Biggers worked at the Hampton Institute Naval School until it was closed, and then John was sent to the Norfolk Navy Yards for the last six months of his naval tenure. These were not wasted years for Biggers. "Gilliard's skill bordered on genius," he said. "He contributed much to my life and art."

Back at Hampton he studied sculpture under Betty Catlett, later to become a noted sculptress. Her husband, Charles White, an outstanding artist, had received a Rosenwald grant to paint a mural at Hampton, and she came with him. White was a great technician, and Biggers watched him closely while he painted. It was a tremendous learning experience. "White's talent and skill were so great that several promising students just quit art when they watched him work," Biggers said. "They knew they could never approach what he was able to do."

Biggers got his teeth into art for the first time at Hampton. He began to produce drawings and paintings which brought him the feeling of fulfillment and became a part of the major corpus of his work. At Hampton he painted two murals, about eight-by-twelve feet, which were important to him. One called *Dying Soldier* depicted a black soldier dying on a battlefield while visions of his boyhood passed on the canvas above his head. The other, entitled *Community Preacher* showed a minister preaching about Africa with his sermon reenacted in African scenes above his head.

Willard Townsend, president of the United Transport Workers

of America and a member of the Hampton board, acquired these two monumental paintings. They hung for years in his office in the union's headquarters in Chicago, but later, after Townsend's death, they were given to an institution in Liberia. Biggers does not know exactly where they are.

It was after John Biggers returned to Hampton from the navy that he met Hazel Hales, a girl from Fayetteville, North Carolina. "We came from the same kind of background," Biggers said. Hazel was an accounting major. She and John were immediately attracted to each other, but marriage then was impossible. She had yet to finish her training, and John had years of education still ahead of him.

This education was not to be at Hampton. In 1946 Victor Lowenfeld left to join the faculty of Pennsylvania State University, and John Biggers followed him. At Penn State he earned all his degrees—Bachelor of Arts, Master of Science, and Doctor of Education. In addition to acquiring the necessary training for a career in art education, he did a lot of drawing and painting. He painted several murals, two in the Burrow's (Education) Building. One dealt with plenty; the other with scarcity and poverty. The subjects in these murals are neither black nor white, just people. There were only eleven black students at Penn State at the time, and Biggers got away for a while from his preoccupation with Negro subjects. "You paint what you are around," he said.

In addition to Victor Lowenfeld, several professors at Penn State influenced John Biggers strongly. One was William Bixby in education. Another was Ed Abrasom in sociology and anthropology. ("He helped me understand the whole social spectrum of history.") Yet another was Hugh Davidson, who taught statistics. ("His approach to mathematics added another dimension to my appreciation of aesthetics.")

At Penn State, Biggers watched the great muralist Varnum Poor paint frescoes in the old Main Building. "It was a wonderful experience."

With Hiram Draper Williams, now an established artist of importance, Biggers worked under Ed Abrasom's direction on a "still film" for the navy department on the subject of racial attitudes. Biggers took a black family and Williams a white through all sorts of situations to demonstrate racial reactions. "It was an exciting project.

The still film can be a powerful medium with great impact.''

In the meantime Hazel had completed her training at Hampton and was working as an accountant at Florida A&M College in Tallahassee. In December, 1948, in the middle of John's last year of residency at Penn State, she came to Pennsylvania and they were married. She returned immediately to her job in Florida so John could finish out his year (It was not until 1954 that he returned to receive his doctorate).

John went to Florida in June, 1949, to collect his bride. Their first real honeymoon was spent that summer in Montgomery, where John taught at Alabama State Teachers College. In August they went to Houston, where John had accepted the challenge of organizing a department of art at Texas Southern University for Negroes.

Hazel is a lovely, serene woman of unusual intelligence and sensitivity. ''She has made my world secure,'' John said. Her belief in his art is so strong that she has always been willing for him to cut loose from everything else and take his chances as an artist. Several times he has been tempted, but his work at Texas Southern was far too challenging and rewarding for him to let go of it, a fact which has enriched the lives of a whole generation of young black artists in Texas.

Formidable obstacles confronted John Biggers at Texas Southern. There was little understanding among the administration and the faculty as to what an art department should be. Many thought of it principally as a free source of posters, graphs, and showcard letterings. They also wanted their portraits painted and could not understand how a man who could obviously paint and draw such fine heads was not interested. To this day he accepts no such commissions.

The only other member of the TSU art department that first year was Joseph Mack, a classmate of Biggers at Hampton Institute. The next year there was added to the faculty the man who, next to Biggers himself, has been most responsible for the growth and influence of the department—Carroll Simms, native of Arkansas, a graduate of Cranbrook Art Academy in Bloomfield Hills, Michigan. At Cranbrook, Simms studied under Bill McVey, later of Rice University, and Berthold (''Tex'') Schiwetz, an unusually talented understudy of Walter Millis and a brother of the beloved Texas artist E. M.

("Buck") Schiwetz. Simms, a sculptor and ceramist, studied in London and Sweden under fellowships and also spent a year in Nigeria.

The first problem of the new art department was getting students. Young black Texans in the early 1950s had seldom been exposed to art in any form in their segregated public schools. "We had to actively recruit boys and girls in order to acquire the ten students necessary for the department to survive," Biggers remembers. Soon, however, the word got around that something really exciting was taking place, and students began to flock to art classes, their numbers significantly augmented by public school art teachers.

At first Carroll Simms's work was seriously handicapped by the lack of a kiln. In the third year of the department's existence, however, Mrs. S. M. McAshan, an unusually perceptive Houston civic leader and philanthropist, gave a fine ceramic kiln to the department, probably the single most important gift that the department has ever received.

From the outset Biggers and his associates took their art to the community and began a program of mural painting which was to become one of the most distinctive features of the department. The first murals were in temporary buildings, soon destroyed. Then came the first off-campus murals, two sixty-foot-long productions by John Biggers and Joseph Mack in the Eliza Johnson Nursing Home. They depict many phases of Negro life. In the garden of the home is an eloquent piece of statuary by Carroll Simms, *Old Couple Fishing*.

There followed a succession of Biggers's murals in a number of off-campus buildings—a mural in the Blue Triangle Branch of the YWCA depicting Negro women in American life; a six-by-twenty-four-foot mural in Carver High School in Naples, depicting the development of Negro education in East Texas; a mural in the Longshoremen's Temple (Local No. 872) which speaks of the life of longshoremen; an unusually beautiful mural in the W. L. Johnson Branch of the Houston Public Library entitled *Birth from the Sea* which came out of Biggers's African experience. There is even a sprightly mural in a veterinary clinic. Perhaps the finest of all Biggers's murals, one which shows the world of life as a great balanced system of nature, is in the Science Building at TSU.

Carroll Simms was as active as Biggers in bringing art to the community, creating fountains, ceramic murals, and a sculpture of heroic proportion in front of the Martin Luther King, Jr., Humanities Center.

However, Biggers and Simms—and their department—have existed primarily for the sake of students. The result has been a remarkable student involvement in art. In the new Art Center, built in 1961, there are hundreds of examples of superior art by students—easel paintings, drawings, prints, weaving, sculpture, and an incredibly wide variety of ceramics. Many of them are beautiful indeed and intensely individualistic. All bear eloquent testimony to teachers who demand that their students learn first the fundamentals—drawing, methods, materials—and then turn them loose to do their uninhibited "own things."

A unique feature of the Texas Southern Department of Art is the mural program for students. For decades the halls on three floors of the Administration Building, even the staircases, have been divided into segments and turned over to seniors to paint murals. Some murals have obviously been more successful than others. After a few months those which do not pass the test of repeated viewing are painted over, and those segments are assigned to other students. It is a great challenge to a student to be given a chance to paint a mural which may become a permanent part of a busy building, viewed by thousands each year. The mural project has brought about an unusual relationship between artists and their fellow students and teachers. "Mural painting comes naturally to blacks," Biggers says. "We like to do things big, to spread ourselves."

There is not room in this piece on John Biggers to tell much about his individual students. Many have gone to solid achievement in art. Many have become teachers and have carried the gospel of art to schools throughout the region. For about eight years the number of art majors has ranged from 80 to 110 students. Some of them have been touched with greatness. Most of them have found self-fulfillment which has enriched their lives and enabled them to live at peace in a bewildering world.

One such student was Kermit Oliver, who came from a small East Texas town and had learned to paint still lifes in a Catholic school. "His talent leaped forward the first week," Biggers said. "He had a God-given gift to draw. He studied the techniques of the old masters and really took off. He is a practicing artist of unusual virtuosity and complete faith in himself. He is an eloquent painter.''

Among many other talented and dedicated students are Calvin Hubbard, Harry Vital, Leon Renfro, Harvey Johnson, and Trudell Mims Obey. Johnson, Renfro, and Vital have remained on the TSU staff to assist Biggers and Simms in their work. ''Their talent is exceptional,'' Biggers states. ''They are creative artists and teachers who are committed to the reaffirmation of the aesthetics of faith, honesty, and perseverance of black people of all ages and of American democracy.''

But back to Biggers and his own career as an artist. Little by little, despite the demands of the art department, he produced a succession of eloquent paintings and drawings which have won many awards, hung in many shows, and built for him a strong national reputation. His paintings and drawings have won prizes at the Museum of Fine Arts, Houston, the Dallas Museum of Fine Arts, and the Negro National Art Exhibition in Atlanta, to name but a few from a long list. One-man shows of his art have been presented in the galleries of some twenty-four leading museums and universities throughout the nation, and his work has been represented in countless other shows. To list all the shows in which Biggers's work has appeared, the magazine articles by and about him, the lectures which he has made, and the honors which have come to him would require many pages. His illustrations have appeared in many books, most notably *Aunt Dicey Tales* and *Dog Ghosts* by J. Mason Brewer, *Cross Timbers* by Edward Everett Dale, an edition of *The Good Earth* by Pearl Buck, and *I, Momolu* by Lorenz Graham, the latter the story of an African childhood.

It was not, however, until 1956, when John and Hazel Biggers went to Ghana and Nigeria under a UNESCO fellowship, that he discovered his roots and, in so doing, found himself. ''It was the greatest experience of my life,'' he said.

Prior to his journey to Afirca, Biggers's art had been preoccupied with the suffering of his people. There, however, he found beauty and dignity and the triumph of the human spirit. He returned to Houston filled with new enthusiasm and new purpose. His work became a joyous expression of his inner feelings. He returned immediately to full-time teaching but, little by little, he recorded his African experience in a series of powerful conte crayon drawings. In

1962 they were published by the University of Texas Press in the book *Ananse: The Web of Life in Africa.*

This writer cannot speak of *Ananse* without resorting to the first person. I was director of the University of Texas Press when J. Mason Brewer, the Negro folklorist, introduced me to John Biggers, and I met with him frequently while work on *Ananse* was in progress. Out of it also came a friendship which has enriched my life.

Ananse is primarily a book of pictures, warm, eloquent, appealing not only in their interpretation of African scenes and peoples but in their universality. The first draft of the text was stilted, self-conscious. I told John to let himself go completely, to pour out on paper what he really felt about Africa. He did. The resultant text is a perfect counterpart to the drawings. It is an exultant song of the human spirit, a celebration of life which is as old as the world and as new as tomorrow's sunrise. Witness this passage for instance:

> We began the trip southward to Lomé in the late afternoon, while the sun was sliding down the western horizon. As we drove through rolling, palm-crowned hills we met long lines of people coming home from the fields. I felt flowing over me that feeling of love and serenity experienced in every land when mothers, fathers, and children return home in the evening, after a day's toil, to comfort each other, to relax, to laugh and play.
>
> Especially were the African women impressive. They walked in single file—hundreds of them—their heads crowned with hand-woven baskets loaded with produce from the earth: yams, cassavas, corn, pineapples, groundnuts, peppers, and pawpaws. They walked quickly, gracefully, determinedly—bringing food and warmth to their families.
>
> Many of them were stripped to the waist, their bosoms embracing the evening glow. Young maidens, mature women, old matriarchs—all walked up from the valley of pregnant earth, breasts protruding with green-gourd firmness, or gently dropping with melon fullness, or sagging with time-wrinkled service and sacrifice. But they all held their backs and shoulders erect, these earthly goddesses of fertility, as they walked without hesitation upon life's sacrificial altar.
>
> The burnished-gold sun burst upon them and glorified

them. Gold shot from their bodies and richocheted from the fertile black earth; the light blinded us. And out of the same valley—the valley of the morning, it seemed—came more black silhouettes, like columns of marching soldier ants—growing into bold contours of human flesh and cloth fiber as they approached us—passing us by, as time does, for we could embrace them for only a moment—then leaving us behind, marching onward across the plain in silhouettes of tomorrow—vanishing into the night. These African women are daughters of the moon, queens of the fertile earth, mothers of toil and sorrow, descendants of Eve tramping through life's Garden of Eden, as countless generations before them had tramped and were trampled on, bearing their burdens and gifts with pride. As I watched this magnificent procession of warm, red sorrow march into the cool blue of the northern skies it seemed to me that the leafy crowns of the tall palm trees grew still, that the evening no longer moved, that the nugget of gold fire hesitated in its downward plunge. But flocks of black crows cried out, startling me, and I realized that darkness was upon us.

This had been a golden day in our own time; Mother Africa had embraced me. Deep emotion, carried within me from early childhood, rose like a flood tide as I reflected on Africa's ageless drama, on her continuing human tragedy, on her quiet evening beauty.[2]

I succeeded in interesting an editor on the staff of *Life* magazine in doing a feature on *Ananse* and took to New York with me, by train, a half dozen of Biggers's original drawings, the smallest about three-by-four feet. I wrestled these monster drawings in and out of taxi cabs and elevators and then found myself in a conference with *Life*'s art editor and the magazine's African specialist, whose names I have mercifully forgotten. *Life*'s art features in those days were devoted principally to abstract art of the far-out variety. The art editor sniffed at the paintings and said, "Good drawings, but are they art?" The African specialist objected because there were no pictures of new hosptials, schools, bridges, etc., the symbols of modern progress in Africa. "We don't want to depict Africa in terms of primitive people," he said. The interview ended quickly.

John Biggers was years ahead of his time. Less than ten years later America's black leaders and all national media were telling blacks that they should discover their roots in Africa and that there was much of dignity and beauty in their African heritage. This was, of course, the theme of *Ananse*.

Ananse bridged the gap between Africa and the United States for John Biggers. At long last he had found his roots. Most of his drawings were made from field sketches, sometimes supported, for detail, by photographs, but many of the people lived only in the artist's memory. When he was working on the finished drawing of the Nigerian Queen Mother, John was astonished to find that he was actually recreating the face of "Miss Blanche" McNeill, a neighbor in Gastonia, a second mama who had both whipped him and fed him as a boy. "We carry images in our subconscious minds," he said.

What his *Ananse* trip meant to Biggers personally is best expressed in his own words:

> At the beginning of our tour I had experienced the discomfort, the uneasiness that an outsider always feels. I did not know from which tribal culture my forefathers were torn; I did not possess linguistic ability for communication. I soon realized, however, that having to identify with all Africans could be an asset instead of a liability, for the future of Africa depends to a great extent on dissolving intertribal dissensions. I also realized that I was probably a composite of all West African tribes anyway, because economic and sociological pressures in America during past centuries had eliminated the many tribal factions and had solidified the Negro into a common group.
>
> But now let the dead past take care of itself. A new dawn challenges this world and demands the salt of every one of us. There can be no doubt of our sodality, for in each of us we reflect one another's image, and our composite image mirrors the tragedy and the comedy of the whole human race.[3]

Ananse, although its time had not yet come, attracted a moderate amount of national attention and received uniformly good reviews. "The African rhythms, patterns, and occasional grotesqueries John Biggers observes are most eloquently pictured," commented the New York *Times.* "The strained faces of the Accra fishermen, the graceful striding of the women, the bizarre shapes of indigenous vegetation—these and other familiar spectacles are memorably depicted.''[4]

Ananse went through two printings in its original hardcover edition, went out of print for a time, and then was reprinted in a handsome paperback edition in 1979 with a foreword by Barbara Jordan. "His poetic depiction enables the reader to visit a place and people under the tutelage of a gentle guide of talent and acute perception," she wrote. "Because of this man and his enthusiasm 'culturally deprived' youth became artistically privileged. *Ananse* serves to lessen the cultural deprivation of a wider audience."[5]

John Biggers's faith in the sodality of the human race was put to severe test in the 1960s, as student and faculty unrest grew at Texas Southern and "brotherhood" became a word reserved for one's race rather than for all mankind. The atmosphere changed subtly as did the students' attitude toward their work. The joy of work and achievement was smothered under low-hanging clouds of discontent.

John and Hazel Biggers had a brief respite from turmoil in 1965-1966, when John taught at the University of Wisconsin as guest professor. Certainly there was great unrest on the campus at Madison too, but it scarcely touched their lives. It was a good year in many ways, academically peaceful and relatively undemanding. At its conclusion Biggers was urged to accept a permanent appointment to the Wisconsin faculty at a salary vastly higher than the one he commanded at TSU. He did not consider the offer for a minute. "At Wisconsin," he said, "I was just another art professor. At TSU I shared the lives of my students and felt that we were helping them to know themselves, to find their way in life."

In the 1960s, as all recall, pressure was put on every university in the nation to add blacks to their faculties. John Biggers, a noted artist in his own right, a teacher of solid accomplishment, and the holder of a doctorate from a leading university, was a prime target for the raiding expeditions which stripped so many black colleges of their best-qualified teachers. John lost count of the number of times he was approached by universities throughout the nation—"I guess it was about 200"—but he told them all that he was not interested. "I can do more for my people, and for myself, here," he said.

During all this time the student storms were brewing. They

finally broke in 1966 over the campus at TSU, culminating in violent episodes which left one Houston policeman dead and three students wounded. The campus was a powder keg waiting for almost any spark to ignite it. Faculty members were almost as bitterly frustrated as the students.

John Biggers was selected by the faculty and the student body to head a committee to investigate, and seek to avoid, confrontations between students and police. Many other problems were dumped in the committee's lap. It was a thankless, soul-draining task. Many animosities, problems, and frustrations came boiling to the surface.

John, who yearned passionately for peace and who held firm in his own life to the old-fashioned values, tried to understand and articulate the grievances and desperation of students and faculty. The situation was complicated by some who had come to positions of leadership and who used their power for exploitation, attempting to turn every situation into personal gain.

On the whole John Biggers's committee performed faithfully and well. God only knows what would have happened at TSU without it. Eventually this ad hoc committee merged with the local chapter of the Texas Association of College Teachers, which has performed some valuable service, but which, Biggers thinks, has been insufficiently concerned with academic ineptness and poor performance. Nor has there been much concern about the political system which perpetuates incompetence and mediocrity in governing boards and administrations.

Twice John and Hazel had to put off another trip to Africa, for which he had a grant from the Danforth Foundation, because of the situation at TSU. In 1969, however, they finally made it, spending most of their time in East Africa, where they added a whole new collection of priceless visual images to their store. Another book probably would have resulted in a few years, but John was tired and torn by the problems he had left behind in Houston. He returned from the trip in poor health. It was soon discovered that he had contracted tuberculosis of the throat. There were other complications. For four years he fought illness, working most of the time but desperately hampered by physical inadequacy. His own work suffered. In the late 1960s and the early 1970s, he produced only one drawing, a powerful charcoal rendering of the head of a black man, larger than life, with tortured eyes searching the horizon. It was emblematic of his people.

Now, his health and vitality restored, he has plunged again into work, both with his students and with his own art. In 1979 Biggers completed thirty years at Texas Southern. Several times he has thought of retiring to devote his entire energies to his art, a project which Hazel heartily endorses, but thus far he has been unable to tear himself away from his work at Texas Southern. Retirement, when it comes, will be almost like beginning again. The future is bright for him, but perhaps not so bright for his people.

"It has been said that the past fifteen years have been a period of black liberation and, in some respects, this has been true," Biggers says. "One of the worst problems we face now is exploitation of blacks by blacks. Many of the people who should be our leaders are our exploiters, their individuality degenerated into egotistical madness. This malady can't be cured by separation of the races. All people, regardless of color, who hold high ideals must work together to achieve them. In any multiracial society you can get the best out of people only by working together, not separately. This is the only way in which the unbridled exploitation which followed the liberation of the sixties can be held in check. We must work together, but if blacks lose their identity they will be lost.

"My philosophy as a teacher has always been concerned with the self-identity of students. We must understand who we are and what we are. To do that we must understand our roots. We can't know where we are going unless we know where we came from, and where we are now.

"An important part of self-identity is realizing our relationship with family—the immediate family, of course, but beyond that the extended family—the community, all mankind, all races. Nothing worthwhile and beautiful was ever built on hatred.

"Just as he identifies with himself the artist must identify with the materials with which he works. Only through identity with himself and his materials can he achieve reality. We encourage our students to express themselves with true individuality, to 'do their own thing' without inhibition, but first they must learn the basics of art. They must learn to draw. Unbridled individuality is born of arrogance and egotistical selfishness, not to mention ignorance.

"You must achieve competence before you can do your own

thing in art or in life. There is a tendency nowadays to place so much emphasis on individuality of expression that criticism of fundamentals meets with hostility. The artist must endure and profit by the criticism of others and, above all, by self-criticism. Artists, indeed all men and women, must achieve individual expression in their work, but their relationships with others must be communal. This is the only way we can survive in the kind of world in which we live.

"One of the highest examples of civilization can be found in the Gothic period with its unity of life and aesthetic expression. The Gothic cathedral represented religion, art, knowledge—the highest aspirations of mankind. When you look at a Gothic cathedral you see a true miracle."

The last five years have brought increased recognition and appreciation for John Biggers and his work. His paintings and drawings have appeared in literally dozens of exhibitions of black art from coast to coast. Perhaps the most important was "Two Centuries of Black American Art 1750-1950" in which three of his works appeared. It was shown in 1976-1977 in the Los Angeles County Museum, the High Museum of Atlanta, the Dallas Museum of Fine Arts, the Detroit Institute of Art, and the Brooklyn Museum. This show formed the basis of a book by the same name published in 1976 by Alfred A. Knopf.

Black art has been a subject of national and international interest in recent years. Biggers's work has been discussed and illustrated in ten books and dozens of articles in periodicals ranging from *Reader's Digest* to publications in Sweden and Finland. A Biggers family group appears on the cover of J. Eugene Grigsby, Jr., *Art and Ethics,* and nine other Biggers drawings and etchings are included in it, together with an extensive interview with Biggers and a discussion of his art. In this interview Biggers was asked for his interpretation of black art. He replied, "To me it means that people must reflect their struggle, their history, their search for their own identity and for spiritual values. They must affirm their own life . . . . To me this is what black art is."

His purpose in going to Texas Southern, Biggers later told Grigsby, was "to develop a community center of art, which meant training teachers and craftsmen and to create a shrine for our neighborhoods."

Grigsby comments: "The success of the 'shrine' that John Biggers went to Texas to build, the quality of his own work, and the quality of his teaching can be judged by the recognition each has received, and this has been considerable. The affirmation to which John Biggers refers was admirably summed up by Germaine Greer on a television talk show: 'To be without tradition is about the most degrading thing an artist faces.' "

Although most of Biggers's national recognition has taken place during the recent surge of interest in Black Art, perhaps the most important was the chapter devoted to his work by the noted artist and critic Elton C. Fax in *Seventeen Black Artists*.

Comparing Biggers's work to that of Norma Morgan, Fax writes:

> . . . the people he draws, and the settings he puts them in are, like hers, very real, very earthy. The difference is in attitude. Where Norma Morgan treats decay and black erosion with a passionate truth, Biggers is equally passionate on his interpretation of a world bursting with vitality and living energy. Because John Biggers combines that approach with a sense of absolute commitment to his personal beliefs, his peak performances yield extraordinary results.[7]

Quoting Biggers as saying "I learned a long time ago that self-dignity and racial pride could be consciously approached through art," Fax comments that "John Biggers' own creations are powerful testimonials to that statement."[8]

The last five years have seen Texas Southern University in a constant state of turmoil, punctuated by many changes in administration, demi-scandals, charges and countercharges, and the development of an atmosphere which made it most difficult for dedicated teachers to do their jobs. One of the most traumatic events of this period involved the destruction, completely without warning, of a number of the "permanent" students murals in Hannah Hall. The principle purpose of this destruction was to provide long windows in the hall through which passersby might watch the university's new computer! Administrative absentmindedness rather than hostile intent was probably responsible for this tragedy, but John Biggers and many others could not be consoled. Biggers thought of resigning but was urged by many artists and friends to remain at his post. One of the more eloquent letters he received at this time was from Jean Lacy, painter and sculptor associated with the Dallas Museum, which concluded:

"We as artists and prophets must continue to confront a depersonalizing world by refusing to be depersonalized by it. We must find meaning and importance in this terrible act and use it for our own productivity and expression and, yes, survival.

"There are many walls yet to be conquered."

Biggers found some small comfort in the fact that most of the destoryed murals had already been photographed for reproduction in *Black Art in Houston: The Texas Southern University Experience*, written by Biggers and Simms with the editorial assistance of John Edward Weems and published by Texas A&M University Press in 1978. This lavishly illustrated book, much of it in full color, is an inspiring record of the work of Biggers, Simms, and their students throughout the years of the making of their "shrine."

In addition to *Black Art in Houston*, the late 1970s brought other memorable experiences to John Biggers. Nearing completion now is his most ambitious mural (in the TSU Student Life Center), which measures fifteen feet high by sixty-two feet long. Biggers's style in this mural is freer and more impresssionistic than in other murals. The theme is "family unity" and reflects the artist's longheld belief that the family is the most important unity in a democratic society.

Simultaneously John Biggers is working on a mural for the internationally known Houston Music Hall, a commission approved by the City Art Commission and by the mayor and city council. Seven-by-twenty-one feet in size, it is being painted on canvas and will be installed in the foyer of the Music Hall. Titled *The Rites of Passage*, it depicts the progress of man through birth, baptism, childhood, adolescence, maturity, old age, and finally "passage" to another life. It is a visual interpretation of Negro spirituals.

Also in the same foyer will stand a ten-foot tall sculpture, *Guitar Solo* by Carroll Simms.

In January, 1980, two major retrospective shows of Biggers's work opened almost simultaneously. One, containing seventy pieces, was at the Institute of Texan Cultures in San Antonio. The other, of forty pieces, was at Laguna Gloria Art Museum in Austin.

In the fall of 1978 John Biggers's native state of North Carolina honored him in ways which touched him deeply. In Raleigh, Governor James B. Hunt, Jr., presented him with a special award for outstanding achievement by a North Carolina artist. On the evening of the same day, he was honored at a dinner, attended by scores of relatives and old friends, in his home town of Gastonia; he was presented with a key to the city.

Speaker at the Gastonia dinner was Susan (Mrs. S. M.) McAshan of Houston to whom Biggers ascribes a role of supreme importance in the realization of the Houston dream; through the years she made possible such things as the building of the first kiln, the publication of *Black Art in Houston,* and the mural for the Houston Music Hall. Her faith in "the Texas Southern Experience" and the men who brought it about has never wavered.

John and Hazel Biggers live in a charming home on a beautiful tree-shaded street in Houston. Furnished throughout with quiet taste, it is in reality a small museum. Hanging on the walls are paintings by John and other artists, all with personal meaning to the Biggerses. A beautiful collection of African sculpture and other artifacts symbolize the link with the Biggerses' African heritage which has so enriched their lives and has enabled them to know themselves.

Into their home in 1952, John's mother came to live. She immediately took over the kitchen and would scarcely let Hazel in it. She fed the birds and squirrels and soon established an intimate relationship with them which drew them in large numbers to the Biggers's yard.

Cora Biggers remained strenuously active until the age of eighty-eight; when John became so ill after his second African journey, she sort of went to pieces. On March 21, 1975, she died.

Cora Biggers's funeral was held in Saint Paul's Baptist Church in Gastonia, where John and his siblings had worshiped as children. It was a big family funeral, attended by children, grandchildren, and a horde of great-grandchildren. Her grandsons were pallbearers, her granddaughters flower girls. Her brother Bruce Whitworth, eighty-six, a retired railroad man still active in home construction and in farming, and a devoted Biblical scholar, spoke. "We don't want no hollering and carrying on, no flapping of arms," he told the mourners. "Nobody wants to be in that coffin. We are going to do this right." He developed the theme of self-reliance and love.

The sermon proper was preached by Cora's son Sylvester Biggers, a full-time Baptist minister in Durham. He talked movingly about Mama's all-embracing love, about her firmly held belief that the body was a holy vessel, not to be violated.

When she was laid to rest beside her husband, Paul—that remarkable one-legged preacher, teacher, carpenter, bootmaker, and farmer—Bruce Whitworth dropped on her coffin a handful of dirt which he had brought from the old family place in Bessemer City.

"The family," John Biggers says, "Is the most important thing in the world. First, of course, your own, but equally important the family of man."

NOTES

1. This essay is based primarily upon interviews by the author with John Biggers. Thus, most of the quotations are from those interviews.

2. John Biggers, *Ananse: The Web of Life in Africa* (Austin, 1962), 17-18.

3. Ibid., 31.

4. *New York Times Book Review,* Mar. 11, 1962.

5. John Biggers, *Ananse: The Web of Life in Africa* (Paperback ed., Austin, 1979).

6. J. Eugene Grigsby, Jr., *Art and Ethnics: Background for Teaching Youth in a Pluralistic Society* (Dubuque, Iowa, 1977), 136.

7. Elton C. Fax, *Seventeen Black Artists* (New York, 1971), 267.

8. Ibid.

The Contributors

Alwyn Barr is professor and chairperson of the Department of History at Texas Tech University. In the field of black history, his publications include *Black Texans: A History of Negroes in Texas, 1528-1971* (1973) and several articles in journals such as *Phylon* and the *Journal of Negro History*.

Olive D. Brown served Huston-Tillotson College as head librarian and in other administrative capacities for over thirty years until her recent retirement.

Robert A. Calvert is associate professor of history at Texas A&M University. He is coeditor of *Chicano: The Evolution of a People* (1973) and the author of essays on black history in the *Southwestern Historical Quarterly* and in Ben Procter and Archie P. McDonald, *The Texas Heritage* (1980).

Michael L. Gillette is chief of the Oral History Program at the Lyndon Baines Johnson Library and Museum. He published an article in the *Southwestern Historical Quarterly* on the NAACP in Texas, which is the topic of his dissertation at the University of Texas at Austin.

Bruce A. Glasrud is professor and chair in the Department of History at California State University, Hayward. He is coeditor of *The Northwest Mosaic: Minority Conflicts in Pacific Northwest History* (1977) and of *Promises to Keep: A Portrayal of Nonwhites in the United States* (1972) and is author of articles on black history in *American Studies*, the *Red River Valley Historical Review*, and the *East Texas Historical Journal*.

Michael R. Heintze is a member of the administrative staff of Texas Lutheran College. He has published an essay on the NAACP and the ownership of property in the University of Texas at Arlington, *Essays in History* (1974), and has completed a dissertation at Texas Tech University on black private colleges in Texas.

Paul D. Lack is professor and chairman of the Department of History at McMurry College. He has additional essays on black history forthcoming in the *Southwestern Historical Quarterly* and the *Red River Valley Historical Review.*

Ann Patton Malone is presently research director for the Wiregrass Georgia Rural History Research Project for Georgia Agrirama, the state agricultural living history museum. Previously, she directed the South-Central Texas Slavery Research Project for the Winedale Museum of the University of Texas at Austin. She has published essays related to black history in the *Southwestern Historical Quarterly* and in Bill C. Malone and Judith McCulloh (eds.), *Stars of Country Music* (1975).

Victor H. Treat is assistant professor of history at Texas A&M University. He has presented papers, including ones on black history, at meetings of the Texas State Historical Association.

Frank H. Wardlaw was the founding director of three university presses—South Carolina, Texas, and Texas A&M—before he retired in 1978. He is the author of a book and of several articles which have appeared in journals such as *Saturday Review* and *Harper's.*

George Ruble Woolfolk is professor and head of the Department of History at Prairie View A&M University. In the field of black history, he is the author of *Prairie View: A Study in Public Conscience, 1878-1946* (1962), *The Free Negro in Texas, 1836-1860* (1976), and articles in the *Journal of Southern History* and the *Pacific Northwest Quarterly.*

Index